Developing IP-Based Services

Solutions for Service Providers and Vendors

The Morgan Kaufmann Series in Networking

Series Editor, David Clark, M.I.T.

Developing IP-Based Services: Solutions for Service Providers and Vendors
Monique Morrow and Kateel Vijayananda

Telecommunications Law in the Internet Age
Sharon K. Black

Optical Networks: A Practical Perspective, 2e
Rajiv Ramaswami and Kumar N. Sivarajan

Internet QoS: Architectures and Mechanisms
Zheng Wang

TCP/IP Sockets in Java: Practical Guide for Programmers
Michael J. Donahoo and Kenneth L. Calvert

TCP/IP Sockets in C: Practical Guide for Programmers
Kenneth L. Calvert and Michael J. Donahoo

Multicast Communication: Protocols, Programming, and Applications
Ralph Wittmann and Martina Zitterbart

MPLS: Technology and Applications
Bruce Davie and Yakov Rekhter

High-Performance Communication Networks, 2e
Jean Walrand and Pravin Varaiya

Computer Networks: A Systems Approach, 2e
Larry L. Peterson and Bruce S. Davie

Internetworking Multimedia
Jon Crowcroft, Mark Handley, and Ian Wakeman

Understanding Networked Applications: A First Course
David G. Messerschmitt

Integrated Management of Networked Systems: Concepts, Architectures, and their Operational Application
Heinz-Gerd Hegering, Sebastian Abeck, and Bernhard Neumair

Virtual Private Networks: Making the Right Connection
Dennis Fowler

Networked Applications: A Guide to the New Computing Infrastructure
David G. Messerschmitt

Modern Cable Television Technology: Video, Voice, and Data Communications
Walter Ciciora, James Farmer, and David Large

Switching in IP Networks: IP Switching, Tag Switching, and Related Technologies
Bruce S. Davie, Paul Doolan, and Yakov Rekhter

Wide Area Network Design: Concepts and Tools for Optimization
Robert S. Cahn

Practical Computer Network Analysis and Design
James D. McCabe

Frame Relay Applications: Business and Technology Case Studies
James P. Cavanagh

For further information on these books and for a list of forthcoming titles, please visit our Web site at www.mkp.com.

Developing IP-Based Services

Solutions for Service Providers and Vendors

Monique Morrow

Kateel Vijayananda

MORGAN KAUFMANN PUBLISHERS

AN IMPRINT OF ELSEVIER SCIENCE

AMSTERDAM   BOSTON   LONDON   NEW YORK
OXFORD   PARIS   SAN DIEGO   SAN FRANCISCO
SINGAPORE   SYDNEY   TOKYO

Senior Editor	Rick Adams
Publishing Services Manager	Edward Wade
Senior Production Editor	Cheri Palmer
Developmental Editor	Karyn Johnson
Cover Design	Yvo Riezebos Design
Cover Image	© Jorg Greuel / The Image Bank
Text Design	Mark Ong, Side by Side Studios
Technical Illustration and Composition	Technologies 'N' Typography
Copyeditor	Sharilyn Hovind
Proofreader	Jennifer McClain
Indexer	Ty Koontz
Printer	The Maple-Vail Book Manufacturing Group

Designations used by companies to distinguish their products are often claimed as trademarks or registered trademarks. In all instances in which Morgan Kaufmann Publishers is aware of a claim, the product names appear in initial capital or all capital letters. Readers, however, should contact the appropriate companies for more complete information regarding trademarks and registration.

Morgan Kaufmann Publishers
An imprint of Elsevier Science
340 Pine Street, Sixth Floor
San Francisco, CA 94104–3205
www.mkp.com

07 06 05 04 03   5 4 3 2 1

Library of Congress Control Number: 2002107239
ISBN: 1–55860–779-X

This book is printed on acid-free paper.

For our family and friends

Foreword

by Margot Heiligman
Principal, StrukturTeam

This book enters the realm of Internet Protocol-based (IP) services with knowledge and decisiveness. Lao Tzu has been attributed with the quote "The good traveler has no set plans, and is not intent on arriving." While this may certainly explain the adventure of traveling to new lands, the discovery of the unknown, and the mystique of uncertainty, it cannot apply to the bits and bytes traversing an IP highway. Here, an IP packet's journey is mired with determinates from the start: its origins must be established, its path discernable, its objective and outcome predictable.

As every player in the IP community—from service provider to network manager—would agree, the packets we are optimizing, switching, routing, managing, handling, guiding, sniffing, trading, billing, monitoring, and ensuring today would do no worse than to follow the sage's advice. In fact, if we extend the continuum with IP-based services as a journey and relate IP packets to the voyager, it would support our authors' goals to design a concept for IP-based services that depicts calculated reference models to illustrate specifics in determining where those packets will end up. Examples of such models are laid out through the book, from guaranteed-bandwidth design to voice-over-IP services, with many IP-VPN service architecture examples in between. The authors' objective in producing a guide so comprehensive and organized in its coverage of IP-based services is to create value for service providers whose innovation objectives and the means for achieving them are tantamount. In order to soak up all the material required of the IP business unit, one would be hard-pressed to find a more content-rich source addressing business, technical, and service questions.

The authors go so far as to define *provisioning,* and cover concrete issues facing the service provider, such as adequate IP devices for customers, connections to the various customer networks, configuration of those IP devices in the customer environment, and activation and monitoring of services for the purposes of differentiating the service provider and mitigating risk. Ms. Morrow, with a rich background in International Telecom planning and strategy, has our full attention in drawing from real service provider cases in Chapter 8's case studies.

To extrapolate our metaphor one level further, the traveler's donkey or chariot would be these IP-based services' technological underpinnings, its routers and architecture, a means to an end that is staid and uncompromising. The consciousness or human choices voyaging on Lao Tzu's advice correlate to the IP service provider's business rules to ascertain how priorities are set, plus the service provider's business model and strategy for development.

All of which are dealt with elegantly in this book. This volume expounds the quest of two discoverers, Ms. Morrow and Mr. Vijayananda, whose route has taken them beyond their native countries and their academic roots to approach the practical application of their experience in myriad well-researched examples and to bring to light findings that are articulated in a lively and unequivocal way. The material conveyed about MPLS, for example, is some of the most pioneering in print today. The material covered in Chapter 5 includes the role of MPLS and its advantages in traffic engineering and security for IP-based services, and the role of newcomers such as DSL in the creation of IP-based services built on new business fundamentals due to factors such as local loop data and voice transport. Mr. Vijayananda, with a Ph.D. in computer science and experience in cutting-edge research, offers his deep knowledge in building innovative IP-based service solutions, such as migrating services from IPv4 to IPv6 for customers who require it (through tunneling to take advantage of the address-space shortcomings of IPv4). All of the material here advances the ability of service providers and business managers to offer more choices to customers and serve those customers who are "on the technology cusp," such as those implementing optical networking for merging transport and IP networks for better resiliency.

Most of all, if you are looking to navigate the often-misunderstood realm of "practical" IP-based service development, or simply looking to familiarize yourself with the process for solving customer issues in today's competitive and quickly evolving telecommunications environment, this book provides answers. The product of the authors' professional pursuits, the knowledge contained within this volume does justice to where we are headed, in pushing technology to represent market needs.

Let's fast-forward now, to the moment you've been waiting for—your planned embarkation on a fascinating IP exploit, whether developing a new IP-based service, translating a market need into a set of rules and business cases, building the perfect IP solution, or finding determinants to bring your customer a sought-after, intelligent infrastructure. *Designing IP-Based Services* is the survival kit you'll need to have with you on that journey. Good luck!

Contents

Foreword   vii
Preface   xvii

1 Introduction   1

1.1   Why IP?   2
1.2   History—Setting the Stage for Service Providers   3
1.3   Regulatory Events That Opened Competition   3
1.4   Potential Service Providers—Categories   4
1.5   Services   5
1.6   Customer Requirements and Service Provider and Vendor Goals   6
    1.6.1   Customer Requirements   6
    1.6.2   Service Provider Goals   10
    1.6.3   Vendor Goals   11
1.7   Chapter Review   12

2 Building the Case for IP-Based Services   13

2.1   Nuts and Bolts of Service Development   14
    2.1.1   Definitions of Service and Service Provider   14

2.2   Service Development Process   15
       2.2.1   The Participants   19
2.3   Service Development Dynamics   21
       2.3.1   Politics   21
       2.3.2   Vendor Product Development Cycle   23
2.4   Problems with the Service Development Process   25
2.5   Role of IP in the Service Development Process   27
       2.5.1   Automation   27
       2.5.2   Implementation   28
       2.5.3   Putting It All Together   29
2.6   IP-Based Services   29
       2.6.1   Service Provider Motivation   30
       2.6.2   Customer Benefits   31
       2.6.3   Vendor Interest   32
       2.6.4   Service Examples   32
2.7   Greenfield and Incumbent   34
2.8   Chapter Review   34

3   Greenfield Service Providers: Opportunities and Challenges   35

3.1   Definition of Greenfield   35
       3.1.1   CLECs and Reseller CLECs   36
       3.1.2   Bandwidth Brokers   37
       3.1.3   x Service Providers   37
       3.1.4   Putting the Alphabet Soup Together   40
3.2   Business Aspects   40
       3.2.1   Marketing Plan   40
       3.2.2   Customer Profile and Requirements   43
       3.2.3   Vendor Profile and Requirements   44
       3.2.4   Vendor Selection Process   45
       3.2.5   Feedback Loop   47
       3.2.6   Alternative Technologies   48
3.3   Service Creation Model   49
3.4   Service Examples   49
       3.4.1   Managed Remote-Access IP-VPN   50
       3.4.2   Web Hosting   51
       3.4.3   E-commerce Portal   53
3.5   Service Packaging and Pricing   54
       3.5.1   Managed Remote-Access IP-VPN   55
       3.5.2   Managed Dedicated Web Hosting   56
       3.5.3   Managed E-commerce Portal   57
3.6   What Are the Challenges?   58
3.7   Who Is the Competition?   59

3.8   Being Competitive in Terms of IP-Based Technology   59
3.9   Chapter Review   60

4   Incumbent Service Providers: Opportunities and Challenges   61

4.1   Definition of Incumbent   62
4.2   Business Aspects   62
    4.2.1   Marketing Plan   62
    4.2.2   Customer Profile and Requirements   64
    4.2.3   Vendor Profile and Selection   64
    4.2.4   Alternative Technologies   65
4.3   Service Creation Model   65
4.4   Service Examples   66
    4.4.1   Managed IP-VPN   66
    4.4.2   Managed Web Hosting   67
4.5   Service Packaging and Pricing   68
    4.5.1   Managed IP-VPN   68
    4.5.2   Managed Dedicated Web Hosting   69
4.6   Legacy Infrastructure   70
4.7   What Are the Challenges?   72
4.8   Chapter Review   73

5   IP as a Building Block: Enabling Multiservices   75

5.1   Multiservices   75
    5.1.1   Layer 2 Services   76
    5.1.2   IP-Based Services   77
    5.1.3   Application-Layer Services   77
5.2   Architectural Overview   80
    5.2.1   Core   80
    5.2.2   Edge   81
    5.2.3   Access   81
5.3   Technologies   82
    5.3.1   Multiprotocol Label Switching   82
    5.3.2   Virtual Private Networks   87
    5.3.3   Multicast   89
5.4   Transport Technology Overview   96
    5.4.1   Packet-over-SONET   96
    5.4.2   Ring Topology   99
    5.4.3   Ethernet   102
    5.4.4   Frame Relay   104
    5.4.5   ATM   108
    5.4.6   ISDN   113

5.4.7   DSL   115

5.4.8   Cable Modem   116

5.4.9   Summary   121

5.5   Service Creation   122

5.5.1   Role of MPLS   123

5.5.2   Role of MPLS-VPN   127

5.5.3   Role of ADSL Technology   132

5.5.4   Role of Cable Technology   132

5.5.5   Role of ATM   133

5.5.6   Role of Multicast   135

5.6   Chapter Review   135

6   IP-Based Service Implementation and Network Management   137

6.1   Simple Network Management Protocol   139

6.1.1   Description   139

6.1.2   Components   139

6.1.3   Operations   141

6.1.4   Management Information Base   141

6.1.5   SNMP Version 1   142

6.1.6   SNMP Version 2   144

6.1.7   Security Issues   146

6.1.8   SNMP Version 3   146

6.2   IP-Based Service Implementation—OSS   147

6.3   Provisioning—What Are the Issues?   149

6.3.1   What Is Provisioning?   149

6.3.2   Device Configuration   151

6.3.3   How to Configure the Devices   153

6.3.4   Service Modification   155

6.3.5   Database Information   155

6.4   Network Management—What Are the Issues?   155

6.4.1   Network Management System   156

6.4.2   Network Management Activities   156

6.4.3   How Is It Done?   159

6.4.4   Security Issues: Managing an IP Network   162

6.5   OSS Architecture   162

6.5.1   OSS Components   162

6.5.2   Requirements of the OSS   164

6.6   Chapter Review   166

7   IP-Based Services: Advanced Topics   169

7.1   Quality of Service   170

7.1.1   QoS Parameters   172

7.1.2   Integrated Services Model   174
7.1.3   Differentiated Services Model   175
7.1.4   IP QoS Implementation   177
7.1.5   Creating New Services Using QoS   179
7.2   Voice-over-IP   180
7.2.1   Requirements   180
7.2.2   Components   180
7.2.3   How Does Voice-over-IP Work?   185
7.2.4   Services Using Voice-over-IP   187
7.3   IP Security   189
7.3.1   Concepts and Terminologies   190
7.3.2   How Does IPSec Work?   195
7.3.3   Advantages   198
7.3.4   IPSec versus MPLS-VPN   198
7.4   IPv6   199
7.4.1   Features   200
7.4.2   Advantages   204
7.4.3   Migration Strategy   207
7.4.4   Creating New Services   208
7.5   Local Multipoint Distribution Service   208
7.5.1   Components   208
7.5.2   Advantages   210
7.6   Optical Networking   210
7.6.1   Technologies   211
7.6.2   IP and Optical Networking   213
7.6.3   Generalized Multiprotocol Label Switching   217
7.6.4   Applications of Optical Networks   218
7.7   Chapter Review   220

8 Case Studies   221

8.1   Conceptual Case Study—Greenfield   222
8.1.1   Background   223
8.1.2   Business Aspects   224
8.1.3   Services   227
8.1.4   Service Implementation Model   228
8.1.5   Company Performance   229
8.1.6   Alternatives Considered   229
8.1.7   Vendor Selection Process   230
8.1.8   Technical Aspects   231
8.1.9   Assessing Project Risks   240
8.1.10   Lessons Learned   240
8.1.11   Future Plans   240
8.1.12   Conclusion   241

8.2   Conceptual Case Study—Incumbent   241
    8.2.1   Background   241
    8.2.2   Business Aspects   242
    8.2.3   IP-Based Solution   245
    8.2.4   Services   245
    8.2.5   Service Implementation Model   247
    8.2.6   Company Performance   249
    8.2.7   Alternatives Considered   249
    8.2.8   Vendor Selection Process   250
    8.2.9   Technical Aspects   250
    8.2.10   Assessing Project Risks   253
    8.2.11   Lessons Learned   253
    8.2.12   Future Plans   254
    8.2.13   Conclusion   254
8.3   Real-Life Case Study   254
    8.3.1   Background   254
    8.3.2   Business Aspects   255
    8.3.3   Technical Aspects   259
    8.3.4   IP-Based Solution   261
    8.3.5   Services   262
    8.3.6   Project Execution and Results   269
    8.3.7   Service Implementation Model   270
    8.3.8   Alternatives Considered   270
    8.3.9   Vendor Selection Process   270
    8.3.10   Technical Aspects   272
    8.3.11   Assessing Project Risks   275
    8.3.12   Lessons Learned   276
    8.3.13   Future Plans   276
    8.3.14   Conclusions   276
8.4   Chapter Review   276

Closing Remarks: Remaining Competitive with IP   279

Acronyms   285

Bibliography   293

Index   297

Preface

Looking back at the tremendous growth experienced in the telecommunications and technology sectors followed by the sudden downturn in those industries, analysts are now speculating as to when a resurgence will occur. What may be of more immediate importance to those involved is *how* a resurgence will occur.

Telecommunication carriers began overbuying new infrastructure in the late 1990s, resulting in a high network capacity-to-customer traffic ratio, resulting in a decrease of equipment purchases from suppliers. These large up-front costs and the unexpected shifting of the business environment have forced both enterprise customers and telecommunication companies to look closely at reducing costs, generating revenues, and sustaining overall profitability. One very important way to draw more customer traffic and thus increase profitability and revenue is the creation of new services. It is with this in mind that we have chosen to write a book on Internet Protocol-based service development and deployment, a topic that will be of increasing importance to the survivability of carriers and service providers.

Service providers struggle to create new services for business and residential customers in order to ameliorate flat (if not declining) voice revenue and a reduction in long-term detrimental operating expenses due to multiple networks and operation organizations. Meanwhile, the customer, specifically the business customer, is becoming more and more demanding in terms of service requirements and expectations. The supplier then needs to provide the infrastructure and features needed to meet these demands. One other important factor for this symbiotic relationship is the utilization of technology by each group to meet the combined goals and requirements.

The Internet Protocol (IP) satisfies many of these important requirements. As end-user applications become more and more aligned with the Internet Protocol, it can be the foundation for service development and deployment for achieving service provider goals, customer requirements, and supplier product and technology development. Why IP? For one thing, IP is widely deployed throughout the world. The Internet connects over a million hosts and is based on IP. IP provides common interfaces that are used to deliver services such as Web hosting, Internet access, and the connection of corporate sites to private virtual networks. As a nonproprietary and open protocol, IP can be used to converge voice, data, and videoconferencing onto a single platform.

This book is the result of our own experiences in service development, both as service providers and vendors of service products. We present business and technical views on the subject of creating and implementing IP-based services because we see both aspects as equally important. The challenge of balancing a business view with technical feasibility is not just inclusive to IP, however, but to service development overall.

Audience

The participants in the service development process are key beneficiaries of this information: product managers, business development strategists, network engineering architects, operational support and network management architects, and suppliers' product development managers. We also include customer information technology (IT) architects and their management as sources of these services. Graduate students with a focus on service development in telecommunications and IT management courses may also find this book useful.

Approach

While there are substantial books on the IP, voice services, frame relay and other technologies, we have found none that address the service development process and that specifically bind IP with service development. Furthermore, it is our experience that project managers need to know both the business-engineering aspects associated with service development and deployment and the practical examples found in technological implementations. We have included both aspects of service creation in this book, drawing from our combined perspectives and experiences in this area. It is not necessary to read the book sequentially. In general, the business chapters (Chapters 2, 3, and 4) may be most appropriate for product managers or business analysts. Technical engineers and implementers are the main target readership for Chapters 5, 6, and 7, and a working knowledge of IP is required to understand the technical portion of the book. Both types of readers will benefit from Chapter 8 and the Closing Remarks. Our goal is to present you with a balanced view of service development and deployment based on IP.

We have made a distinction between new competitors and incumbents, because the issues facing these service providers are different. Incumbents are confronted with the problem of deploying new services on legacy or existing infrastructure. They may have multiple networks, such as a public-switched telephone network (PSTN), asynchronous transfer mode (ATM), and digital subscriber line (DSL), and multiple services, such as voice and data services that have been developed over years. Converging these services to a single network is complicated by the existence of different operating support systems to manage these existing networks. New competitors, on the other hand, do not experience this problem. They are trying to compete with incumbents and are confronted with such challenges as name recognition and proving to customers that an alternative service provider can bring value to a customer business.

Book Organization

The book is divided into five parts:

- *The Introduction sets the stage for the principles* espoused throughout the book. We review some historical trends in telecommunications that have attempted to discourage monopolistic practices and encourage competition. We also present common problems and issues associated with service development and upgrades.
- *Chapters 2, 3, and 4 comprise the business section* and detail business elements in service development and deployment. Topics such as shortening the service development cycle and models of development for new competitors as well as incumbents are discussed in these chapters. The focus is on service creation.
- *Chapters 5, 6, and 7 comprise the technical section* and expand on these business models from actual technology examples. Technology discussions related to IP-based provisioning, network management, and advanced technology themes are treated in these chapters. An example of using the technology for service deployment follows each section. The focus is on service implementation.

- *Chapter 8 is the case study section.* This chapter is further divided into conceptual case studies and then includes an actual example from a European incumbent. The case studies demonstrate practical examples of IP-based service development and service upgrades for incumbents as well as new competitors. We take the principles, problems, and issues identified earlier in the book and run through end-to-end examples to tie these themes together. Due to nondisclosure agreements, we are restrained from offering details in the actual case study example, hence the summary format. However, the theoretical conceptual case studies together with the real case should serve to provide a comprehensive overview of the IP-based service development process. Further, there is not that much of a deviation in service development experiences among actual service providers. The European example reflects the approach used by quite a few service providers internationally.

- *In Closing Remarks,* we confirm that IP-based technology is a service enabler by offering our conclusions and citing new technological trends.

Acknowledgments

We have been inspired and supported by quite a few people in this effort. To our friends and family—namely, Sreelatha Vijayananda, Véronique Thévenaz, Sam and Odette Morrow—a big thank you for your support and patience during this process. To our colleagues in the service provider business with whom we have worked and have shared a prolific experience in service development, our deepest gratitude for inspiring this book.

To our esteemed reviewers of the manuscript, Margot Heiligman of StrukturTeam, Y. Reina Wang of AT&T, Dana Dawson of Qwest, Eric Myers of Vignette, and Yakov Rekhter of Juniper Networks, many thanks for your invaluable feedback and keeping us on track for our readers. We also thank our book proposal reviewers, Margot Heiligman, Yakov Rekhter, Bruce Davie, Dana Dawson, Paul Lundgren, Thomas Nadeau, Kurt Mathys, and Geoff Jordan. A special thanks to Yakov Rekhter of Juniper Networks, who was the impetus for this project, always stating that such a book is needed in this industry. To our employers, Cisco Systems, we are grateful for the opportunity to write this book. We also give particular mention to a colleague from Cisco Systems who has been focused on helping service providers to develop IP-based services from a technological as well as a business point of view, Jaak Defour. To the Ph.D. candidate Roland Klueber, we wish all the best on your thesis, "eServices for Procurement-Oriented eMarkets," a leap toward using IP for service activation in the business-to-business marketplace.

The quality of this book and superb encouragement are attributed to our editorial team of Karyn Johnson and Rick Adams of Morgan Kaufmann Publishers. Thank you so very much for your support in this project! We extend our gratitude to Diane D. Cerra, publishing director of Morgan Kaufmann, for believing in the book's vision.

To err is human. This book may have oversights. If there are any such oversights, we take this opportunity to blame the other author.

Lastly, we would like to thank Stephen John Brannon, to whom this book is dedicated. We had the pleasure and honor to work with Steve on numerous service development initiatives. He always inspired us to look beyond what was possible. Steve, we know that you are looking down on us from Internet Heaven.

Monique Morrow, *mmorrow@cisco.com*
Kateel Vijayananda, *kvijayan@cisco.com*

Introduction

The *Internet Protocol* (IP) is widely used to route packets over the Internet and other TCP/IP-based networks. As the unifying protocol between computing and communications, IP provides solutions for merging new technology with legacy platforms or existing infrastructure. This capability is due to the nonproprietary character of IP. IP is open and permits the creation of new services for customers. *Services* are solutions that add value to a customer business; they are developed by providers called *service providers*. Examples of IP-based services are an IP-VPN (virtual private network) offering to an enterprise customer for site-to-site communications, Web hosting, Internet access, and so on. Customer applications are being released or have migrated to IP, such as email, file transfer, Web browsing, and IP telephony. Electronic commerce (e-commerce) companies are using IP for such applications as *enterprise resource planning* (ERP) and *supply chain management* (SCM), which integrate business facets such as manufacturing, sales and marketing, and product and information flow in order to automate daily operations.

The history of IP extends back to the development of the *transmission control protocol/Internet Protocol* (TCP/IP) by the U.S. Department of Defense Advanced Research Projects Agency (DARPA) in 1974. This protocol was to permit diverse computer networks to interconnect and communicate with one another. The motivation for the protocol was a problem that the U.S. Air Force had commissioned the RAND Corporation (an American nonprofit research organization) in 1962 to resolve: how the Air Force could still maintain command and control over its infrastructure after a nuclear attack. The new network was to survive a nuclear attack. The proposal from the RAND Corporation was a packet-switched network.

Paul Baran of RAND wrote:

> Packet switching is the breaking down of data into datagrams or packets that are labeled to indicate the origin and the destination of the information and the forwarding of these packets from one computer to another computer until the information arrives at its final destination computer. This was crucial to the realization of a computer network. If packets are lost at any given point, the message can be resent by the originator.

In 1983, the TCP/IP protocol was deployed on the Advanced Research Projects Agency Network (ARPANET) that later became the basis for what is now the Internet. Today, the Internet connects over 100,000,000 host devices or computers throughout the world.

1.1 Why IP?

Why IP? Service providers also use IP to collapse multiple service such as voice, data, and videoconferencing into a single converged transport environment, thereby reducing recurring operational expenses associated with these separate services. Further, the service provider can use IP-based tools to automate service development and service provisioning. An example is to use the *operations support system* (OSS), which is the nerve center for network management, ordering, billing, and reporting used by a service provider to automate service development and provisioning. Via a Web interface, a customer requests a service, the request is flagged as a new service by the service creation database that is part of the OSS architecture, and the process for developing services commences. This automation of service creation and provisioning is further discussed in Chapter 2.

The combination of automation and service development cycle reduction can decrease time to market of new service introductions. The president of AT&T Labs has asserted that his goal is to reduce the time it takes to deploy new services to 6 months from 12 to 18 months, thereby potentially increasing revenue dramatically.[1] Automating service delivery would also decrease costs by eliminating unnecessary manual processes. There is indeed an opportunity to use IP as a service and business enabler.

When is IP not a solution for service providers? Examples are services that offer dedicated Layer 2 connections only, like leased lines, *synchronous optical network/synchronous digital hierarchy* (SONET/SDH), *integrated services digital network* (ISDN), *digital subscriber line* (DSL), *asynchronous transfer mode* (ATM), or *frame relay*. Layer 2 connections are used to

---

1. Marsan, C. D. "New AT&T Labs Chief Brings Operational Focus," *Network World Fusion* (August 27, 2001).

provide only bandwidth to customers. These customers have the resources to manage their *information technology* (IT) infrastructure and only require bandwidth from service providers. These technologies are not competing with IP, as IP operates at Layer 3. In fact, these technologies complement IP-based services and are often used in the access to provision IP-based services to customers.

1.2 History—Setting the Stage for Service Providers

Prior to the Modified Final Judgment (MFJ) on January 1, 1984, that resulted in the separation of AT&T from its seven original regional Bell operating companies (RBOCs) in the United States, no telecom competitors outside these companies existed. This separation is commonly referred to as AT&T's divestiture of the Bell operating companies. In fact, the MFJ was decreed in order to break up a monopoly. Internationally, post, telephone, and telegraph (PTTs) are still largely subsidized by national governments.

A trend toward privatization of these government entities is currently under way. A common thread, however, is that these incumbents have had years, if not centuries, of existence, which has resulted in a virtual lock on the market in terms of telecommunications services. With such longevity in the market, to transform from a slow-moving bureaucracy to a dynamic business requires time and patience. The universal telephone service with its 99.999% availability has been a phenomenal achievement of these incumbent operators, and they have long depended on the sure revenue from this voice service.

The reason to open the telecommunications sector up to competition is to offer customers a choice in service providers. But the choice is null if one cannot have the expected services for a good price. The true beneficiary of competition should be the customer.

1.3 Regulatory Events That Opened Competition

The Telecommunications Act of 1996 in the United States was to implement a pro-competitive national policy. The goals of this communications policy were to foster competition by opening local service to additional players, permitting the RBOCs to provide long-distance voice and video services, deregulating cable fees, revising broadcast ownership regulations, and protecting the universal voice service. By passing this act, Congress had also acknowledged the possibility of developing innovative services in the data area, namely, the Internet.

At the heart of the act was freeing up the "last mile" of copper or fiber connecting a customer to an operator (also called the *local loop*). In addition to the MFJ of 1984, the Telecommunications Act of 1996 was to induce competition in order to offer value-added services to the customer. Section 271 of the act consists of a 14-point checklist that serves as a guideline for competition with both local and long-distance services. Despite this checklist, the reality today is that the impact of the Telecommunications Act of 1996 has been minimal. Due to mergers and acquisitions, four of the seven original Bell operating companies no longer exist. Many incumbents have attempted to prove full compliance to the checklist, however, their applications only described a plan toward compliance rather than an actual demonstration of fact.

Competitive local exchange carriers (CLECs), formed as a result of the Telecommunications Act of 1996, are battling to survive. These are alternative service providers to the incumbents. Being new entrants, CLECs and other alternative service providers are referred to in this book as *Greenfield service providers*. Examples of these providers are AOL Time Warner, IP Communications, and x service providers (xSPs).

On the international scene, the situation is not that much different than in the United States. In countries where PTTs have embarked on the road to privatization and competition is welcome, unbundling the local loop is still a challenge. In some cases, incumbents have obtained a deferral from governmental regulatory agencies. Incumbents in these countries have argued that the playing field for competition is not fair to their own business profitability, and therefore gives an unfair advantage to the competitor. (This subject is further discussed in Chapter 4.)

This history helps us to understand the dynamics behind the service provider environment. Understanding the backgrounds of the incumbents as well as the challenges confronting both incumbents and new competitors in this industry is critical to comprehending the current business situation. Regulation with a goal to introduce more competition is one aspect of the current situation, however, the focus of this book is not on regulation but rather on service development and deployment for all players in the market.

1.4 Potential Service Providers—Categories

Identifying service providers and their individual focus helps to clarify the challenges that they face in developing and deploying new services. The service providers may be classified as follows:

- *Incumbent local exchange carriers* (ILECs) and *incumbent PTTs* who dominate Layer 2 transport domains and access such as leased lines, ISDN, DSL, frame relay, SONET/SDH, and ATM. Services from these providers tend to be homogeneous, with focus on voice as a commodity. ILECs control about 90% of the access lines in the United States. Examples are the former RBOCs and their derivatives, such as

SBC Pacific Bell, SBC Southwestern Bell, SBC Ameritech, BellSouth, and Verizon.

- *Competitive local exchange carriers* (CLECs) are similar to ILECs and incumbent PTTs in that the service approach is a commodity—for example, voice service to residential and business customers. Some CLECS do have their own backbone and manage access to the customer. Unlike ILECs, CLECs do not dominate Layer 2 transport and access domains. *x service providers* (xSPs) offer specific services such as host service providing, applications service providing, and so on. (CLECs and xSPs are discussed further in Chapter 3.) Applications service provider examples include Digital Island (part of Cable&Wireless) and digex.
- *Interexchange carriers* (IXCs) offer long-distance access. Legacy players have included AT&T and Sprint. Qwest and Level 3 Communications pose competitive threats to these incumbents.
- *Cable companies* offer commodity services over cable. Examples are AOL Time Warner in the United States and UPC in Europe.
- *Bandwidth brokers* have a focus on offering massive and cheap bandwidth to everyone, reflecting a "carrier's carrier" model. Some examples are Qwest and Level 3 Communications.

In examining the challenges and motivations of these providers to develop new services based on IP, we have divided them into two major categories: Greenfield service providers, representing new-entry providers, and incumbents. *Greenfield* is a term used in telecommunications to describe something new, such as a new backbone. Greenfield service providers and incumbents are discussed in Chapters 3 and 4, respectively.

1.5 Services

Services are solutions for customers with an agreed level of support, such as availability, performance, and reliability. IP-based service examples are Internet access, e-commerce portal management, Web hosting, a corporate *virtual private network* (IP-VPN), voice-over-IP (VoIP), videoconferencing, and so on. Developing services depends on the requirements of customers, service providers, and vendors. An example of the interaction of the three is discussed in the next section.

Services can be bundled or unbundled. Bundles are a type of service packaging often used in a managed service. An example of a bundle would be offering a combination of managed service offerings such as IP-VPN, Internet access, and Web hosting. However, bundles are not a requirement for a managed service offering. A Greenfield service provider may use bundle packaging to secure the customer relationship. For example, it becomes more difficult for a customer to user multiple service providers with bundles as the Greenfield service provider becomes the key source of most of these services. Service and service packaging are themes found in Chapters 2, 3, and 4.

1.6 Customer Requirements and Service Provider and Vendor Goals

In setting the stage for using IP to develop and deploy services, we need to understand the requirements of the three main participants: the customer, the service provider, and the vendor. These requirements form the foundation of the case studies in Chapter 8, and we refer to them throughout the book to show their relationships to the service development and technology deployment examples using IP.

1.6.1 Customer Requirements

The requirements of the customer vary, depending on the needs of their applications and the services that they buy from the service provider. Some of the common requirements are

Connectivity

Throughput

Quality of service: guaranteed bandwidth, minimal delay, and minimal delay variation (jitter)

Security

High availability (99.999%) of the service

Service-level agreement reports

Multiservices using a single connection

Connectivity

Connectivity refers to IP connectivity between two sites that are separate. It is a basic requirement. Typically, customers have several geographically scattered sites and need connectivity between them to exchange information. Depending on the needs of the customer, the connectivity can be either a full mesh between all the sites or a star topology with the main site (typically the head office) having connectivity to all other sites.

Throughput

Once connectivity is available, the link capacity *(throughput)* between sites is the next requirement. The link capacity required for a site depends on the volume of traffic from and to the site. Small sites (regional offices)

require less throughput than the head office. As the volume of traffic increases over a period of time, customers upgrade the link capacity of the connection to a site or between two sites. Monitoring the link utilization is necessary to make the decision to upgrade the link capacity. The ability to dynamically order bandwidth and have it provisioned within 15 minutes is also a requirement of the customer.

Quality of Service: Guaranteed Bandwidth, Minimal Delay, and Minimal Delay Variation (Jitter)

By default, IP is best-effort and makes no guarantees of the throughput on a physical connection when it is shared by several IP connections. Today, IP-based applications have more requirements compared to basic connectivity provided by best-effort IP. Some of these applications require a guaranteed minimum throughput. It is not enough that information can be transferred between sites, it must also be exchanged within a certain period of time. Since the physical connection between sites can be shared by multiple IP connections, it is necessary to guarantee the bandwidth to connections (or a class of connections) that have minimum bandwidth requirements.

Today, there are several real-time IP-based applications that are time-sensitive. Voice and video applications like videoconferencing not only have bandwidth requirements but are also sensitive to delay and variation in delay. It can be very annoying to hear somebody speak very slowly, to hear the voice drag, or to see a fuzzy video picture because of the delay. Hence, it is not enough if the data packets from these applications are ultimately delivered, they must also be delivered on time.

Security

Security concerns fall under two categories: network security and data security. *Network security* means that the network is accessible only to authorized people and from authorized locations. Customers do not want unauthorized people accessing their network (and hence accessing their confidential data). Physically isolating a network can provide some sense of security, however, this is not enough to prevent intruders or hackers from logically connecting to it from remote sites. It is necessary to secure a customer network both physically and logically to ensure that intruders cannot connect (logically or physically) to it.

Data security is related to contents of the data packets transported over an IP network. Customers are becoming more and more conscious of data security. With the rapid emergence of applications like e-commerce, e-banking, and e-trading, confidential information is commonly exchanged over private networks, as well as public networks like the Internet. Steps must be taken to ensure the integrity and confidentiality of the transported data. Typically, a service provider network provides connectivity for several customers. Since the same backbone network is used to transport data packets from multiple customers, it is even more important to ensure network and data security in order to win the confidence of the customers who use the service provider network to build their own private data networks.

High availability customers require that the network services are highly available. *High availability* means that the network services are not interrupted due to failure of individual components or parts of the network. The network services with high availability include connectivity and quality of service.

Service-Level Agreement Reports

An additional customer requirement is the ability to monitor in real time the *service-level agreement* (SLA) via a secure Web interface to the service provider. Billing and reporting, therefore, should be made available in real time to the customer via a secure Web interface. A typical SLA that customers are interested in is the availability of the links between sites. They may want to check the availability of the service during the preceding month in order to verify that the service provider is adhering to the contract. Another SLA that is of interest is the throughput, or link utilization, which affects capacity planning. When the link utilization exceeds a threshold value for a certain duration, it is time to upgrade the capacity of the link to a higher speed.

Multiservices

The end customer, specifically the business customer, requires a single-service, rich-access line. Rather than multiple access lines for each desired service—for example, data, voice-over-IP, videostreaming, and so on—the customer desires these services over one link. The result should be an attractive service price and a wealth of feature options that include quality of service and implement a class-of-service differentiation. The customer requirement also includes any-to-any connectivity between sites. The customer does not want to wait six weeks or three months for such a service option.

Requirements of a Sample Customer

We now present a sample customer and their requirements. This example represents the requirements of a typical customer and is examined once again in Chapter 8 to validate the relevance of IP-based services for this customer.

Consider a large corporation (Anonymous Inc.) with a head office located in one city and several large regional offices located in different cities. They need connectivity between the head office and regional offices for their voice, video, and data requirements (see Figure 1.1). The

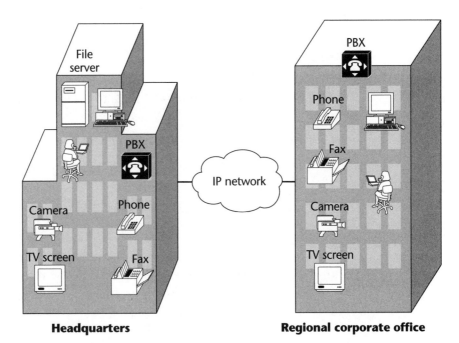

Figure 1.1 Requirements of Anonymous Inc.

videoconferencing facility is used to hold daily meetings between the teams located in the regional corporate offices and the head office. This eliminates the time required to travel between the offices to attend these meetings. The private branch exchange (PBX) is used to provide voice services. Data servers are located in the head office and are accessed by all the users in the regional offices.

Some of the requirements of Anonymous Inc. are

- Any-to-any connectivity for video, voice, and data applications
- Bandwidth for video, voice, and data
- Guaranteed bandwidth for data transfer between sites
- Minimal delay or jitter in video and voice applications
- Data security to ensure that the confidentiality of the data transferred between sites is not compromised
- Network security to prevent hackers from accessing their data network
- High availability of network service between all sites to ensure that voice and video applications can be used during office hours and that data from all the regional offices can be backed up at the central site every day
- SLA reports on link utilization. Anonymous Inc. would like to monitor the utilization of links for each regional office and upgrade the

links to higher speed when the utilization exceeds a certain threshold value over a certain period of time.

1.6.2 Service Provider Goals

Service providers have a number of goals to meet in order to make their business profitable:

Short development and deployment time of IP-based services

Scalable and stable backbone (core) network

Multiservices using the same network

Ease of network operations

Vendor support

Short Development and Deployment Time of IP-Based Services

Developing new services is necessary to remain competitive in the market. In the data networking world, customer requirements keep changing rapidly, so service providers are forced to be innovative and offer new services to meet those requirements. As a result of rapidly changing customer requirements, gauging the right service development time cycle is challenging for the service provider.

Scalable and Stable Core Network

Scalability and reliability are key themes for service providers in developing services and supporting a large number of customers. Scalability is an issue for core and edge networks. A *scalable core network* must support traffic from multiple services. The service provider must be able to offer these services to many customers without having to add new equipment to the core network. As long as the core network is scalable, it permits the service provider to offer many IP-based services (to more customers) using the same network. A *scalable edge network* can aggregate traffic from multiple customers. The addition of new customers must not result in a proportional increase of edge devices.

A reliable network does not fail as a result of single point failures. That is, failure of any single component (device or link) does not result in loss of connectivity within the network as a whole. Redundancy is used to protect the network, so customers will not be affected by component failure.

Multiservices Using the Same Network

Voice and data networks are two of the different types of networks owned by service providers. Typically, a service provider would like to reduce the cost of maintaining these networks and at the same time be able to offer all the services required by their customers. IP can be used to converge these different services, such as voice-over-IP, IP-VPN, and videoconferencing based on IP.

Ease of Network Operations

An efficient *network operations center* (NOC) plays a key role in running and maintaining a large IP network that supports several IP-based services. Good *network management system* (NMS) tools can assist the operator in the NOC to manage the network, detect and diagnose faults in a timely manner, and take preventive action to avoid network outages. NMS tools are also important for provisioning new customers and upgrading to meet the requirements of existing customers. Provisioning large numbers of customers in a short period of time is the key to rapid deployment of new IP-based services and having a competitive edge in the market.

Vendor Support

Vendor support is necessary to get the technologies to roll out services in a timely fashion. Ideally, vendors work with service providers to develop the products they need. The service providers add input to product development, and there is a relationship between the vendor's product life cycle and the service provider's service life cycle. (This relationship is further explored in the next chapter.)

Two conceptual case studies and one real-life case study representing actual examples in the industry are discussed in Chapter 8. These case studies focus on both the business and technical aspects of developing and deploying IP-based services. Examples are used to highlight the requirements of customers and the goals of service providers.

1.6.3 Vendor Goals

Vendors, or suppliers, must understand the services to be developed and deployed so as to synchronize technology enhancement and needed features with both the service provider and the end customer. Often there is a lack of synchronization between these parties that results in immature technology and unavailable features. Exchanging information requires that the service provider, end customer, and vendor be partners. The vendor goals are

Ensuring product mapping to the service offered by the service provider

Aligning technology with product availability

One example of vendor support toward product and service development is a strategic partnership that fosters the exchange of personnel between vendors and service providers. This can be an engineering exchange program in which service provider engineers work on-site at the vendor's product development facilities, testing products and services for feasibility and use in their own environment. Feedback is quick, since the engineers are working directly with the product and service developers. Conversely, a vendor developer can work on-site with a service provider's engineering team to understand how the products are deployed and can use the information for further product development or enhancements. An engineering exchange program provides rich feedback to both parties. The implementation of such a program requires a nondisclosure agreement for both sides, as the engineers will be working in the center of product and service development. Another example of vendor support is to directly inquire about service provider requirements as a step to product development. Service providers can also agree to evaluate preproduction releases of products.

Taking the customer requirement of multiple service features offered on a single access line requires that both the vendor-specific infrastructure and the technology are capable of supporting this need. In the next chapter, we will examine the product and technology development life cycle in the supplier environment and the impact that this life cycle has on service development and deployment.

1.7 Chapter Review

IP is a widely deployed protocol and can be used to develop and deploy new services such as voice-over-IP and videoconferencing. In order to stay competitive, service providers must understand not only the business drivers and requirements of their customers, but also the dynamics that affect their customers' customers, as they move down the chain of value-added service relevance and impact. Vendors also need to understand the service provider business model and its impact on end customers in order to contribute to the technology required for IP-based services. Chapters 2, 3, and 4 focus on the business aspects of service development and its impact on Greenfield and incumbent environments. Chapters 5, 6, and 7 offer practical technological examples reinforcing these business aspects. Both the business and the technical examples converge in Chapter 8 in case study scenarios. Are you ready for the journey?

C H A P T E R

Building the Case for IP-Based Services

Service providers are confronted with growing challenges from deregulation, new competition, cost pressures, emerging technology, and a constant requirement to develop and deploy new services due to customer demands. Customers are driven to reduce their own costs and maximize their business revenue due to fluctuations in the economy. This presents an opportunity for service providers to deliver value-added services that will help reduce customers' costs. To develop and deploy these value-added services, service providers require organizational adaptability, flexibility in the processes that are used, and an understanding of the processes, tools, and participants that are involved. Processes such as a customer request for a new service (service creation) and delivering a single service for a set of customers are discussed in this chapter.

Participants in the service development process include the customer, who originates a service request; the product manager, who is responsible for service revenues; sales and marketing staff, who need to sell and position the new service; engineering and operations staff, who conduct technical feasibility tests on the new service and integrate the network management, reporting, and billing into the operations support system (OSS); and, finally, the vendors, who provide the products needed to develop and deploy the service. These roles are highlighted in this chapter, along with the associated organizational politics that can affect the process.

There is a relationship between the vendor's product development cycle and the service provider's service development cycle. For example, lack of a product can delay a service, and correspondingly, lack of service provider requirements and technology can delay a product. IP-based technology can be used to improve service development by reducing the amount of steps in the initial service creation process and by automating the information exchange between participants during the service development process. (Details are discussed in Chapter 6.)

2.1 Nuts and Bolts of Service Development

Service development comprises the *service creation* and *service implementation* processes. Service creation can be just an idea and represents the beginning of the service development process. Service creation can be either an actual request from a customer or a hypothetical scenario pondered by the service provider: What if the company were to launch a particular service? Who would be the customer? Who would be the target market? Service implementation (also called *service delivery*) is the provisioning of the service to the customer. The service can be delivered as per a delivery process such as a customer order, followed by fulfillment of the order by the service provider operations team (which includes service and network management). The service provider uses the OSS to deliver the services.

Why develop services? Defining and developing services based on available products and technology is a complex task; however, the alternative, delivering and maintaining customized solutions, is simply not scalable for a provider. Several questions need to be considered if a service provider is to go forward with a new service: What are the drivers? Does the customer drive the process? Is the process service-driven? What role does an idea have in the process? Exploring these questions is the focus of Section 2.2.

2.1.1 Definitions of Service and Service Provider

A *service* delivers solutions to customers that can have an impact on the customer's business (such as cost reduction), and is characterized by a service-level agreement (SLA). The SLA defines service features—such as availability (how often the service is operational), provisioning time (the speed that a service can be delivered), and quality characteristics (such as committing to the priority delivery of voice over data file transfers)—in a contract between the customer and the service provider. Via the SLA, the service is measurable and controllable, and failing to deliver an agreed-upon SLA typically results in a credit to the customer by the service provider. Services are most often developed for use by a large number of customers, resulting in an economy of scale—that is, the service can be deployed with joint resources and processes, such as using a single network to develop and deliver multiple services. A *value-added service* is a service that differentiates itself from other services by, for example, instead of offering only voice, offering a palette of services such as Internet access, Web hosting, e-commerce, voice-over-IP, and videoconferencing. Thus, a value-added service addresses a variety of customer requirements and results in a high return on investment, adding value to both the customer and the service provider.

Delivering a service is the function of the *service provider,* who assumes the risk to develop and deploy the service. There is a value-added chain associated with the service provider role that starts with the technology supplier and ends, at the top of the chain, with the business provider. The service provider function is in the middle of the chain. If you are a service provider, it may be interesting for you to understand the business growth opportunity you have. As a telecommunications company, what does it mean to claim to be "a full-service provider"? If you are a customer, understanding the business scope of your service provider may impact what services you can expect—for example, are you contracting for rented technology from your service provider but are responsible for the actual service yourself?

The *technology supplier* is the equipment manufacturer—of operating systems, software, routers, switches, workstations, and so on. The *technology provider* integrates the equipment into the service, transferring the technology for turnkey solutions. The service provider, then, transforms both the products and the technology into services. The business provider arranges for customers to outsource business processes that are not part of their core commercial activity, such as accounting and payroll processing.

2.2 Service Development Process

The service development process can be depicted as passing through a series of *tollgates,* from service creation to full-service implementation. Each tollgate has an input and an output. The process can be stopped at any point if there is insufficient input to continue. The tollgate concept provides business case accountability as well as structure for managing the process itself. (A marketing plan is linked to the business case in the service development process but not explicitly described in this section; marketing plan details are discussed in Chapters 3 and 4.)

Figure 2.1 depicts a service development process example using six tollgates. Let's take a look at the steps and decisions required during the process.

Tollgate 1 is the idea that can be presented in the form of a paper proposal and responds to a service fit in the company product portfolio. The portfolio identifies potential customers and determines whether or not there are service cannibalization issues that the service provider needs to

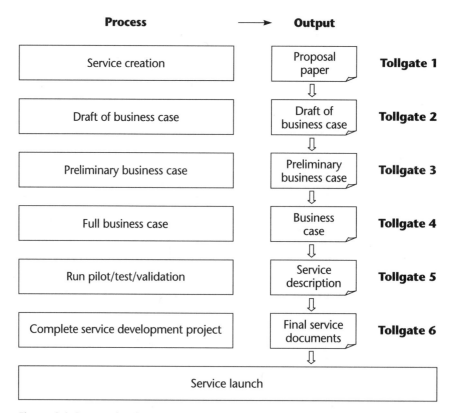

Figure 2.1 Service development and tollgates.

worry about: *service cannibalization* is the erosion of an existing service as a result of introducing a new one. *Service positioning,* how a service provider will position a new service in the market, is also very important early in the service development process. The decision to proceed from tollgate 1 to tollgate 2 is an indication that there is an opportunity in the market for the service. This indication is general and unconfirmed by market research; an example would be an overview of market trends.

The output for tollgate 1 is input to a business case draft for tollgate 2—for example, a technical feasibility overview that confirms the availability of the technology and products required for the new service. The decision to proceed from tollgate 2 to tollgate 3 results from the confirmation that the service is unique.

The output for tollgate 2 is input to a preliminary business case for tollgate 3. Examples of such input include competitive analysis; *strengths, weaknesses, opportunities,* and *threats* (SWOT) *analysis;* marketing goals, strategy, and budget; and revenue potential, all of which are part of the marketing plan and present the competitive landscape of the market for the new service. (These are further discussed in Chapters 3 and 4.) The decision to proceed from tollgate 2 to tollgate 3 is a business judgment that the service provider can earn revenue from the new service.

The output from tollgate 3 serves as input to the full business case for tollgate 4. Examples of such input are (1) why the company will develop the service, (2) what tools are necessary for service development, and (3) how the service will be developed and with what resources. Tollgate 4 is the most critical phase in this service development model because the business case identifies the risks the company must assume in order to develop and deploy the new service. The decision elements affecting whether to proceed from tollgate 4 to tollgate 5 are attractiveness of the business case, identification of a pilot customer, realistic service launching date, and resource availability. In short, can the service provider develop the service? Table 2.1 summarizes the key issues associated with tollgate 4, the business plan.

The output for tollgate 4 is input for tollgate 5, the pilot, testing, and service validation phase. These examples can be seen in Table 2.1 under "How will the service be developed?" Inputs are resources to develop the service, customers willing to pilot the service, required vendors, risks associated with the service development like failing to launch on time, and the financial model that identifies the cost of developing the service and the potential revenues. (Examples of financial models and service pricing can be found in Chapters 3, 4, and 8.)

Tollgate 5 specifies the service, service-level agreement, service price, service delivery process, OSS architecture, service management, lab, testing, and customer pilot results. New service training for the service provider's operations, sales and marketing, and engineering teams are provided during tollgate 5.

The decision elements affecting whether to proceed from tollgate 5 to tollgate 6 are lab test results confirming that both the technology and product are feasible for the service; customer pilot results confirming that the customer has signed off on the service pilot; the service management announcing that it has integrated the OSS architecture successfully; and, finally, the service delivery organization being successfully trained for the new service.

We are now close to full-service launch at tollgate 6. The output from tollgate 5 to tollgate 6 includes service reliability and performance as a result of the testing, completion of service training, completion of marketing and sales plans, and completion of service delivery documentation, such as the operations manual, engineering manual, and service implementation manual. Tollgate 6 output includes service fact sheets, technical white papers, service description, service price, and contract templates. (Service packaging, pricing, and financial models are described in Chapters 3, 4, and 8.) The service can now be launched!

We have just explored a service development process. If you are a service provider, this process may be familiar, as it is used in several provider

Table 2.1   Tollgate 4—business case factors.

Element	Description
Why develop the service?	
Issues	Identification of customer impact
Business architecture	Participants, their roles, processes they perform
Business rules and assumptions	Explanation of how the service will find acceptance by customers, along with an indication of how fast it will penetrate the addressed customer segment
Benefits	List of qualitative and quantitative benefits (for service provider, customers, and partners)
Business opportunity	First quantitative assessment of the business potential (market potential, customer potential, etc.)
What tools are necessary?	
Service provider processes to satisfy the explicit/implicit customer need	Which service provider processes are required to deliver the service and how
Technical IT architecture	Which applications and activities are required; indication of the level of modifications to the system environment
Organizational chart for implementation	Who is required to participate for a successful service development
Competitive analysis	Brief overview of competitors
How will the service be developed?	
Resource requirements and plan	Project time schedule, including tollgates 4 and 5
Marketing plan	Target market, service pricing
Interdependence chart	Gantt identifying critical paths
Partnership concept (optional)	Strategic customer relationship
Pilot partner shortlist and the approach to win them	Early service adopters
Risk assessment	What the business impact is to the customer if service is not delivered on time
Financial model	Includes revenue drivers, revenue, profit, net present value

environments. If you are a customer, you now realize what is involved in service development and can see what function you have in this process. Namely, you can drive service development. The following section identifies the players and their roles in the service development process.

2.2.1 The Participants

Service development participants include the customer, the service provider, and the vendor: the customer requests the service of the service provider, who in turn provides product and technology requirements to the vendor, who delivers these products and technologies to the service provider, who then develops and provisions a service for the customer.

Customers drive the requirements for services, and services are developed for their specific needs. An example might be to add IP-based products to the service portfolio and to provide services like Web hosting and e-commerce. Customers are generally interested in lowering their operational costs in hardware and software maintenance. The service provider thus needs to understand how the total cost of hardware and software ownership in a customer environment impacts the customer's business, in order to offer value-added services.

Vendors supply products that will be used to develop and deploy a service. Obviously, technology is necessary for developing products, and service providers and vendors can both play a part in driving technology standards in such forums as the International Telecommunications Union (ITU) and the Internet Engineering Task Force (IETF).

Now, what can go wrong in these relationships? If the service provider does not communicate requirements accurately, or if the vendor misunderstands the requirements, then the result is a product that the service provider cannot use, and a customer who has no service. For successful service deployment to occur, service providers need to clearly identify product requirements to vendors. In response, vendors need to listen carefully to these requirements and offer a stable product in the time frame requested. Should a technology not exist, both parties have an opportunity to jointly develop the technology. There are risks for both parties, however, and they can be equally challenging to overcome. Vendors risk releasing products that service providers will not buy, and service providers risk having products released that do not align with their own requirements because they failed to provide the necessary input to these vendors or vendors did not understand the requirements. As seen to be true with customers and service providers, communication is also critical between vendors and service providers.

What about the service provider organization itself? The key players here are the chief executive officer (CEO) and the sales and marketing, product management, finance, engineering, operations, and service management departments.

- The *CEO* of a service provider organization sets the vision for the company, outlining what the business focus is—for example, to be number one in value-added services in the domestic market and to use IP-based technology to automate collaborative tools for the supply chain, e-commerce, and training.
- The *sales and marketing staff* communicates end-customer requirements for service development to product management.
- *Product management* looks at the service from a profit-and-loss perspective and leads the service development process and service life cycle (depicted in Figure 2.2). The service life cycle is implemented in phases similar to service development, but includes service enhancements and retirement. A *service enhancement* is a feature added to a service, such as *quality of service* (QoS) added to a basic IP-VPN service for voice-over-IP. It is not necessary to implement the entire service development process for an enhancement.

The last phase in the life cycle is to retire a service. A signal to retire a service is when it has become a commodity, that is, widely available in the market from competitors. If the only differentiation at that point is price, then similar services will flood the market at lower and lower prices, thus eroding business margins for the

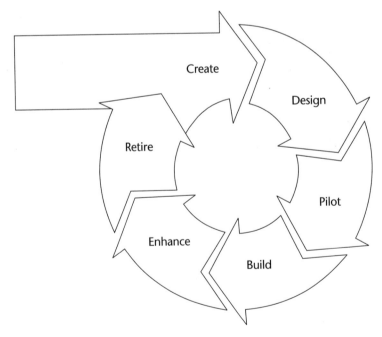

Figure 2.2 Service life cycle.

original service provider. This means that the company will make less money on each dollar of sales, thus adversely impacting overall business profitability. The product manager is responsible for directing the service life cycle and working with marketing to position the company's services.

- The *financial department* provides accounting support for both receivables and payables. Logistics and human resources are part of the finance function. In service development, this department offers input as to the cost of additional resources and capital investment. It can also direct changes and process management. *Process management* describes how an individual and/or group manages its workflow activities. Ultimately, customer satisfaction is more than just achieving service specifications; it is focusing on ways to please the customer.

- The *engineering department* selects the architecture that is used to develop services. This team performs technical feasibility studies and works with vendors in technology and product testing. The team has a leading role in customer pilots and works closely with operations.

- The *operations department* administers the network configuration management, fault management, and change management. The group also maintains IT systems that are used to manage databases. Operations will look at vendor products for manageability in the service development process.

- *Service management* is responsible for customer support, help desk and call center functions, billing and reporting, capacity planning, and security. This department is in charge of the OSS architecture and manages customer SLAs.

2.3 Service Development Dynamics

In this section, we explore those dynamics that can either hinder or facilitate the service development process. One such area is politics. Politics between organizations and companies can be a nightmare if not managed properly. Another source of tension can be due to the vendor's product development cycle and its effect on the service provider's development cycle. Is the vendor pushing a product? Is the service provider pulling a product? Who stands to gain? What about the customer?

2.3.1 Politics

In a service provider environment, particularly at an incumbent company, politics are due largely to legacy organizations (departments or subsidiaries) having control for a period of time. An example of a legacy organization is voice, which has traditionally been a source of revenue for providers. Data services like Internet access are offered by a separate organization within the company, transmission by yet another. These organizations do not necessarily communicate with one another, because there has been no requirement to do so.

Changing regulations have opened the markets. Since 1998, long-distance voice revenues have consistently declined in the United States. The need to compensate for this loss with a new value-added service, such as bundled data and voice-over-IP, has resulted in an environment of change within these provider companies, as they transition from the traditional telephony focus to IP.

The transmission group manages the Layer 1 and Layer 2 services, such as leased-line, frame relay, and ATM, and often views IP as a transmission medium. The transmission and voice groups together participate in the ITU to develop telecommunications standards. Conversely, the IP-based services group has functioned separately, providing Internet access and following IETF initiatives for standards development. The groups have distinct cultures, often called *bell head* (traditional culture) and *net head* (Internet culture).

Each group has established relationships with vendors that are competitors. This can be an obstacle in product selection for service development. The result is that one group and vendor will play against another group and vendor, creating havoc in the service development process. We term this *group mobbing,* and it is negative for a company: such chaos results in management intervention to resolve the deadlock, as well as delays in the service development. Service development organizations must recognize these distinctions and address the issues from the beginning. Examples of these differences are highlighted in Table 2.2.

Sometimes customers themselves are involved in these politics. For example, a vendor that has a good relationship with a customer may prod that customer to pressure the service provider into delivering a service with the vendor's product. The customer will dangle a business contract to the service provider in order to leverage the product selection.

What can a service development organization do to prevent such politics? Recognizing that the politics exist is the first step. Involving all parties in the service development process with clear communication regarding goals, project scope, and deliverables is the second step. As will be seen in Chapter 8, a success factor in both the conceptual and real-life case studies is the communication by the CEO, which can transform a company and its business focus. This transformation often means a cultural change is required to support the new corporate model. A company needs to recognize the cultural distinctions between the two groups we've discussed and integrate the best of both worlds into a new organization ready to develop and deploy services jointly.

Table 2.2 Cultural differences between traditional groups working with telephony and transmission (transition state) and newer groups working with IP technology (IP state).

Transition State	IP State	Service Development Consequences
Hierarchical	Flat	Organizational clash if not managed
Centralized decision making	Distributed decision making	Result can be composite of two worlds
IP not yet integrated as core business	IP is core business	Transition group needs to be integral part of voice-over-IP service development initiatives
IP integration must be evolutionary	IP is revolutionary—the quicker the better	For an incumbent, evolutionary is essential due to legacy issues
Emphasis on processes	Avoidance of processes	A little of both—for example, an improved service development process
Standards = ITU	Standards = IETF	Both are essential
Emphasis on wholesale services	Emphasis on retail and value-added services	Market and product-positioning issue

2.3.2 Vendor Product Development Cycle

The vendor product development cycle is represented in tollgate 1, which identifies technical feasibility and product availability. At the very beginning of the service development process, service creation, the team is already exploring technical alternatives and reviewing product choices. How does a vendor develop products? Who provides the input? Factors affecting product development include technology availability, market requirements, and vendor competition.

- *Technology availability.* If a technology is available, products can be developed using it; if a technology is not available and a product is required, then vendors tend to deliver a proprietary solution while working in standards organizations to drive this proprietary architecture for acceptance by other vendors and service providers. Clearly, getting acceptance of a proposed architecture will facilitate product development, and for that particular vendor assure an implementation of the product as an industry standard. For example, the development of the *multiprotocol label switching* (MPLS) architecture started with a vendor's proprietary implementation, based on tag switching technology, and resulted in the release of time-to-market products from the vendor while the MPLS standard had been developed (Davie and Rekhter 2000). (*Time-to-market* refers to early product releases to the market while the architecture is still being defined and standardized with a goal to capture customer mind-set toward adopting the product.)

- *Market requirements.* Vendors will poll customers as to their requirements, desired features, business goals, and priorities for development. Internally, vendors will prioritize product development based on potential business opportunity. For example, how committed is the service provider to having a specific product? As the service provider assumes a business risk to develop services, the vendor assumes a business risk to develop products.

- *Vendor competition.* By developing a product, how is the vendor differentiating itself from its competition in features, scalability, and price? It is not enough to be first in the market if the product is not stable. The vendor's motivation is to capture market share and be market leader. Service providers complain that vendors are either too slow or too sloppy: slow in getting the exact product mix when needed and sloppy by releasing time-to-market variants that are not stable. In fact, new product releases are often between 9 and 18 months from the identification of these requirements to the vendor, but are still misaligned with service provider expectations. This may be due to the unavailability of technology, a change in service provider requirements, or a misunderstanding on the part of the vendor. Improving in these areas may set a vendor apart.

The product development cycle is similar to the service development process (see Figure 2.3): The business requirements and opportunities are prioritized for development; a product is designed and then tested internally to validate basic features before customer pilot release; input from the customer pilot are integrated into the product prior to general release; there is usually an internal test run to assure that the basic features are still operational; and the product is then released to the market. Later, vendors will integrate feature enhancements to maintain the product's competitive edge. Finally, the product will be retired as soon as there is market saturation, indicated by large presence of similar products with no differentiation other than price.

Vendors and service providers must work closely together to reduce gaps in product and service development. One way would be for providers to include vendors in the process. Another would be to exchange

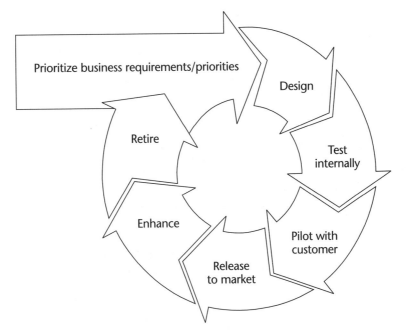

Figure 2.3 Vendor's product life cycle.

product development requirements monthly or quarterly. Vendors need to provide a status of product development as it applies to the process. This is a delicate subject, as this information is confidential and of course cannot be allowed to fall into the hands of a competitor. The issue of confidentiality also applies to a provider when developing a service. Thus, there must be a degree of trust between vendors and service providers that supports both product and service development while maintaining confidentiality. What is important for both parties is being clear about requirements as input from a service provider and product output from a vendor. The result should be a close alignment of the vendor's product to the provider's service.

2.4 Problems with the Service Development Process

In examining the input/output interaction for each tollgate in Figure 2.1, we do not see time metrics. When asked, the service providers we interviewed stated that it took an average of between 9 and 18 months for a service launch. The sales and marketing teams for some of these service providers feel that this is too long. The general feedback from corporate customers is that service providers tend to be slow when it comes to providing services that address their requirements. The tendency by sales and marketing is to push aggressively for customized solutions so as to close the gaps between customer requirements and a service launch. The result is often friction in the service development team as this group tries to develop and deploy services for a market. So what is the ideal time for a service launch? Let's look at the process itself.

The reason for the longer time periods (up to 18 months) to develop and launch services is multifold. While a service provider can influence some factors, if a vendor is not able to provide technology or products, then the launch time frame is out of the control of the service provider. However, the service provider can exert pressure on the vendor to provide the required products and technology within the time frame by not buying products unless the schedule is met.

One of the main reasons for delays is service implementation. Service providers generally do not have the right tools and processes to speed up this phase of service development. Most of the tasks in service implementation are done manually and are prone to errors; valuable time is lost in correcting manual errors and finding the right information. For example, the lack of tools to manage IP addressing can result in incorrect provisioning of customer devices in the service provider network. Consequently, the service will not be implemented and customers will not have connectivity. Inaccurate information exchange between service development participants can be another reason for a delay in implementation. For example, the IP addressing plan for a customer's network implementation might be transmitted from the sales department to the provisioning department as a hard copy, which is then lost. Due to the loss of the hard copy, the customer network cannot be implemented.

The second main cause of delays is the lack of automation in information flow between the tollgates. This increases the time required for each tollgate, because valuable time is lost searching for documents. For example, the engineering team might develop a technical solution based on the number of customers that have to be supported by the service. Inaccurate information about the number of customers given by the marketing department to the engineering department can result in a technical solution that may not scale as the number of customers increases. In this example, automating the flow of information between the departments will help the technical team keep up to date on the number of customers and develop a solution that will scale as needed.

Finally, to avoid delays, a service provider may need to define the scope of the deliverables. For example, a preliminary business case, business case draft, and business case can be converged to the business case with clearly defined deliverables. This action requires evaluating the efficiency of the processes and looking at ways to improve them. IP-based technology can improve the implementation issues, but the service provider defines the scope.

2.5 Role of IP in the Service Development Process

We have examined the service development process, as well as dynamics such as politics and the vendor product life cycle. We have also looked at some problems associated with the process. We now explore the following questions: Can automation or implementing IP-based tools improve the process? What will be the business impact of such an improvement?

IP has a role in service provisioning and service upgrades. A common thread is automation—IP-based technology is used to automate these functions. The OSS architecture is a composite of these functions and is central to service development and delivery. Here, we examine the role of IP in each of these functions.

2.5.1 Automation

Automation can help speed the service development process by addressing those factors that delay the process, such as information exchange. For example, the service product manager and marketing manager can use a Web interface to create a service and produce both the marketing plan and business case electronically. The documentation output of the tollgates can be updated and exchanged electronically among the service development participants.

While automation can address some of the problems highlighted earlier, success factors for this automation include the work and research needed for input such as the business case and the marketing plan, as well as the accuracy of the information itself. Active engagement is required with the customer, the market, and the vendor. An engagement example would be a customer advisory board within the service provider organization. Participants could be strategic (leading) customers representing designated market segments. Such an advisory board could provide input to the service development process, specifically to the business and marketing plans.

Scope of Process Deliverables

One area for improvement is to define the scope of the process deliverables—for example, tollgate 1 is the service proposal or request by the customer, and tollgates 2, 3, and 4 from the original tollgate process can now be converged into tollgate 2 for the business case and marketing plan. Tollgate 3 comprises the product manager's service description and the pilot documentation with ready-for-service launch at tollgate 4. Figure 2.4 depicts this example.

In describing the outputs of the process deliverables, tollgate 1 identifies customer requirements and benefits while tollgate 2 responds to the

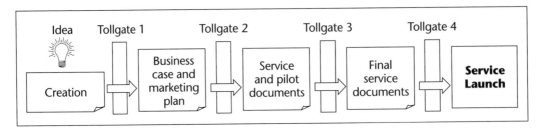

Figure 2.4 Scope of process deliverables.

business case attractiveness and the marketing strategy. Tollgate 3 assures that the service elements are ready, training has been completed, and the pilot customer has signed off on the service pilot; tollgate 4 leads to the full-service launch with the marketing, product brochures, and contract templates in place.

2.5.2 Implementation

Another area where automation can be used to improve the service development process is in service implementation. Once the service has been launched, it needs to be provisioned, and IP-based technology can be used to automate the workflow.

The problematic nature of manual processes can be seen in service provisioning. For example, a customer sends an address plan in a spreadsheet format. The service provider operations group receives it, and an operator then manually enters the addresses for routers that need to be installed at the customer site. Suppose an address is typed incorrectly in a router configuration. The router will be shipped to the customer location but will fail to become active. Time will be spent troubleshooting the problem until the operations group realizes its error. The router will then be sent back for a reconfiguration of the address and once again sent to the customer location for installation. The contracted provisioning window has now slipped, thus resulting in a breach of contract between the service provider and the customer. Sound like an exaggeration? Unfortunately, this problem is very common.

With automation, the information is entered at a single entry point. This information can be either correct or incorrect. If incorrect, it is easier to trace the problem back to the single entry point. Using automation, in the previous example, a customer could provide the address plan via a Web interface to the service provider's operations group. The provisioning tool would enter the address in a database and generate the router configuration automatically. Thus, the benefit of automation is efficiency in service delivery to the customer.

Service Upgrades

Service upgrades are another activity that must be automated in order to reduce delays in service implementation; IP technology can automate the process. An example of a service upgrade would be an increase in bandwidth: Via a Web interface, the customer orders an increase in bandwidth. The order is flagged for a bandwidth increase by the service upgrade engine that is part of the OSS architecture. The request is routed electronically to the capacity-planning engine to determine capacity availability. If capacity is available, the bandwidth is increased for the customer. Upon completion, a notification is sent electronically to the billing engine to invoice the customer for the increased bandwidth. After the change has been made in the billing engine, the customer receives an electronic notification from the provider that the service upgrade has been completed. The customer is able to validate the upgrade via an online report displaying the bandwidth increase and the new service price.

If capacity is unavailable, then the customer is notified by the reporting engine about the current status. The time elapsed between the online order and delivery of the upgrade is between 15 minutes and one hour. Without this automation, a customer can wait from 24 hours to three months.

OSS Processes

Figure 2.5 depicts OSS business processes and interfaces. Provisioning is part of the service delivery process in OSS. Other OSS process interactions include service usage, which impacts billing and financial accounting, service assurance, which manages the SLAs, and service creation, for the generation of a new service. Automating these OSS processes is key to reducing delays in the service development process.

2.5.3 Putting It All Together

IP-based technology is important in automating service development, provisioning, and upgrades. Key business issues include the time it takes to launch a service, provision for an existing service, and activate an upgrade. It is critical to minimize human errors associated with manual processes. Maximizing workflow is the real effect of automation in a service provider environment.

2.6 IP-Based Services

Moving from service development to the actual services, we ask, What is the motivation to develop IP-based services? What are the customer

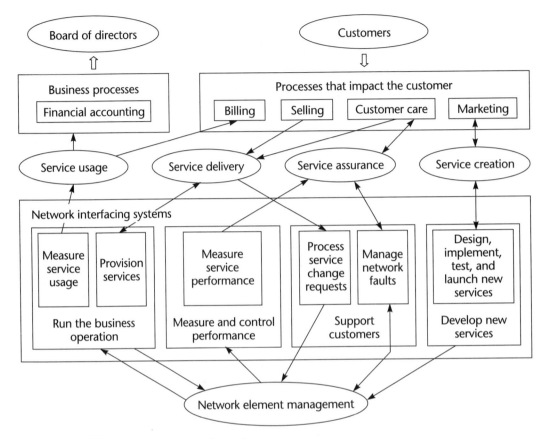

Figure 2.5 OSS business processes and interfaces.

benefits? What interest does a vendor have in them? This section examines the reasons for developing IP-based services.

2.6.1 Service Provider Motivation

The main reason for a service provider to develop and deploy IP-based services is to gain revenue. In common business language, this translates to making money. One example of the shift from voice to IP-based services can be found in North America, where incumbents have experienced a decline in long-distance voice revenue since 1998. For one major U.S. incumbent, this decline translated into a $14 billion loss in long-distance voice from 1998 to 2001.

Conversely, the North American market (as well as the international market) has seen an increase in data traffic over the same period. This trend is attributed to an emphasis on e-business applications and cost reduction driven by enterprise customers. Examples are *customer relationship management* (CRM) and converged voice and data. Enterprise customers are pressured to operate their businesses efficiently and keep costs under control. Consequently, service providers worldwide are looking for revenue generation opportunities to replace voice (which has become a commodity) with a value-added service that fulfills customer requirements.

Reducing operational expenses is another motivation for service providers to construct an IP-based infrastructure. Service providers have multiple networks and OSS capabilities for various services, such as PSTN for voice and frame relay and ATM for data. Multiple networks create operational complexity and costs for service providers, thus, converging services to a single infrastructure will reduce costs and complexity.

Platform simplicity and value-added services are objectives for service providers, with the most important goal being to garner revenue from the new services. Both objectives can be achieved via IP-based technology. This transition is evolutionary for service providers with legacy infrastructures.

2.6.2 Customer Benefits

What are the drivers for IP-based services from a customer perspective? For customers, a value-added service describes the capability to extend requirements, such as quality of service for voice, on top of a base service that can be delivered simply, quickly, and for an uncomplicated service cost. Without IP-based services, customers contract for data services via frame relay and voice via PSTN, from different organizations within the service provider company. The provisioning for these services may vary, perhaps depending on a combination of bandwidth availability and effects from manual processes, like configuration errors. In this case, the customer will receive multiple invoices, depending upon the services, and may need to track these multiple invoices (often manually). The result is that the customer can lose track of the costs and impacts of these services; the lack of clarity is a problem.

IP-based services make the process simpler. They permit customers to request service enhancements, for example, data service based on IP, such as a corporate IP-VPN, voice-over-IP, or a videoconferencing-over-IP package via a Web interface. With IP-based services, the customer can receive a bundled service package for data, voice, and videoconferencing. The billing for this package may be at a fixed price, depending upon the bandwidth and SLA that the customer has requested, and the customer will receive a single invoice. Customers can also view service reports via a Web interface in real time and can track the service impact on their business. Finally, the provisioning will be less complex, since it is automated.

2.6.3   Vendor Interest

Vendors are interested in developing a platform that can be used by service providers to build IP-based services. A vendor's goal is to be the market leader in a service provider segment. Service providers can consider market leadership as a factor for vendor selection. Alternatively, as customer requirements drive the service development process, vendors are concerned about offering end-to-end products that will be used to deploy these value-added services. Suggesting product solutions to end customers is also a vendor activity. The desired result is that customers will, in turn, request the service provider to implement these product solutions and put them into a service package.

2.6.4   Service Examples

IP-based service examples include *LAN connection-over-IP;* corporate IP-VPNs; metro Ethernet-access services like *Ethernet to the business* (ETTB) or *Ethernet to the home* (ETTH); Internet access with managed firewall for security; and remote access for telecommuting developed on top of a corporate IP-VPN. LAN connection-over-IP may be a managed router service where the requirements are high bandwidth (155 Mb/sec or more) and any-to-any connectivity. Contrast this service with *LAN connection-over-frame relay,* where the topology is typically a hub and spoke and there is a limitation to available bandwidth, typically not more than 45 Mb/sec. The any-to-any pricing for a LAN connection-over-frame relay can be prohibitive for the customer. (An example of these differences can be found in Chapter 8.)

The customer may order a corporate IP-VPN for a base intranet service. A base service package may be to provide an "any-to-any" connectivity in the form of Layer 3 VPNs. The service is managed by the service provider. The end customer purchases a committed access rate based on IP. The service provider then manages the service, provisions the customer's equipment, ensures Layer 3 connectivity between the customer's VPN sites, and assures that there is no VPN leakage between other customers as part of the security offering.

The customer may request voice-over-IP as an addition to the IP-VPN service. The service provider then adds it to the service bundle. The service provider can offer metro Ethernet services to customers who want to extend their LANs remotely. An example is a gigabit Ethernet service offered on a per port basis; although a metro Ethernet service is Layer 2, it can be offered as an enhancement to IP-based services.

Moving up the value-added chain, service providers can offer Web hosting and managed server packages to customers. The price will depend on bandwidth and hard disk requirements. These services can also be bundled for price simplicity (for the customer).

Finally, a service provider can be a business provider by offering e-commerce services such as *business-to-business* (B2B) or *business-to-consumer* (B2C). B2B exchanges are transactions between companies, such as price negotiation, product specification, and delivery targets. B2B involves supply chain management. Examples of B2B service benefits are reducing paperwork cost and efficient inventory management. B2C applies to any company that sells products or services to consumers. Examples are online retailers like Amazon.com and online services like banking, travel, and health information. B2C is often attributed to the ailing dot-com phenomenon. Figure 2.6 depicts the business provider model.

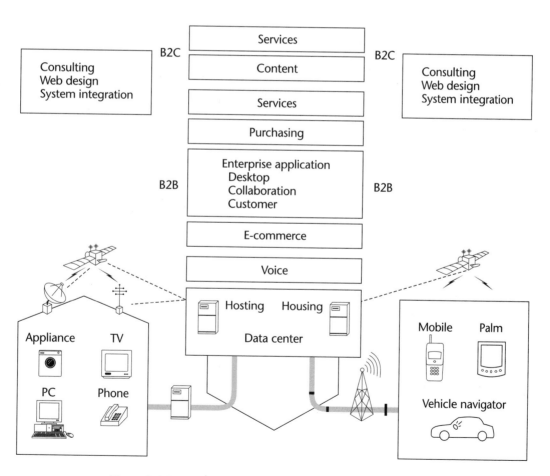

Figure 2.6 Business provider model.

2.7 Greenfield and Incumbent

How do IP-based services apply to a Greenfield service provider? One advantage that a new service provider has is a lack of legacy infrastructure and business engineering processes. The Greenfield player can build an IP-based company from the beginning and does not need to address the transitional, cultural, and organizational issues that an incumbent does.

For an incumbent, IP-based services offer a new revenue opportunity and a replacement for lost revenue in long-distance voice. Incumbents typically have legacy issues, such as multiple networks, but can migrate toward a single-platform, multiple-service infrastructure. The incumbent can transform itself to an IP-based company. We take a look at Greenfield and incumbent challenges in Chapters 3, 4, and 8.

2.8 Chapter Review

The key objectives for a service provider are rapid service introduction and improved quality of service at a lower cost, ultimately resulting in revenue. These objectives can only be achieved using IP-based technology for service development and delivery automation. IP-based technology reduces service layer complexity and its associated operating costs. Finally, customers benefit from IP-based services by having value-added service packages, quicker provisioning cycles, and clear pricing.

As a customer, you can influence the service development process by communicating your business priorities to your provider. As a vendor, you can influence the process by releasing products that are essential to the provider's architecture. As a service provider, you can determine your business direction by listening closely to your customers and clearly communicating requirements and priorities to your vendors.

Greenfield Service Providers: Opportunities and Challenges

This chapter explores Greenfield service providers and their business potential for developing IP-based services. It investigates reasons why a Greenfield service provider would deploy IP-based services, identifies alternative technologies to these services, gives examples of IP-based services and pricing, examines the challenges and competitors for a Greenfield provider, and highlights the benefits for implementing IP-based services. Becoming and remaining competitive drives any company. How can IP-based technology help a Greenfield service provider seize and retain a competitive edge?

3.1 Definition of Greenfield

The term *Greenfield* describes a neophyte service provider as opposed to an established or incumbent service provider. Greenfield service providers are new entrants in the telecommunications market. As alternatives to incumbents, they can provide customers with different service choices, such as applications software for payroll or expenses. These entrants often focus on specific customer segments, such as small to medium enterprises

35

or particular customer geographic locations. An incumbent is likely to concentrate on multiple customer segments, such as large enterprises as well as small to medium enterprises and multiple geographic locations. Service differentiation and the time to market are key factors (but not the only ones) of the success of Greenfield service providers.

Greenfield providers are in the business to offer value-added services. "Value-added" can mean different things to different communities of interest. As an example, in the IT community, value-added is associated with network access, as in a *value-added network* (VAN). For financial analysts and business managers, value-added equates to a financial performance measure, as in *economic value-added* (EVA). In keeping with the theme of this book, value-added describes an enhancement to customer productivity as well as service provider productivity using IP-based technology.

Greenfield service providers may be classified as follows: *competitive local exchange carriers* (CLECs), reseller CLECs, bandwidth brokers, and *x service providers* (xSPs), where x may be application, management, Internet, or a combination of these service provider types. These categories are discussed in the next section. The classification identifies the business emphasis of these various Greenfield service providers, which helps in assessing the applicability of IP-based services to these companies.

3.1.1   CLECs and Reseller CLECs

In the United States, a CLEC competes with incumbent carriers by providing its own network. The availability of *unbundled network elements* (UNEs) is significant to CLECs. A UNE is any facility or equipment used to provision a telecommunications service as well as its features, functions, and capabilities. The *local loop* is the most important UNE available to a CLEC, as it connects the *incumbent local exchange carrier* (ILEC) switches to the ILEC's customers. The local loop provides the capability for CLECs to connect their switches to ILEC switches, thus providing CLECs access to ILEC customers.

Being a reseller is another option for CLECs. Per the Telecommunications Act of 1996, any telecommunications services ILECs offer at retail must be available to CLECs at a wholesale discount. The CLEC avoids an investment in switches, fiber-optic transmission facilities, or collocation arrangements by being a reseller. A CLEC may decide on being a reseller, providing its own switching infrastructure or a combination of both approaches.

Examples of CLECs include U.S.-based cable operators AOL Time Warner, IP Communications, and Birch Telecom. CLECs provide services such as local telephone service, long-distance telephone service, dial-up Internet access, *integrated services digital network* (ISDN), *digital subscriber line* (DSL), and Web hosting.

3.1.2 Bandwidth Brokers

The term *bandwidth broker* has different meanings—for example, it applies to a manager of network usage within a domain that provides reservations for resources and negotiates reservations with other domains. In this context, a bandwidth broker sets a policy for IP-based routers as defined by the Bandwidth Broker Advisory Council (BBAC). This group is part of the Internet2 Initiative to build a test bed for new IP-based quality-of-service (QoS) technologies.

For Greenfield service providers, bandwidth brokers are providers that offer bandwidth as a service. The bandwidth is sold as large connectivity pipes, where the minimum connection may start as T1/E1. Other carriers would be the typical customers for bandwidth brokers. Examples of bandwidth brokers include Qwest and Level 3 Communications.

3.1.3 x Service Providers

This section reflects the development of service providers with a specific business focus for customers. Some of these terms have been used interchangeably, adding to the confusion as to what "x" truly denotes for the customer. In addition to being a particular type of xSP, a Greenfield service provider can also be a combination of these service providers. What are the common xSPs and their business focuses?

Application Service Providers

Application service providers (ASPs) offer customers access to software applications and provide support over the Internet. ASPs are *independent software vendors* (ISVs) that deliver access to applications such as accounting, data warehousing, document management, e-commerce, legal services, medical services, real estate services, retail services, and customer training over the Internet. ASPs permit customers to avoid support overhead by outsourcing the installation and management of an application to an ASP. Some examples of ASPs are Corio for *enterprise resource planning* (ERP), cMeRun for desktop applications like word processors and spreadsheets, NetLedger for accounting and financial applications, and PeopleSoft for collaboration and e-business applications.

Management Service Providers

Management service providers (MSPs) offer network management and application-monitoring services to multiple customers over a network on a subscription basis. MSPs deliver system management services, while ASPs deliver business applications to their customers. Both MSPs and ASPs offer service delivery via an Internet or network connection based on IP.

Examples of MSPs include InteQ, offering 24/7 monitoring and reporting for customer IT infrastructures; and Coradiant, which provisions customers' mission-critical locations and manages, maintains, and monitors those sites from a network operations center. Other MSPs are Internet Security Systems, providing outsourced managed security services such as security assessment, intrusion detection, and life cycle security consulting; and Nuclio Corporation, which offers design, implementation, 24/7 management, monitoring, and Web-based reporting on customers' server-based operations.

MSP customers are enterprises, ASPs, and emerging dot-coms, and they typically own servers, operating systems, and applications. Services include remote application and monitoring support, database backup, maintenance, recovery, and firewalls and other security applications.

Host Service Providers

Host service providers (HSPs) provide space and services to host Web-based content for customers. HSP types are shared, dedicated, and co-location. Shared hosting provides a hosted site or content to a customer that is shared with other sites. Via dedicated hosting, customers access their data from a server that is leased or rented from their service provider. With co-location, a customer selects a server, installs the software, and then places the server in an HSP facility using floor space provided by the HSP. HSPs offer dedicated Web-hosting services. Examples of HSP companies include Verio, Hostway, Interland, and InetU.

Storage Service Providers

Storage service providers (SSPs) offer data storage and management services to customers. The customer is charged based on storage size (in megabytes or terabytes) required for the data. SSPs also provide enhanced services such as backups and data replication. Examples of SSPs include 1Disk, Conxion, EMC, ManagedStorage International, and LiveVault.

Wireless Service Providers and Wireless Internet Service Providers

Wireless service providers (WSPs) and *wireless Internet service providers* (WISPs) offer fixed wireless broadband and mobile Internet connectivity to customers. They can offer broadband connections to their customers directly as opposed to doing so via ILECs or CLECs. This capability is due to the nature of wireless technology itself. IP does play a role in wireless networks. Wireless IP, also known as *cellular digital packet data* (CDPD), is a standard for providing data service over cellular voice networks at speeds of up to 19.2 Kb/sec. For emerging third-generation wireless networks (3G), the use of packet-oriented protocols such as IP are being reviewed for packet data and data rate on demand. Examples of WSPs and WISPs include Nextel Communications, Craig Wireless International, and MKL.Net (RealEthernet wireless service).

Internet Service Providers

Internet service providers (ISPs) provide Internet access to their customers. They purchase bandwidth from *network service providers* (NSPs) that have direct connectivity to the Internet. ISPs sell this bandwidth in discrete chunks ranging from dial-up modem access, ISDN, and DSL to private-line speeds T1/E1 and T3/E3. ISPs in the United States are often segmented into tiers: A tier-one ISP may have either its own national backbone or over a million subscribers. A tier-two ISP may possess its own regional backbone, providing national or state access to its customers, and may have over 50,000 subscribers. Tier-three ISPs constitute the majority; they have less than 50,000 subscribers and offer only local services. Some examples of tier-one ISPs are America Online (AOL), EarthLink, United Online, and Microsoft.

Network Service Providers

Network service providers (NSPs) are often referred to as *backbone providers*. NSPs sell bandwidth and network connectivity to ISPs, ASPs, HSPs, and MSPs. NSPs offer direct access to the Internet as well as to *network access points* (NAPs) and *metropolitan access exchanges* (MAEs). Examples of NSPs include Sprint, UUNET (Worldcom), Genuity, Level 3 Communications, Qwest, Telia, and AT&T.

Other Service Providers

E-commerce service providers permit companies to sell products and services over the Internet and to accept payments via online credit card authorization. Amazon.com is an example of an e-commerce service provider.

   Content service providers (CSPs) offer data and information that is available via a Web server. An example is Streetmail.

   Gaming service providers (GSPs) provide online gaming services. An example is Sega Online.

   Vertical service providers (VSPs) offer industry-specific application hosting to customers in a specific vertical market, such as health care, manufacturing, financial service, or retailing. A VSP is a type of ASP that offers customers the ability to use Internet technologies and applications without the customer requiring know-how or resources. For example, a retailer might contract with a VSP to configure and administer its online shopping cart as well as its inventory and payment-processing applications. The customer thus avoids hiring its own administrators to do this service. Examples of VSPs include BlueStep for Web-based collaboration and content publishing services; Dorado.com, which focuses on the mortgage industry; Invesmart for Internet-based retirement financial services; and Novopoint, which provides virtual exchange for food ingredients like sugar, baking products, and so on.

3.1.4 Putting the Alphabet Soup Together

The common characteristic of these various service provider environments is an emphasis on service and service delivery via IP-based technology. The service can be Web hosting, using an IP-based network to provide data backup and archiving, or offering Internet access and services such as email, domain names, or an e-commerce portal for the sale of goods. The potential for being innovative and seizing the competitive edge is great for Greenfield service providers; examining this potential is the focus of the following sections.

3.2 Business Aspects

In today's business environment, developing and provisioning a service requires that it generate revenue. This fact becomes even more apparent in a high-tech industry. Good technology is insufficient in itself to create a successful company. In this section, we look at the business aspects for developing and provisioning IP-based services within a Greenfield service provider environment.

As the approaches for a marketing plan can vary between companies, we highlight key factors associated with a marketing plan, such as customer, vendor, service provider interaction, services, packaging, and pricing examples. We also examine a general methodology in assessing the requirement of IP-based services. Although there are variations for cost justification within companies, we classify some approaches to assessing the fiscal impact of IP-based technology on a Greenfield service provider's budget and offer examples of services and pricing. (Technical implementation scenarios are examined in Chapters 5 and 6.)

3.2.1 Marketing Plan

A marketing plan is important to every company's success. A first-rate IP-based service is not in itself enough for a Greenfield service provider unless it is marketed well. In fact, marketing can make or break a good service. This section examines a marketing plan outline for a Greenfield service provider and assumes that a market study (research) has been done for input to the market plan. The research confirms the service niche, answering the questions, Is there a need for the new service?, and What company types and market segments will benefit from this new service?

A marketing plan consists of the following sections:

Plan summary

Situational review

Strategic opportunities and threats

Goals

Strategy

Budget

Controls

Each of these components is discussed a bit more in the following pages.

Plan Summary

The marketing plan commences with a summary. This part is usually written last, since it summarizes the other sections. A well-written summary is important, as it may be the only section read by external parties such as bankers and venture capitalists when the company is requesting funding support.

Situational Review

The situational review identifies the competitive landscape and may consist of other subsections such as the market, customer order process, and competition.

- *Market subsection:* Identifies the overall market size for IP-based services, as well as the characteristics and buying patterns of customers for this type of service. Being specific about the quantity of businesses that exist under the target market, the amount of potential buyers, and why these buyers would contract for this new IP-based service are the focuses of this subsection.
- *Customer order process subsection:* A high-level view of how customers will contract for the service and interact with the Greenfield service provider. Will the customers use a Web interface for ordering the service? Fault reporting, billing, and service-level reporting may be addressed in this subsection.
- *Competition subsection:* Identifies competitors and states why the new IP-based service is different. Specifies how much of the market the Greenfield service provider intends to capture, either as a percentage of the target market or the number of customers.

Strategic Opportunities and Threats

This section is what is commonly termed in marketing language as *SWOT,* or *strengths, weaknesses, opportunities,* and *threats.* The Greenfield service provider analyzes the competition and its own IP-based service offering in depth. Performing a SWOT analysis is the output for this section. Such an analysis identifies a point-counterpoint description of strengths and weaknesses, and the results are integrated into this section. An example is offering an IP-based service with differentiation for voice and data, for an additional cost. It is a value-added service to a basic IP-VPN for data only. The additional revenue is a strength for the Greenfield service provider. The weakness in the positioning may be that other providers offering free or cheap service may be able to counter with a lower price.

Goals

Marketing goals identify the number of expected customers, market share, and gross profit. Other goals may be new IP-based service awareness and brand awareness. An example of market goals may be as follows:

1. Greenfield service provider's basic IP-VPN service price at 56 Kb/sec per month/per site is $200; the company's goal is $250,000 gross profit in planning year one.
2. Capture 5% of the target market or 10,000 customers during planning year one.
3. Generate sales revenue of $1 million in year one and a monthly recurring revenue stream of $200,000 per month by the end of year one.
4. Conduct a wide-scale advertising program to build new IP-VPN service awareness and to gain additional customers.
5. Expand sales channel potential by 5% monthly.
6. Increase average ticket size to $200 per IP-VPN site by incrementally selling value-added services such as voice, videoconferencing, and higher-speed connections.

Strategy

The marketing strategy is the most detailed section of the marketing plan and determines the marketing budget. The marketing strategy may consist of the following subsections: target market, positioning, product, service, price, method to contract new customers, promotion, and advertising.

- *Target market subsection:* Describes the niche that the Greenfield service provider will be marketing to.
- *Positioning subsection:* Describes how the Greenfield service provider will position the new IP-based service in the market, such as value-added with quality of service and a premium price.
- *Product subsection:* Describes the IP-based services that the provider will sell. Examples are IP-VPN service, Web hosting, and e-commerce portal management.

- *Service subsection:* Describes how the Greenfield service provider will interact with the customers in terms of service levels.
- *Price subsection:* Identifies the pricing schedule for the new service. The unit and frequency of billing is defined under price (e.g., per account, per month).
- *Method to contract new customers subsection:* Provides more details to the situational review in terms of signing up new customers. A discussion of the sales force and their role in signing up customers is included.
- *Promotion subsection:* Identifies *how* the Greenfield service provider will promote its new IP-based service.
- *Advertising subsection:* Describes *where* the Greenfield service provider will promote its new IP-based service and outlines the marketing campaign.

Budget

The highlights of the spending plan are described in this section. A complete marketing budget is inserted as an appendix to the marketing plan. The metrics of the spending plan are discussed in the marketing budget (e.g., spending as linked to percentage of sales).

Controls

This section describes methods to assure that execution of the marketing budget is managed—for example, spending within the budget. An example of a market control statement would be that the Greenfield service provider will monitor sales and performance on a monthly basis. The monthly budget may be used as a tool for monitoring.

From the marketing plan, the Greenfield service provider is ready to examine requirements, customers, and vendors more closely. The marketing plan provides the road map for these new IP-based services. The next sections identify customer and vendor requirements and further highlight a feedback loop between customers, Greenfield service providers, and vendors.

3.2.2 Customer Profile and Requirements

What type of customer purchases services from a Greenfield service provider? On a macro-level potential, Greenfield service provider customers can be from the small-to-medium enterprise sector. Large enterprises tend to contract with established service providers, particularly incumbents. Name recognition and the fact that large enterprises are most risk-averse when it comes to trying out a new provider are examples of why large companies lean toward incumbents for service.

Greenfield service provider customers are more open to an alternative provider. Some of these customers do not have the know-how and/or resources to manage services such as Web hosting, e-commerce portals, IP-VPN, Internet access, and so on and look for opportunities to outsource these tasks. Thus, an opportunity exists for Greenfield service providers to tap into this set of customers.

Greenfield service provider customers require the following:

- *Service simplicity and transparency,* meaning that if a service is managed, the service should not be complex for the customer, and it should be simple to order. Transparency applies to the service billing. The bill should be easy to understand.
- *End-to-end service ownership,* meaning that the service provider owns the SLA and its deliverables for the customer. Specifically, the service provider avoids third-party dependencies for end-to-end service ownership or, if such a dependency exists, this is transparent to the customer. An example of such a dependency is subcontracting to another service party for long-distance service.
- *Providing solutions that decrease total cost of ownership* for the customer. This factor affects the customer's IT infrastructure purchase decision for hardware and telecommunications system, as well as administering the IT infrastructure. The service provider has an opportunity to target services and solutions that will aid in decreasing such costs for the customer. Customers are often pressured to manage these cost structures within their own companies.
- *Secure and resilient services,* meaning that services, whether IP-VPN or server co-location, should not violate customer data integrity or application availability.
- *Risk reduction of operational and catastrophic failures;* this is a subset of the previous point, in that the service should be available and operational failures should be transparent to the customer.

To summarize, an opportunity exists for a Greenfield service provider to develop and provision a service that will reduce customer costs, be easy to use, improve resiliency, and enhance service availability. Before examining how IP-based technology can be used to address these customer requirements, let us look at the vendor, or supplier, and its role within a Greenfield service provider environment.

3.2.3   Vendor Profile and Requirements

The vendor, or supplier, profile for Greenfield service providers could be either a new technology entrant or an established vendor for whom positioning emerging products and technology are key strategies. Greenfield service providers tend to be open to innovative solutions or new product introductions, particularly those that are IP-based. This is due to the specific business focus of these providers, such as ASPs, ISPs, e-commerce service providers, and so on, where the use of IP is a base for services and provisioning. Some Greenfield service providers construct and own their own backbone infrastructures to deploy new services. These providers tend to be open to evaluating new technology and products for installation in the backbone.

Vendors for Greenfield service providers must understand the following:

- *Greenfield service provider's business model:* This means that in order for a vendor to position technology and products, the vendor needs to know the business focus of the Greenfield service provider. This fact is certainly not limited to Greenfield service providers. The vendor focus for a Greenfield service provider may differ from that of an incumbent in that Greenfield providers do not have the challenge of dealing with existing infrastructures and business-engineering processes to develop and deploy IP-based services (what is often termed *legacy*).
- *The factors that affect life cycle management* within a Greenfield service provider environment. This is required in order to drive hardware purchase decisions because of the tactical buying behavior of the Greenfield service provider. The vendor needs to understand the compelling aspects that drive IP-based service development and deployment within these Greenfield environments. This information affects product development given the availability of technology required to deliver these products.
- *The business viability of the Greenfield service provider,* so as to assess risk in product development for this provider. This point is related to the first bullet but with an emphasis on due diligence for product development. How long will the Greenfield service provider exist? Are new products targeted only for Greenfield service providers? These questions impact the vendor's business model. On the one hand, Greenfield service providers are apt to evaluate new products earlier than incumbents, thus providing valuable feedback to product development. On the other, the longevity of Greenfield service providers affects strategic partnership decisions between vendors and these providers. It is a sensitive balancing act for both parties.

Summarizing these points, the Greenfield service provider is a potential early adopter of emerging products and technology. The vendor needs to understand the Greenfield service provider's business model in order to assess both risk and opportunity for new product development.

3.2.4 Vendor Selection Process

Determining factors that impact the vendor selection process for Greenfield service providers is the next step toward IP-based service development and deployment. What are the recommended strategies? Single vendor? Multiple vendors? What are the pros and cons? A Greenfield service provider's requirements of a vendor are similar to customer requirements: products and solutions that contribute to the provider's business and reduce cost; that reduce operational and catastrophic failures; and that are secure and resilient. The Greenfield service provider selects a vendor strategy that defines the relationship between the provider and the vendor.

After agreement on a vendor strategy, the Greenfield service provider launches a process called a *request for information* (RFI) to solicit information from various suppliers about product availability, technology availability, future developments, business model, reference customers, and so on. This process can run parallel to determining a vendor strategy. The vendor strategy and RFI constitute the vendor selection process.

Vendor Strategy

Vendor strategy is characterized by the approach a provider will have toward suppliers. This translates to adopting either a single-vendor or a multiple-vendor strategy. A single-vendor strategy means that the Greenfield service provider works with only one vendor for its products and solutions. The benefit of this approach is a reduction in managing multiple suppliers that can be complex if not handled carefully. Examples of complexity include platform interoperability assurance and finger pointing among vendors when interoperability problems arise. Another benefit is that the supplier and service provider can develop a closer relationship that contributes to both product and service development. A drawback to the single-vendor strategy is the dependence upon only one supplier: What is the longevity of the supplier? What happens if the supplier goes out of business? Does the product implement a vendor-proprietary solution that prohibits platform interoperability should this become a requirement for the service provider? Another drawback can be product pricing: Is the vendor offering competitive product pricing? Or is the vendor taking advantage of the single-vendor relationship to inflate their prices?

A multiple-vendor strategy means that the Greenfield service provider will work with more than one vendor for its products and solutions. The benefit of this approach is that the key risk associated with a single-vendor strategy—business longevity—is minimized. A drawback might be the complexity of working with multiple vendors to assure platform interoperability. Another drawback might be that vendors are apprehensive in sharing nondisclosure information because of the relationship the Greenfield service provider has with potential competition. This information may impact the service provider's business model as it addresses future product development strategies and directions. What changes in the network infrastructure or applications does the Greenfield service provider need to consider, given the direction of product and technology development? Table 3.1 summarizes the pros and cons of single-vendor versus multiple-vendor strategies.

Once the Greenfield service provider has decided on its vendor strategy, the vendor selection process commences with an RFI. The RFI can provide valuable information, as it is an indication of what is available in the supplier market.

Request for Information (RFI)

The Greenfield service provider indicates in its RFI the problem and service opportunity it wishes to solve. Once it receives responses, it reviews and prioritizes them. Factors that affect the prioritization may be whether or not the supplier is a market leader, applicability of products to solutions and services, customer references, network management solutions, technology and product maturity and availability, pricing, platform interoperability, support of open standards, and so on. Vendor selection within a Greenfield service provider organization may be quicker than selecting a vendor within an incumbent environment. This is due largely to the legacy infrastructure factor that an incumbent must consider as part of its vendor selection process. (Incumbent-related issues are discussed in Chapter 4.)

To summarize the vendor selection process for Greenfield service providers: Deciding on a vendor strategy is the first step; launching an RFI is the second step; evaluating and prioritizing the RFI results, and assuring that there is a fit in the service provider's business model concludes the steps.

3.2.5 Feedback Loop

Identifying a feedback loop between customers, vendors, and Greenfield service providers is possible from the previous sections. The feedback loop confirms the key interactions that contribute to product and service

Table 3.1   Single-vendor versus multiple-vendor strategies.

Single-Vendor Pros	Multiple-Vendor Pros
Avoids complexity of managing multiple vendors	Avoids dependency on single vendor
Facilitates relationship for product and service development	Encourages platform interoperability
Dependent on vendor for fair product pricing	Can use relationship with other vendors to manipulate product offering and pricing

development. When taken altogether, customer requirements, vendor understanding, Greenfield service provider goals, and the vendor selection process are interfaces that affect the product's life cycle, the technology availability, and the Greenfield service provider's service life cycle. (These interfaces have been highlighted in Chapter 2 in the context of service creation.) Figure 3.1 depicts this feedback loop between customers, Greenfield service providers, and vendors. Essentially, customers provide requirements to the Greenfield service provider that serve as the base for product and service development. The service provider translates these requirements into an RFI as part of the vendor selection process. Vendors respond with appropriate products and solutions. Examining alternative technologies to IP for service development is the next step for Greenfield service providers.

3.2.6   Alternative Technologies

How does a Greenfield service provider offer services like Web hosting without IP? How does it offer Internet access and Internet-based services without IP? Or an e-commerce portal for selling books? Layer 2 technologies such as frame relay, DSL, ISDN, ATM, and leased lines are used to

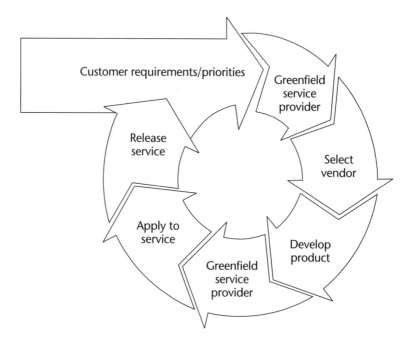

Figure 3.1 Service and product feedback loop.

provide access to the customer from a service provider. Quite a bit of existing services within Greenfield service providers in fact are based on IP.

If the Greenfield service provider is building its backbone infrastructure, the same questions apply. Convergence of voice and data into a packet-based backbone as in an IP-based infrastructure is a reality. Greenfield service providers who intend to build a backbone do not have the complex issues associated with multiple networks and services that incumbents have.

These issues impact provisioning. For service automation, what is the alternative to IP-based technology? How can a customer service order, implementation, billing, and reporting be done without IP-based technology? IP-based technology is pivotal to service automation, as discussed in Chapter 6.

If Greenfield service providers are deploying IP-based services today, then what is the value-added proposition to continue to do so? The question hits at the heart of a Greenfield service provider's existence. The fact that most such providers are deploying IP-based services highlights the market requirements for these services. The real challenge for a Greenfield service provider is avoiding the commoditization of IP-based services. This theme is explored further toward the end of the chapter.

3.3 Service Creation Model

Greenfield service providers can use IP to create services such as corporate VPN, Internet access, Web hosting, e-commerce portals, and so on. Creating value-added enhancements like voice-over-IP or videoconferencing on top of a corporate IP-VPN are key examples of implementing IP for service creation. The Greenfield service provider can develop an IP-based service package like standard IP-VPN with Internet access, adding Web hosting, voice-over-IP, and videoconferencing to extend the service value proposition to customers.

3.4 Service Examples

The discussion's emphasis has been on generic processes such as defining customer requirements, vendor understanding, and the vendor selection process. Using IP-based technology to develop and enhance services and to be and remain competitive is explored in the rest of the chapter. What are IP-based service examples for a Greenfield service provider? In the context of the customer requirements identified earlier, this section gives a few IP-based service examples, such as managed IP-VPN, Web hosting, and an e-commerce portal. This section explores a bit more deeply how these examples satisfy customer requirements and examines the impacts of these services on a Greenfield service provider, such as revenue creation and up-sell potential.

3.4.1 Managed Remote-Access IP-VPN

Cost is a factor affecting the decision of a customer to contract for a VPN service that is IP-based. Customer scenarios include telecommuting and migrating from a frame relay service to an IP-based VPN service. This section looks at a telecommuting example, while the migration from frame relay to IP-VPN is explored in Chapter 4. This example is for a managed service for which the Greenfield service provider manages the customer's infrastructure and routing. In an unmanaged service, the customer manages its own infrastructure and routing. The unmanaged service is focused on bandwidth and bandwidth availability.

For those customers who operate their own private remote-access service, the initial investment is in the remote-access infrastructure such as a *modem pool* or *network access server* (NAS). Telecommuting is a main driver for a company to offer remote access to its employees. Employees are working either from home or from a hotel if traveling on business. Companies experience an increase in recurring long-distance toll charges as the amount of telecommuters increases. To monitor these charges, companies in the United States use a toll-free number. The problem is that these calls are, in fact, not toll-free. The charges are transferred from the telecommuter to the telecommuter's company. Adding other cost factors, such as remote-access infrastructure maintenance, depreciation, and support personnel, to the overall cost of managing this service privately, the recurring cost of administering the service may not be so attractive for a company.

An alternative is to replace the private service with a managed IP-VPN service that is secure, available, and cost-effective. Determining what is attractive also requires that the customer provide information such as how long it will take for the customer to recover costs and the time frame for a return on investment. These numbers vary and may depend on such factors as current amount of telecommuters, projected amount of telecommuters, number of simultaneous telecommuters online, company network topology and bandwidth usage, call hours by type (e.g., local/domestic, etc.) over a period of a month and per telecommuter, and finally a description of the customer remote-access network infrastructure.

In determining whether or not a managed remote-access IP-VPN service is an attractive alternative to the customer's private remote-access service, a Greenfield service provider may determine a basic return-on-investment comparison. An example is a company with 500 employees. Three hundred of these employees work from home (for a mix of local and toll calls), 30 hours per month per employee. Two hundred of these employees require access when traveling (use of a toll-free number and international calls averaging 25 cents/minute), 10 hours per month per employee. There are five branches connected via frame relay to corporate headquarters. Each branch administers its own modem pool. The company is considering a managed IP-VPN service available in all five sites in preparation for a site-to-site VPN. DSL will be used as the access transport from these sites to the Greenfield service provider's location.

The company has been paying approximately $65,388 per month to operate its private remote-access network. A managed remote-access IP-VPN service (basic no-service differentiation) may be priced at $50 per month per employee, or $25,000 per month, representing a savings of $30,388 per month, or approximately 47%. An initial investment of $45,000 can be recovered in three months. This new service builds the foundation for a future site-to-site, managed IP-VPN service that extends beyond remote access. Table 3.2 summarizes the comparison between a managed IP-VPN service (remote access) and a privately administered corporate service.

This is an example of the type of interaction between a Greenfield service provider and its customer. There are other variables that impact the return-on-investment calculation, such as the monthly charge for the managed remote-access IP-VPN service. The example shows that the monthly telecommunication costs dominate the monthly remote-access costs for a customer. These costs can be attributed to the margin that exists between the managed IP-VPN access charges and the premium that can be assessed for managed IP-VPN services. The private remote-access support represents a significant recurring charge for the customer. The opportunity for a Greenfield service provider to offer a managed service is great. Even more attractive for both the customer and the provider are the benefits from a managed IP-based service.

In the context of customer requirements, cost reduction is certainly possible with a managed IP-based service, as demonstrated in the return-on-investment example. For the Greenfield service provider, this represents a new revenue creation opportunity. The security requirement can be met via the implementation of a firewall and other similar devices by the Greenfield service provider. Understanding recurring costs of the customer is key to demonstrating the financial viability of a managed IP-VPN service within the customer environment.

3.4.2 Web Hosting

Web hosting is another example of an IP-based service. This section looks at a specific implementation of this service, called *dedicated Web hosting*. A Greenfield service provider offers customers a dedicated server or multiple servers, depending on the customer requirements, as well as dedicated bandwidth. The provider also offers performance guarantees. The service

Table 3.2   Cost comparison for remote-access IP-VPN service—in-house versus managed by a service provider.

	Administered In-House	Managed by Service Provider
Total telecommuters	500	500
Local usage (hours/month)	1000	1000
Toll-free number/international usage (hours/month)	1000	1000
Monthly telecommunication charges	**$50,000**	**$0**
Customer remote IP-VPN access	$0	$9000
Customer backbone IP-VPN access (T1)	$0	$1000
Monthly connectivity charges	**$0**	**$10,000**
Remote-access equipment maintenance 15 hours/month at $100/hour	$1500	$0
Company in-house support 15 minutes per user per month at $100/hour	$12,500	$0
RAS equipment depreciation (Five 50-port RAS servers purchased at $50,000, fully depreciated over 36 months)	$1388	$0
IP-VPN remote access ($50/user)	$0	$25,000
Monthly infrastructure charge	**$15,388**	**$25,000**
Total monthly cost	**$65,388**	**$35,000**
Savings per month		**$30,388, or 47%**
Months to recover investment		**3**

target is small to medium enterprises that lack a staff to manage their servers. A managed Web-hosting service can address those customers who do not have the resources, specifically in-house know-how to administer and manage servers. Bandwidth, space, customer service, reliability, upgrade options, speed, and price all impact a customer's decision to select a Greenfield service provider that offers such a service.

- *Bandwidth:* The customer needs to consider the type of connection the Greenfield service provider has to the backbone, such as T1/E1, T3/E3, and so on. If a Greenfield service provider offers a T1 connection to the Internet, this means that it can only permit 1.544 Mb/sec. This bandwidth is dedicated to the customer in this example.

Bandwidth is derived from the amount of disk space required to administer a customer server (e.g., 100 MB).

- *Determining space:* The customer knows what kind of server it requires for the amount of disk space and the amount of files to maintain.
- *Customer service:* The type of support available to the customer, such as 24/7 coverage reachable by phone, email, and fax.
- *Reliability:* This can be provided by server backup options in case of failure. The Greenfield service provider also provides a report displaying server uptime.
- *Upgrade options:* If a customer environment is growing, a Greenfield service provider may offer upgrade options to accommodate this growth.
- *Speed:* This is associated with the server. Customers want to ensure that data access is not slow. Bandwidth does impact data access, but if the server speed is slow, the customer will experience slow response times when surfing for information. Testing the site permits customers to confirm service performance.
- *Price:* Pricing for managed Web-hosting services that are dedicated can vary. Variables include bandwidth, server infrastructure, and the SLA package. Greenfield service providers that are new in offering this service tend to price low so as to build up their customer base. Thus, a lower price does not necessarily mean that the service is substandard. Conversely, a higher price may reflect service add-ons such as VPN management or email.

A Greenfield service provider interested in offering managed Web hosting requires the resources to do so. These resources are people and the infrastructure. There are host service providers (HSPs) whose main business focus is Web hosting as a service. It is also possible for a Greenfield service provider such as an ISP to offer Web hosting as a value-added service. There are customers requiring such services, and in the context of cost reduction within a customer IT infrastructure, Web hosting is a revenue-generating opportunity for Greenfield service providers.

3.4.3　E-commerce Portal

E-commerce by definition is selling or buying something electronically. This relationship can be between businesses, commonly called *business-to-business* (B2B), or between a business and a consumer, referred to as *business-to-consumer* (B2C). In B2B, the relationship is among vendors, distributors, and other businesses. These groups are further segmented into verticals and horizontals. *Verticals* are B2B sites that are focused on a specific industry, such as retail. *Horizontals* are sites that provide products, goods, and materials that are not dedicated to a particular industry. Retailers are typically B2C companies.

The Greenfield service provider has an opportunity to offer a managed e-commerce portal service. The target customer could be from a small to medium enterprise that has accepted the potential for doing business over the Internet but lacks both the know-how and infrastructure to do so. In a managed Web service, the scope is often limited to such features as quantity of email accounts, file transfers, and so on. Providing a managed e-commerce portal service means offering an online store or commerce-enabled Web site where goods and services are described and can be selected by the customer (the enterprise company's customer).

The Greenfield service provider offers an electronic payment capability, which means the online processing of credit cards. This may require an agreement between the service provider and the enterprise customer releasing the provider from liability due to credit card fraud. The portal includes an electronic order and shipment tracking feature. The enterprise customer is able to track orders and shipment of goods to its own customers. Customer service is perhaps a call center managed by either the enterprise customer or a third party.

For its managed service, the Greenfield service provider offers service guarantees, such as portal availability and server performance, to the enterprise customer. These guarantees are translated into an SLA. This service is similar to Web hosting, with the exception that it is focused on e-commerce portal management. The same options available for managed Web hosting, like a shared, dedicated, and co-located server, are also available for e-commerce portal management.

An opportunity exists for a Greenfield service provider to offer this IP-based service to customers requiring a managed e-commerce portal service. It can be an enhancement to an existing, managed Web-hosting service and can help the customer reduce overall costs by lowering or avoiding IT infrastructure costs and in-house support costs.

3.5 Service Packaging and Pricing

The IP-based service examples of managed remote IP-VPN, managed dedicated Web hosting, and managed e-commerce portals have the potential to generate new revenue for Greenfield service providers. More important is that these services also provide solutions for customers in terms of cost reduction of IT infrastructure. Applying return on investment to compare the potential between the new IP-based services and a customer's private implementation is a step toward calculating the benefit of such services for the customer. Service pricing and packaging is another step for the Greenfield service provider. The following examples apply to the services that have been presented in this chapter and serve to guide the Greenfield service provider in pricing and packaging. As these are managed services, the service packages can be bundled. (Service pricing and packaging are part of the marketing plan.)

3.5.1 Managed Remote-Access IP-VPN

A base, managed remote-access IP-VPN service considers factors such as bandwidth access, customer equipment, and service level for pricing. One approach is to define a base IP-VPN remote-access service and offer value-added enhancements on top of it. The value-added enhancements result in a premium service classification, for an increase in pricing. An example is to offer an "always on" access via DSL to a customer's VPN and include Internet access. The DSL access provides downstream speeds for up to 1.5 Mb/sec and upstream speeds of up to 128 Kb/sec. This access is connected to the customer's home, as the customer is a corporate telecommuter. The customer receives an IP address, 15 MB of personal Web space, 10 email accounts, 25 hours of dial-up access per month when traveling, and 24/7 customer support. The Greenfield service provider also provides the equipment for the customer's premises. The pricing for DSL and managed CPE may be approximately $50 per month. Add $15 for the 25 hours of dial-up access for a total of $75 per month per user at a customer enterprise.

A service enhancement such as videoconferencing may be added to this base remote-access IP-VPN service. A Greenfield service provider hosts videoconferencing facilities on its premises and offers the software to the customer. The service is available via a Web interface. The customer's personal computer is equipped with a camera, and the customer can then set up and manage a videoconference with a Web-based management tool on demand and as long as it wants. With this enhancement, the Greenfield service provider can upgrade bandwidth to customer locations for customers subscribing to this service. The provider offers the service at a fixed fee of $400 per customer site with unlimited users at that location. IP-based videoconferencing can help the customer manage the costs associated with travel. With it, meetings and training can be conducted remotely.

The Greenfield service provider can offer managed remote-access IP-VPN and IP-based videoconferencing as bundled services. Bundled options may have discounts based on quantity of customers, customer locations, bandwidth, service levels, and contract duration. A customer may ask the Greenfield service provider about the availability of bundled options. Table 3.3 depicts the pricing for the managed remote-access IP-VPN service and the IP-based videoconference enhancement.

The managed remote-access IP-VPN service and IP-based videoconferencing enhancement provide solutions to the customer that reduces IT infrastructure and support costs and creates efficiency in the work

Table 3.3   Pricing for enhanced services.

Managed Remote-Access IP-VPN	IP-Based Videoconferencing
DSL access; downstream speeds of up to 1.5 Mb/sec and upstream speeds of up to 128 Kb/sec; managed CPE; 24/7 customer care	IP-based videoconferencing
IP address; 15 MB of personal Web space; 10 email accounts; 25 hours of dial-up access per month	Managed videoconferencing facilities; user software; on-demand videoconferencing; unlimited usage and connection; 24/7 customer care
Price: $75 per month per user	Price: $400 per month per site, unlimited users

environment. With an innovative IP-VPN service enhancement such as IP-based videoconferencing, customers can improve contact with telecommuters, provide e-learning, hold project meetings and design reviews, and so on. The benefits for a Greenfield service provider are the creation of service relationships that foster the development of value-added services and, of course, the creation of revenue.

3.5.2   Managed Dedicated Web Hosting

Server capacity, server speed, and bandwidth requirements are key components to pricing for a managed, dedicated Web-hosting service. A Greenfield service provider may offer a customer the option of dedicated bandwidth or paying per gigabyte of data transfer, to include the ability to burst to additional bandwidth. A basic server package may include a server with 64 megabytes of memory, hard drive with 8.4 GB of capacity, LAN connection card for Ethernet or fast Ethernet (10/100 network interface card), floppy drive, specified bandwidth option, and an operating system that supports Web server, file transfer, email, and domain name server capabilities. The service can include options for additional services, such as daily backups and installation of customer-provided software. Other options available to the customer may be more memory, faster central processing unit (CPU), and tape drive.

The pricing for the basic dedicated server package includes a one-time setup fee and a monthly fee. The price will vary according to the dedicated bandwidth required by the customer. For example, at 56 Kb/sec, the setup fee may be $300 and the monthly charge $100. The customer avoids purchasing the infrastructure and having to hire dedicated personnel to manage the server, so the price is therefore attractive. Table 3.4 depicts an example of managed, dedicated Web-hosting pricing and packaging for a basic offering. This pricing is for dedicated bandwidth and includes 24/7 customer care.

Table 3.4 Pricing for managed, dedicated Web-hosting service.

Bandwidth (Kb/sec)	Setup	Monthly Cost
56	$300	$100
128	$300	$115
256	$300	$145
768	$340	$550
1536 (T1)	$340	$900
2 T1	$450	$1600
3 T1	$450	$2400
4 T1	$450	$3200
5 T1	$450	$4000
6 T1	$450	$5000

An attraction for customers is that premium service including additional bandwidth can be offered with *step pricing*. This means paying incrementally for more value-added service options. The Greenfield service provider benefits from this approach, since it can offer more service enhancements and thus gain revenue. The key for the service provider is packaging the service. What is the basic package for a managed, dedicated Web-hosting service? What is the premium package? What are the options? What is the time frame to provision these services and options?

3.5.3 Managed E-commerce Portal

Managed e-commerce portal service may vary depending on whether or not the customer has limited products, multiple products, or unlimited products to sell electronically. These factors impact server capacity requirements. The amount of traffic that the customer requires for the e-commerce portal also affects the service pricing. For a managed online store or a commerce-enabled Web site that is administered by a Greenfield service provider, the service can be packaged to reflect the number of products—for example, standard, premium, and premium-plus.

All services may include database software, security software, online credit card billing and ordering software, online reporting, one static IP address, multimedia application support, Web control panel with individual customer password, and so on. The Greenfield service provider may offer 24/7 customer care, service-level guarantees for portal availability,

Table 3.5   Pricing for managed e-commerce portals.

Standard	Premium	Premium-Plus
750 MB of Web space Up to 10 GB of Web traffic 50 email accounts Server choice Secure area for payments and back-office support	750 MB of Web space Up to 25 GB of Web traffic 90 email accounts Server choice Secure area for payments and back-office support Online catalog Shopping cart	750 MB of Web space Up to 30 GB of Web traffic 120 email accounts Server choice Secure area for payments and back-office support Online catalog Shopping cart
Setup: $50 Monthly fee: $35	Setup: $55 Monthly fee: $40	Setup: $60 Monthly fee: $45

throughput (pages come up quickly), and daily backups. For customers with limited products or who wish to offer a pay-as-you-view service, the standard service would be appropriate.

An example of a standard package is to offer 750 MB of Web space, up to 10 GB of Web traffic, 50 email accounts, server choice, secure area for payments, and back office support. The customer pays a one-time setup fee of $50, then $35 per month. Table 3.5 depicts examples of packaging for standard, premium, and premium-plus services for managed e-commerce portals.

Greenfield service providers can offer a managed e-commerce portal service as part of their IP-based service portfolio. This service is an extension of the managed Web-hosting service. For customers needing to use the Internet for selling and buying goods and lacking the IT infrastructure to do so, managed e-commerce portal service provides a solution. The customer can focus on its core business and use the Internet to extend its business reach beyond geographic borders. Greenfield service providers need to measure the value of this service to its customers. Are customers generating revenue by using this service? What is the value of this service to the customer's business? Answers to such questions serve as input to help develop additional value-added services based on IP.

3.6 What Are the Challenges?

The key challenge for a Greenfield service provider is service differentiation. Specifically, Greenfield service providers need to work with customers and vendors to develop value-added services based on IP. This means looking at opportunities to enhance offerings such as IP-VPN by adding voice-over-IP, videoconferencing, and so on. A Greenfield service provider that focuses a business on a specific niche such as Web hosting may face challenges as this market becomes saturated with other HSPs. This applies to any service provider. Commoditization of IP-based services is another challenge to a Greenfield service provider; it means that service differentiation no longer exists due to the saturation of other service providers in the market. Then the only differentiation is price.

To counter these challenges, Greenfield service providers can emphasize value-added IP-based services. The value proposition for the customer, such as reducing total cost of infrastructure ownership or enhancing customer revenue, is critical to the success of service providers. IP-based services and enhancements that address customer requirements are key to revenue generation for Greenfield service providers.

3.7 Who Is the Competition?

Incumbents are the main competitors of Greenfield service providers. They have existing resources like backbone ownership, IT infrastructure, and personnel. Some Greenfield service providers do not own their backbone and are required to lease services from incumbents. This factor can impact end-to-end SLA ownership for a Greenfield service provider customer, since the service level depends on a third party.

Other Greenfield service providers are also competitors. ISPs offer Web-hosting services and are in competition with HSPs. Conversely, HSPs may offer Internet access and so be in competition with ISPs. There is not a lack of competition. The key, however, is being and remaining competitive in terms of IP-based technology.

3.8 Being Competitive in Terms of IP-Based Technology

Provisioning is the key to being competitive in terms of IP-based technology. Greenfield service providers may offer a plethora of IP-based services and enhancements, but without IP-based provisioning, their competitive edge is lost. Think about the impact of a Greenfield service provider that commits to a service being provisioned within 15 minutes or the customer receives a credit. IP-based service provisioning affects the customer's business. A customer that must wait for a service to be provisioned may be incurring costs that this service is to replace. To seize and maintain a competitive edge with IP-based technology, Greenfield service providers can offer both value-added services and a value proposition by automating provisioning. Manual provisioning incurs both errors and delays, thus resulting in customer frustration. IP-based technology is pivotal to the success of both the customer and the Greenfield service provider.

3.9 Chapter Review

Greenfield service providers are certainly in the business of offering IP-based services, whether a managed remote-access IP-VPN, managed Web hosting, or a managed e-commerce portal. Success factors include a good marketing plan, a focus on addressing customer requirements, and using IP to create services as well as automate provisioning. These factors all contribute to being competitive for Greenfield service providers. The role IP plays for incumbents is the subject of the next chapter.

4

Incumbent Service Providers: Opportunities and Challenges

Incumbents have traditionally earned revenue in transporting bits from one location to another. Transporting bits as in voice has become a commodity; long-distance voice revenues have been declining in the U.S. market since the Telecommunications Act of 1996. In order to compensate for this revenue loss, incumbents need to offer value-added services such as corporate virtual private network access with videoconferencing, Internet access, integrated local and long-distance voice, Web hosting, and e-commerce.

Unlike the Greenfield service providers, incumbents are confronted with legacy infrastructures that reflect separate networks and services. They have constructed separate networks that correspond to a specific service, such as a public-switched telephone network (PSTN) for voice, private leased lines, and frame relay and asynchronous transfer mode (ATM) for data services. Each network possesses a management, provisioning, billing, and reporting system that consists of separate operations support systems (OSSs), often managed by different organizations in the company. The challenge for the incumbent is to converge a network like PSTN, based on *time-division multiplexing* (TDM) circuit switching, with a packet-switched network based on IP. (TDM is discussed in Chapter 5.) This chapter identifies the issues associated with a legacy infrastructure and explores the reasons for an incumbent to develop and deploy IP-based services, the most important of which is to be competitive and profitable.

4.1 Definition of Incumbent

Incumbents consist of incumbent local exchange carriers (ILECs), former Bell operating companies often referred to as the *Baby Bells;* traditional American interexchange carriers (IXCs), and post, telephone, and telegraph companies (PTTs). PTTs are government-operated communications companies in other countries. Incumbents have a monopoly in the telecommunications market due to years of existence—for example, ILECs in the United States control an estimated 90% of the access lines. This is significant, since the owner of the access lines generally rules the telecommunications industry: these access lines compose what is termed the *last mile,* or *local loop,* and are used to connect to the end customer, thus representing the greatest revenue source for the service provider. The nearer to the customer, the more complex and diverse the network becomes, since service intelligence like billing and reporting functions is often located at the service provider network edge, and the network edge supports multiple access technologies, such as leased lines, DSL, frame relay, and ATM.

4.2 Business Aspects

For an incumbent, developing and deploying IP-based services have business aspects, such as creating a marketing plan that, among other things, identifies the services to be developed and the packaging and pricing of those services. This section identifies the business aspects as they apply specifically to an incumbent environment—for example, unlike a Greenfield service provider, an incumbent may develop a marketing plan that focuses on entering a market dominated by Greenfield service providers (such as Internet access). Incumbents have the advantage of name recognition over Greenfield service providers, as they have been in the telecommunications market for years; as a result of this name recognition, large enterprises typically are customers of incumbents.

4.2.1 Marketing Plan

In developing and deploying IP-based services, an incumbent's marketing plan focuses on defending local and long-distance voice services as traditional revenue sources, while capturing additional revenues from new IP-based services such as corporate IP-VPN, videoconferencing, voice-over-IP, Web hosting, and e-commerce. For new IP-based services, the focus of the plan is to attack the competitive landscape dominated by Greenfield service providers and to project a new image of being innovative. This image is important because incumbents have been traditionally perceived by customers as slow to develop new services.

Marketing Goals

Examples of marketing goals that an incumbent can develop for basic IP-VPN service with Internet access are as follows:

1. Market basic IP-VPN with Internet access at 256 Kb/sec for a service price of $400 per month per site. The company's goal in planning year one is $450,000 gross profit.
2. Capture 10% of the target market or 20,000 customers during planning year one.
3. Generate sales revenue of $2 million in year one and a monthly recurring revenue stream of $350,000 per month by the end of year one.
4. Conduct a wide-scale advertising program to build new converged IP-VPN and Internet-access service awareness and to gain additional customers.
5. Expand sales channel potential by 10% monthly.
6. Increase average ticket size to $350 per IP-VPN site by up-selling value-added services such as voice, videoconferencing, and higher-speed connections.
7. Defend against competitive encroachment of traditional local and long-distance services by integrating the services into value-added bundles like basic corporate IP-VPN and Internet access with local and long-distance voice services.

Marketing Strategy

An example of an incumbent's marketing strategy is to target both large enterprises and small to medium enterprises as customers for the new IP-based services. The name recognition of an incumbent facilitates the introduction of these new services to large enterprises, which tend to contract with incumbents because of risks associated with Greenfield service providers (e.g., lack of business longevity, and unproven performance).

However, for an incumbent to attack the competitive landscape of Greenfield service providers, it needs to set itself apart from those providers. Rather than a me-too strategy, incumbents can capitalize on innovative image positioning and their own business longevity. This differentiation can result in a value-added proposition for customers translating to services that will address their requirements for cost reduction, offered by service providers who have been (and may be) around longer than the alternative providers. For service positioning, an incumbent can emphasize geographic reach, as incumbents tend to own their own (often national) backbones. Finally, for pricing, an incumbent can stress that the new IP-based services are value-added, not basic voice and data transport. To summarize, a marketing plan for an incumbent service provider needs to highlight such factors as innovative image, business longevity, geographic reach, and the value-added proposition.

4.2.2 Customer Profile and Requirements

Large enterprises tend to be existing customers of incumbents, because alternative providers are rather new in the telecommunications market and because incumbents focus on large enterprises for the substantial revenue opportunities. Small to medium enterprises are also customers of incumbents, but are typically more open to considering an alternative service provider. For incumbents, penetrating the small-to-medium enterprise customer segment with new IP-based services is an opportunity to attack Greenfield service providers. One incumbent marketing strategy is to erode the Greenfield service provider's traditional services, such as Internet access, Web hosting, e-commerce, and so on.

An incumbent's customer requirements are as follows:

- *Value-added services* like corporate IP-VPN with voice, videoconferencing, and Internet access, meaning that the incumbent does not just provide transport for voice and data. These services should all be secure and reliable.
- *Wide geographic reach* for these value-added services is required by large enterprises.
- Value-added services should reduce customer IT infrastructure costs and result in profitability for the customer.
- Customers require flexible pricing and packaging for these value-added services (e.g., bundled services).

To summarize, an incumbent has an opportunity to develop IP-based services that extend geographically and positively impact a customer's business. Exploring the vendor profile and requirements within an incumbent environment is discussed in the next section.

4.2.3 Vendor Profile and Selection

An incumbent's vendor profile emphasis is on being an established rather than a new technology supplier. Incumbents have multiple networks and services that have evolved over a period of many years, and as a result of the existence of these multiple networks, changing vendors can be problematic from a network infrastructure support viewpoint.

Vendors for incumbent service providers need to understand the following:

- The incumbent service provider's business model and the impacts of legacy infrastructure and multiple business engineering on the service provider's business. A vendor can provide products and solutions that may move the various networks to a converged platform to deploy multiple services.
- The IP-based service portfolio that the incumbent intends to develop and deploy so as to position the necessary products required for these new services.

Incumbents, due to their history, tend to have a multiple-vendor strategy and rely on requests for information (RFIs) to obtain information about vendors' product availability, technology availability, future development, customer references, and so on in order to select vendors to provide products and solutions for a new service. Incumbents emphasize the requirement for platform interoperability because of their multiple networks. One approach for an incumbent is to insist that vendors provide platforms that are open and nonproprietary.

To summarize these points, a vendor for an incumbent needs to provide products and solutions that both address legacy infrastructure issues and facilitate the introduction of IP-based services. (Legacy infrastructure issues are discussed later in this chapter.)

4.2.4 Alternative Technologies

The existence of multiple networks in an incumbent service provider's environment prompts a question as to alternatives to IP-based technology. The circuit-switched voice network is TDM-based, and incumbents have transported data over Layer 1 and Layer 2 networks like leased lines, DSL, frame relay, and ATM. The alternative for an incumbent is to continue to provide multiple services over multiple networks. However, as we will see later, this is expensive for the service provider. Incumbents require a solution that reduces the operation expenses associated with maintaining multiple networks: IP-based technology can be used to consolidate multiple services to a single platform and develop value-added services.

4.3 Service Creation Model

Incumbent service providers can develop and deploy IP-based services, such as a corporate IP-VPN with Internet access and Web hosting, and create value-added enhancements to those services, such as voice-over-IP and videoconferencing. Additionally, incumbent service providers can bundle integrated local and long-distance voice into the IP-based service offerings. Capitalizing on bandwidth increases due to value-added services such as videoconferencing or Web hosting provides another revenue opportunity for incumbents, since they can charge more for the bandwidth.

4.4 Service Examples

Two value-added service examples—IP-VPN and managed Web hosting—are discussed in this section to demonstrate the impact of IP-based services on both the customer and the incumbent. The managed IP-VPN service is an alternative to traditional access offerings such as remote access, frame relay, and leased lines. Offering differentiated services such as Internet access and voice will be the focus of the first service example. (The cost savings opportunity for a remote-access service is already pointed out in Chapter 3.) A managed Web-hosting service opportunity for an incumbent serving small to medium enterprises is the focus of the second example. (Chapter 8 offers detailed scenarios for the development of these services.)

4.4.1 Managed IP-VPN

An IP-VPN service can be managed or unmanaged. In an unmanaged IP-VPN service, the customer manages its on-site equipment or router that connects to the service provider network and is responsible for the Layer 3 routing between locations. The service provider essentially offers bandwidth to the customer. This type of customer possesses the technical know-how to manage the network infrastructure.

In a managed IP-VPN service, the network infrastructure that connects the customer network to the service provider network is administered by the service provider (i.e., the customer outsources this responsibility to the service provider). The customer may lack either the know-how or the needs to manage the network and may have pressure to reduce IT infrastructure costs. In the following example, the incumbent offers a managed IP-VPN service to a large enterprise that is national and has points of presence throughout the country; there is a requirement for any-to-any connectivity between all of the customer's locations.

The alternative to a managed IP-VPN service is to use frame relay to transfer customer data between sites. For any-to-any connectivity, a frame relay implementation can be expensive for the customer (this is highlighted in Chapter 8). For customers that have a hub-and-spoke topology—that is, connectivity between a central location and remote locations—frame relay may be an alternative. The value-added proposition for an incumbent service provider is to offer an IP-VPN service that supports differentiated services such as Internet access, voice, and videoconferencing. The customer typically needs to order four access lines to support each of these services, one line for corporate VPN, a second line for

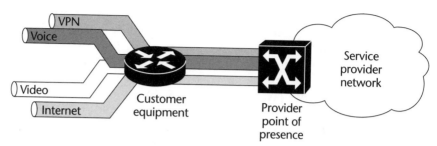

Figure 4.1 Ubiquitous IP plug.

Internet access, a third for voice, and a fourth for videoconferencing. Rather than four different links for these services, an incumbent service provider can offer a single access line that supports them. The incumbent can position this service as a ubiquitous IP plug. (The term *ubiquitous* has been used in the telecommunications industry to describe the universal presence of the telephone network.) This value-added service can potentially result in cost savings for the customer. Figure 4.1 depicts this example.

An example of potential savings is as follows. Assume that the four services below are deployed using four access lines that cost the customer approximately $3200 per month:

8 voice channels (512 with pulse code modulation)

512K VPN access

256K Internet access

128K videoconferencing

The incumbent service provider can offer these services with a single access line at T1/E1 for approximately $1115 per month. This is for access only and represents approximately a 65% savings for the customer. (The managed IP-VPN packaging and pricing is discussed later in this chapter.) The benefit for the incumbent service provider is to gain and retain customers with this service offering.

4.4.2 Managed Web Hosting

An incumbent can offer managed Web-hosting services to small to medium enterprise customers that do not have the resources, people, or IT infrastructure to administer the servers. The services can include a load-balancing option that balances Web traffic across dedicated customer servers so that traffic is evenly distributed among servers. For customers who have multiple dedicated servers that the incumbent manages, this feature impacts server performance such that traffic does not congest a server. The load-server balancing feature can assure that, in the event of either a server or an application failure, the failure is detected and within seconds fail-over to the next available server occurs without service interruption to the customer.

An incumbent can offer managed Web-hosting connectivity options that depend on the network access methods and bandwidth, such as Ethernet, fast Ethernet, gigabit Ethernet, leased lines, and frame relay. The customer identifies the traffic requirements based on the customer applications, and these requirements determine the bandwidth needed to support the Web-hosting service. An incumbent service provider can offer 24/7 coverage for the customer, as well as options such as network management and intrusion detection for servers connected to the Internet. The benefit to the customer for this value-added service is cost reduction and cost avoidance by outsourcing the Web server management to the incumbent service provider. The benefit to the incumbent service provider is additional revenue from the new service.

4.5 Service Packaging and Pricing

This section provides examples of service packaging and pricing for IP-based services. These examples are generic and serve as an overview for an incumbent service provider. Bundled packages are presented here, since the services are managed. The key approach for packaging is service differentiation by offering enhancements to the service that are attractive in price and provide solutions for the customer. To attack a Greenfield service provider, an incumbent service provider needs to emphasize the value-added proposition to the customer, like feature reach, widespread geographic range, business longevity, quick service provisioning, and a guarantee of new value-added services via innovation.

4.5.1 Managed IP-VPN

An incumbent can offer a managed IP-VPN that is site-to-site for a large enterprise; access can range from 56 Kb/sec–64 Kb/sec to T3/E3 via leased lines, DSL, or frame relay. The service includes managing customer on-site equipment (the pricing for the equipment varies depending on the combination of bandwidth and service options needed by the customer). The service has options for Internet access, voice-over-IP, and videoconferencing. Table 4.1 depicts an example of components to consider for managed IP-VPN service pricing and service enhancements.

Service enhancements permit an incumbent service provider to offer a base package like IP-VPN, a premium package with an addition of Internet access, and a premium-plus package that includes IP-VPN, Internet access, voice-over-IP, and videoconferencing. These packages may be bundled to

Table 4.1   Example of components and enhancements for managed
                 IP-VPN pricing.

Managed IP-VPN Components	IP-VPN Service Enhancements
Access method: DSL, frame relay, leased lines Bandwidth: 56 Kb/sec–64 Kb/sec, T1/E1, T3/E3, etc.	Internet access, voice-over-IP, videoconferencing
CPE and features	Can affect choice of CPE
SLA: Emphasis should be on speed for service provisioning.	SLA: Emphasis should be on speed for service enhancements.

the customer and can also include integrated local and long-distance
voice options that are priced according to number of minutes. For example, a basic IP-VPN service may include a certain amount of local and
long-distance voice minutes, a premium IP-VPN may have more local
and long-distance minutes, and the premium-plus IP-VPN may offer even
more local and long-distance minutes.

4.5.2 Managed Dedicated Web Hosting

For managed Web hosting with the load-balancing server feature, price
components include the server type, the bandwidth required for the customer's Web-based traffic, storage requirements for customer data, and additional options such as same-day server backup and data archival. As
with the managed IP-VPN packaging, an incumbent can offer basic, premium, and premium-plus Web-hosting services. A basic Web-hosting service may include server type, appropriate bandwidth, server backup, and
support for Web server, file transfer, email, and domain name server capabilities. A premium Web-hosting service may include the load-balancing
server feature, plus additional server capacity and bandwidth. A premium-
plus Web-hosting service can comprise network management, intrusion
detection, the load-balancing server feature, and additional server capacity and bandwidth.

An incumbent service provider emphasizes value-added service enhancements for its customers. These service enhancements can be bundled to include IP-VPN and local and long-distance voice. The customer
thus receives a comprehensive service package from a single service provider; the potential benefits to the customer are cost reduction and a reduction in the complexity that is associated in dealing with multiple service providers. The incumbent service provider retains the customer by
offering value-added services in bundles that are attractive in price. This is

a single service provider paradigm, and in fact customers may want to contract with multiple service providers for the same reasons that service providers will select a multiple-vendor strategy—that is, not to be dependent on a single provider. The focus of this discussion is how an incumbent can offer IP-based value-added services to customers.

4.6 Legacy Infrastructure

Converging multiple services to a single platform requires an evolutionary strategy for an incumbent that has legacy infrastructure including OSS platforms. One strategy is termed *cap and grow,* which means to maintain existing legacy services such as voice and data over frame relay and grow IP-based services onto a new network infrastructure. This strategy requires that the incumbent build a new network.

For some incumbents, investing in a new network infrastructure may not be possible, so a second strategy is to add features to the legacy infrastructure that supports IP-based services, such as Layer 3 routing capability on ATM switches. This strategy requires the incumbent to maintain the legacy infrastructure with IP-based technology features added to it and integrate features in the OSS platforms to support these IP-based services—for example, network management, configuration management, performance management, and so on. This is complex, since the various OSS platforms may be vendor-proprietary and the business-engineering processes to provision the services are dependent on various incumbent service provider organizations. Additionally, upgrades may be required on the legacy infrastructure to support the IP-based features, and network upgrades can be disruptive if not planned carefully.

A third strategy is to build an IP-based network infrastructure, grow new services on the network, and use the legacy infrastructure (Layer 2 networks like frame relay, Ethernet, and ATM) to tunnel traffic over the IP-based network. This strategy allows the service provider to protect its existing investment while building a packet core that is IP-based. The service provider can trunk current Layer 2 customer traffic like frame relay across the IP-based core network; it is a good strategy for an incumbent service provider that is focused on transport and also means that the customer manages Layer 3 routing (IP) between customer sites.

Figure 4.2 shows multiple services and transport technologies that are common in incumbent service provider companies—such as ISDN, ATM, DSL, leased lines, frame relay, voice, global system for mobile communication (GSM), plain old telephone (POTS), plesiochronous digital hierarchy/synchronous digital hierarchy (PDH/SDH), and wavelength-division multiplexing (WDM) (all are described in Chapters 5 and 7). Service examples include IP-VPN, Internet access, and remote access. These services and technologies are mapped to functions of the incumbent service provider

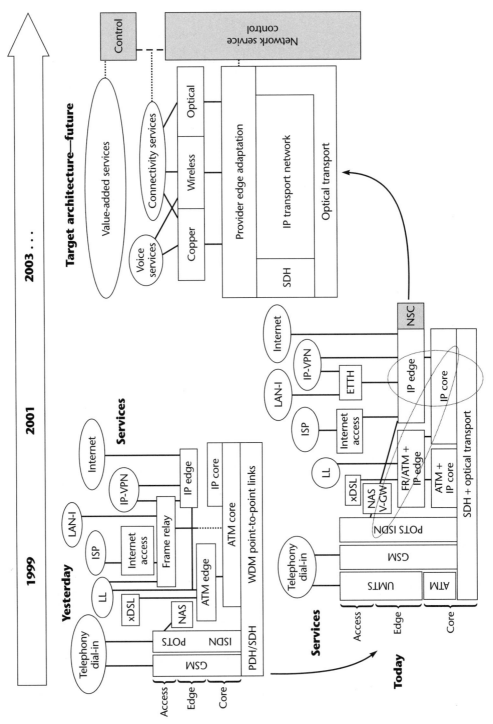

Figure 4.2 Example of evolutionary strategy.

network, such as a core, edge, and access network. Moving from yesterday to today, we see that the optical transport is added to the SONET/SDH core; DSL, frame relay, and ATM are converged to an IP-based edge; remote access (network access server or NAS) connects to an IP-based edge that provides IP-based services such as Internet access, IP-VPN, Ethernet to the home (ETTH), and LAN interconnection for enterprise customers. The emphasis is on evolving multiple services to value-added services based on IP. These strategies permit the incumbent service provider to evolve legacy infrastructure to a packet network based on IP and constitute different approaches to multiple services on a single platform. Figure 4.2 highlights this evolutionary approach for incumbent service providers.

The incumbent service provider has several strategies to address the legacy infrastructure, with an emphasis on migration toward a single platform based on IP. Factors such as operating expenses due to the existence of multiple OSS platforms and the people who administer these platforms can be a liability for legacy infrastructure, as these expenses impact overall profitability.

4.7 What Are the Challenges?

One challenge for an incumbent service provider is to change its business focus from transport only (e.g., voice) to value-added services. As multiple networks collapse to a single platform, the incumbent service provider is confronted with the possibility of downsizing, with the result of job losses. The alternative is not to do anything, but this can result in the loss of customers who then move away from traditional services to IP-based services offered by Greenfield service providers, with a resulting loss of revenue. An incumbent service provider needs to price IP-based services so as to compensate for this loss in revenue from traditional services. By training staff to develop and support IP-based services, an incumbent can address the fear of job loss.

Another challenge is for vendors to offer products and solutions that can facilitate this evolutionary strategy and especially address the complex business-engineering processes associated with managing multiple networks and services. Incumbents are desperate for a solution that will reduce the complexities in managing their legacy infrastructures while evolving their businesses to (1) support multiple services on a single network infrastructure and (2) most importantly, improve service provisioning. Finally, incumbent service providers need to address the cannibalization issues related to introducing new services—it may be necessary to cannibalize existing services in order to develop and deploy new ones. This is part of the marketing strategy, and an incumbent has to decide at which point cannibalization is required for value-added service development.

4.8 Chapter Review

Incumbent service providers have an opportunity to use IP-based technology to reduce their own operating costs by migrating to a single infrastructure and to develop and deploy value-added services quickly to both large enterprises and small to medium enterprises. Incumbents have resources that Greenfield service providers may lack, such as a national backbone network and research labs to evaluate and test new technology. Fostering an image of service innovation and rapidly provisioning the services contribute to a competitive edge for the incumbent service provider. It is most important that these services add value to the customer's business, and incumbent service providers can use IP-based services to do this by offering solutions that enhance the customer's profitability, like IP-VPN and Web hosting.

What is the role of IP-based technology in developing and deploying services? Chapters 5, 6, and 7 discuss the technological details that balance the business aspects of IP-based service development and deployment and give the technical base needed to understand these issues.

IP as a Building Block: Enabling Multiservices

This goal of this chapter is to provide an architectural overview of IP as a building block for enabling multiservices. It first elaborates on what is meant by multiservices, then focuses on IP as a building block for developing services. IP is at Layer 3 of the classic seven-layer open systems interconnection (OSI) communication model (see Figure 5.1). It is necessary to have a discussion regarding the underlying layers (Layers 1 and 2), which provide the infrastructure to build IP networks, in order to understand the issues related to developing IP-based services. The chapter then goes into a technical discussion on various Layer 2 technologies, such as ATM, POS, Ethernet, ADSL, cable, and so on, and topics, such as MPLS, VPNs, traffic engineering, multicast, and so on, that are used today in building IP networks. This is followed by a discussion on how these technologies can help a service provider in creating new services.

5.1 Multiservices

The term *multiservices* has a broad meaning and depending on the context is used to represent several things. In the context of this chapter, this term is used to refer to the following:

- Services that IP uses to deliver data packets: datalink layer services that are independent of Layer 2 technology

- IP-based services like IP-VPN and Internet access
- Application layer services that make use of IP, such as IP telephony, video-on-demand, Web hosting, and so on

5.1.1 Layer 2 Services

Figure 5.1 shows the OSI seven-layer model and the corresponding TCP/IP model. IP is at the network layer and is responsible for delivery of packets in the networks. Data packets are delivered based on the IP address in the packets. The transport layer (TCP) and the application layers depend on IP to deliver packets to the correct destination.

IP depends on the datalink layer (Layer 2) to deliver packets from one hop to the next in the network. (An overview of some Layer 2 technologies is provided later on in this chapter.) Service providers offer a variety of Layer 2 services to their customers, and an IP network can be built using several Layer 2 technologies. Using different aggregation techniques and aggregation devices, it is possible to provide IP service using different Layer 2 technologies.

Figure 5.2 shows some of the Layer 2 networks that are used by service providers to provide IP connectivity. These networks are also referred to as *access networks*. They are used to deliver IP packets from the customer's

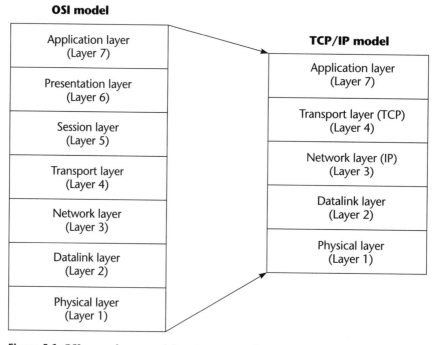

Figure 5.1 OSI seven-layer model and corresponding TCP/IP model.

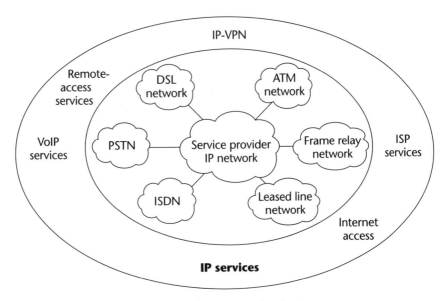

Figure 5.2 IP services using multiple Layer 2 technologies.

premises to the nearest *point of presence* (PoP) of the service provider. The packets then traverse the IP backbone of the service provider to the PoP closest to the destination. From that PoP, the access network is used to deliver the IP packet to the destination.

5.1.2 IP-Based Services

Service providers generally offer several types of IP-based services. The most common among these are VPN services and Internet access. Traditionally, the VPN services were offered using the Layer 2 networks: A group of sites that were part of a VPN were interconnected using a Layer 2 network, and an IP network was built on top of this Layer 2 network. This solution is not scalable because it requires a separate Layer 3 network for each VPN.

Furthermore, it would be even more profitable if the same IP backbone can also be used to deliver other IP-based services, like Internet access. This will help to reduce the number of IP backbones required to deliver services, thereby saving the cost of building and maintaining them.

5.1.3 Application-Layer Services

As seen in Figure 5.1, the application layer depends on the TCP layer, which in turn depends on IP to deliver the packets to the correct destination. In the world of data communication, communication is needed to access or exchange data. Data may be located in a central location or in several different locations. Depending on the nature of the data, and the type of applications that require the data, the *quality-of-service* (QoS) requirements regarding the data communication can vary.

Traditionally, IP networks have provided best-effort services. *Best-effort service* means that the packet may be eventually delivered to the destination, but that there is no guarantee that it will be delivered within a given time period or even delivered at all. IP provided the means for delivering data from a source to one or multiple destinations. The Internet is a classic example of this type of IP network. The transport layer (TCP) provided QoS, such as

- *Guaranteed delivery* in case of packet loss (retransmission)
- *Delivery of packets in correct order* (reordering of packets)
- *End-to-end flow control,* in case of congestion either in the end systems or in the service provider network

Today, best-effort service is no longer enough to meet the QoS requirements of the modern application-layer services. In addition to best-effort, some of the additional requirements are

- *Delivery on time* (low latency)
- *Delivery of packets with minimum loss* (low loss)
- *Delivery of a minimum number of packets* in a given time period (guaranteed bandwidth)
- *Data security*

While the first two requirements can be fulfilled using the transport layer (TCP), the other requirements are dependent on IP and the lower layers used by IP to deliver packets. The QoS offered by IP has a direct relationship to its ability to fulfill the requirements of the application-layer services. QoS refers to the following factors:

Delay

Delay variation

Packet loss

Delay is the amount of time it takes for the packet to reach the destination. *Delay variation* refers to the difference in delay for each packet that is delivered to the same destination. *Packet loss* means that not all packets are delivered to the destination.

Delay depends on the queuing mechanisms used by the network devices to deliver packets when there is congestion in the network. It is possible to compute the minimum delay to deliver a packet from the source and destination based on the information about the physical media and Layer 2 services and the delays in the intermediate nodes in the network. However, network congestion can result in additional delays in the intermediate nodes and increase the end-to-end delay. (*End-to-end delay* refers to the time taken for a packet to be delivered from a source to a destination. It also includes the time taken to retransmit the packet if the packet gets lost in an intermediate node.)

Some of the reasons for packet loss are faults that occur at Layer 2, faults that occur at Layer 1, and network congestion. Faults in Layer 2 (e.g., collision in Ethernet) and Layer 1 (e.g., cyclic redundancy checksum (CRC) errors) can result in packet loss. Network congestion can occur due to lack of resources, like memory to buffer incoming packets and when the sum of the bandwidth of all the incoming interfaces exceeds the bandwidth of the outgoing interface. IP depends on the QoS mechanisms of the lower layers in providing this QoS to the application-layer services.

Figure 5.3 shows some of the common application services that depend on the IP network for data delivery. These applications include voice (telephony), videostreaming, database servers, Web servers, and so on. Some of the applications, like telephony and videostreaming, are time-sensitive applications and require low latency. Others, like database access, are sensitive to packet loss. *Multiservices* in this context refer to QoS requirements of the application-layer services that make use of the IP-based services. The IP network must be capable of satisfying or meeting the QoS requirements of all the application services.

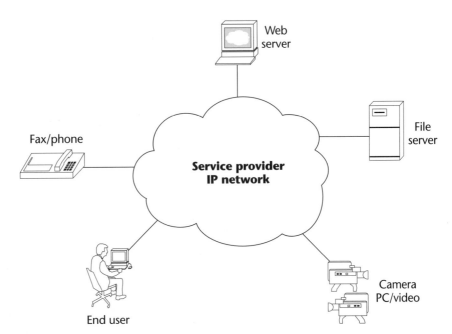

Figure 5.3 Application services that make use of the IP network.

5.2 Architectural Overview

In this section, we provide an overview of the architecture of the service provider IP network. This architecture will make a network stable and also scalable. As discussed in Section 5.1, this IP network must also be capable of delivering multiservices.

Figure 5.4 depicts an architectural overview of the network. The network is built in three layers: core, edge, and access. The *core network* is responsible for providing connectivity between the edge nodes. The *edge network* provides the intelligence that is required to support multiservices. The *access network* provides connectivity between the edge nodes and customer sites.

5.2.1 Core

The core network provides connectivity between the various edge nodes. It should be independent of the customer network in the sense that irrespective of the number of *customer-premises equipment* (CPE) devices that are attached to the service provider's network, the size of the routing

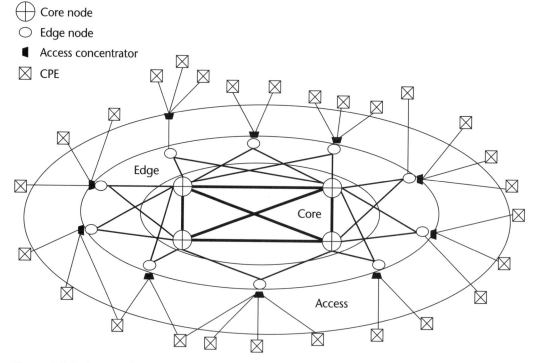

Figure 5.4 Architectural overview of an IP network.

tables of the core network should not be affected. Also, any instability in the customer network should not affect the core network.

5.2.2 Edge

The edge of the service provider network is used to terminate the Layer 2 connection from the CPE devices. The edge device must be capable of connecting to several CPE devices: this capability will help the service provider to build scalable networks and will help reduce the costs of the network infrastructure. The edge device plays an important role, because most of the intelligence that is required to create and provide IP services resides within it. It must also be able to augment the QoS requirements of the IP-based services when the CPE device or access network is not capable of providing them.

The edge device must be a powerful device in terms of its ability to

- Examine the IP packets and switch them based on the packet contents. This decision could be based on the IP address or the QoS requirements of the IP packet.
- Have memory to maintain routing information
- Implement traffic-shaping, policing, and queuing mechanisms to satisfy the QoS requirements

5.2.3 Access

The access part of the network, as the word implies, provides access to the service provider network. Typically, the access network helps to provide connectivity between customer sites and the service provider network. It terminates the Layer 2 connection from the CPE onto the device on the edge of the service provider network, the *provider edge* (PE) device. Various access technologies can be used to provide this connectivity. (Section 5.4 provides an overview of some of the access technologies that service providers use today.)

A very useful device in the access network is the *access concentrator*, which helps concentrate Layer 2 connections (whenever it is possible) from several CPE devices and terminate them on a single interface of the PE device. This type of device is typically used for access technologies that permit multiple Layer 2 connections (and hence multiple Layer 3 streams) on a single physical interface.

The access network plays a significant role in providing IP-based services to customers. Typically, the Layer 2 connectivity from a customer site starts on the CPE and terminates on a PE device. The access network must provide the means to terminate several customer connections on PE devices. This will help minimize the cost of the service provider's edge and core networks and also make them scalable. A large growth in the number of customers will definitely increase the number of devices (i.e., CPEs and access concentrators) in the access network. However, the increase in the number of devices in the access network should not result in a corresponding or similar increase in the number of the PE and core devices.

An interesting topic in this area is the ability of the access network to support the QoS requirements of the IP layer. This includes the ability of access concentrators to support the QoS requirements of the IP layer. One of the QoS requirements is bandwidth. Typically, the access network of a service provider is oversubscribed. What this means is that the total capacity of the access network will exceed the sum of bandwidth requirements of all customers attached to the access network. This oversubscription is normally done under the assumption that all the CPE devices do not use all of the bandwidth all of the time. For example, in an ATM access network, on a 155 Mb/sec link, there might be 100 customers, each of which has a 2 Mb/sec PVC. This results in an oversubscription of 30%. The service provider assumes that the customers may not be using 155 Mb/sec all of the time. However, in a situation where all of the customers start using their connection to the full capacity, it results in congestion in the access network.

At this point, some of the devices in the access network have to drop 30% of the traffic in order to avoid congestion. Access concentrators must be capable of discarding traffic in an intelligent manner, such that a reasonable throughput is achieved at the IP layer. Since IP packets are split into ATM cells, the ATM network must have the intelligence to discard cells from the same IP packet rather than discard one cell from each packet. Assuming that each IP packet is 1500 bytes long, and the ATM network decides to drop one cell from each packet to avoid congestion, the effective throughput achieved at the IP layer is zero.

5.3 Technologies

This section presents a brief description of some of the technologies that can be used by service providers to create new services. Details about service creation are provided in Section 5.5.

5.3.1 Multiprotocol Label Switching

Network layer routing can be divided into two parts: forwarding and control. The forwarding component is responsible for the actual forwarding of the packet from the input to the output across the router or a switch. It depends on a forwarding table and the information in the packet itself to forward the packet. The control component is responsible for building and maintaining the forwarding table. It consists of one or more routing protocols (e.g., open shortest path first (OSPF), intermediate systems-intermediate systems (IS-IS), border gateway protocol (BGP), and protocol-independent multicast (PIM)), which help to exchange routing

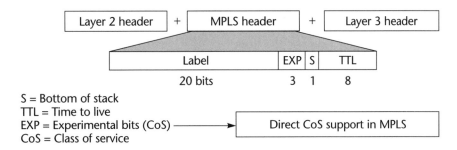

Figure 5.5 MPLS header.

information among the routers and also to convert the routing information into a forwarding table.

In a conventional IP network, as a unicast packet traverses the network, each router extracts forwarding information (destination IP address) from the Layer 3 header, looks up the forwarding table, and then forwards the packet. Header analysis is repeated at each router (hop) through which the packet passes.

In a *multiprotocol label-switching* (MPLS) network, packets are forwarded based on labels. Each IP network that is reachable through an interface is assigned a unique label. A mapping is established between an incoming label (ingress label) and an outgoing label (egress label). This is maintained in the label forwarding information base (LFIB) table. Each node examines the incoming label, does a table lookup, swaps the incoming label for the outgoing label, and then forwards the packet out of the outgoing interface. Labels only have local significance, and they get modified (swapped) as the packet traverses the MPLS network.

MPLS Operation

Figure 5.5 shows the details of the MPLS header. It is located between the Layer 3 (IP) header and the Layer 2 header. The EXP bits and the TTL field of the MPLS header can be copied from the IP header. The S bit indicates whether there is more than one MPLS label in this packet. Packets are forwarded based on the label in the MPLS header.

A protocol is used between the routers in an MPLS network to assign labels to IP network prefixes and exchange label information with other routers. There are two protocols that are currently used, both of which are based on TCP:

Tag distribution protocol (TDP)[1] (TDP port number 711)

Label distribution protocol (LDP) (LDP port number 646)

---

1. TDP is a Cisco Systems proprietary protocol.

Figure 5.6 gives an overview of label switching in an MPLS-enabled IP network. A protocol is used to assign labels to networks that have been learned by the interior gateway protocol (IGP). At the ingress of the MPLS network, an MPLS header is added to the IP packet. At each hop, the packet is forwarded by looking only at the label in the MPLS header. The label is swapped before forwarding it to the next router. At the egress of the MPLS network, the MPLS header is stripped and the IP packet is forwarded out of the egress interface.

Advantages of MPLS

At a superficial glance, it looks as if the main advantage of an MPLS network over an IP network is that the MPLS network can switch packets faster because it forwards them based on labels. However, this is not an advantage for only the MPLS network; IP networks also forward packets based on a label (destination IP address). The advantages of an MPLS network over an IP network are

Stack of labels and packet switching based on the topmost label

Traffic engineering

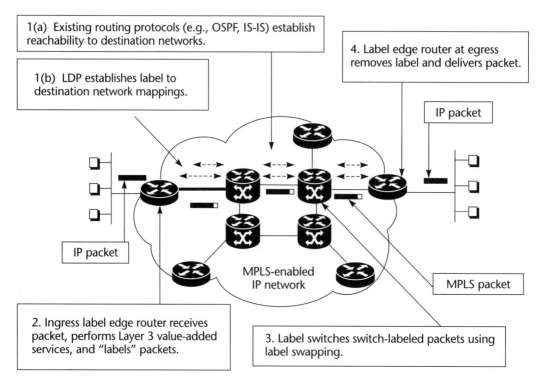

Figure 5.6 Overview of MPLS.

Hierarchical Networks

The stack of labels aids in building hierarchical networks. This means that the core of the IP network can switch packets without any knowledge of the customer networks. This will help to restrict the *routing information base* (RIB) to subnets in the core network to a minimum. Increase in the number of customer networks at the edge of the service provider network has no effect on the RIB in the core. Changes to the RIB in the customer network (instability in the customer network) do not have any effect on the RIB in the core network. This makes the core stable and also scalable.

Figure 5.7 shows an example of how MPLS helps to keep the RIB in the core independent of the RIB from the customer network. The core routers are P_1 and P_2. The edge routers are PE_1 and PE_2. Four customer networks are connected to edge routers. In the core router P_1, traffic destined for network 11.0.0.0/24 and 14.0.0.0/24 are switched based on the same label (the ingress label is 6 and the egress label is 23). This is not possible in an IP network because there is no concept of a stack of IP addresses and all forwarding is based on the IP address of the packet. Irrespective of the number of customer networks connected to PE_2, P_1 will switch all packets destined for networks connected to PE_2, based on the same label. The number of labels used by the core router is independent of the number of customer networks connected to the edge routers.

Traffic Engineering

Since the MPLS labels have only local significance, it is possible to build tunnels (or forwarding paths) in a controlled manner. In other words, it is possible to make a tunnel traverse particular links in the core network. Tunnels can be built from the source to the destination in a controlled manner[2] (also with backup mechanisms in case of link failures). In conjunction with reservation protocols like the *resource reservation protocol* (RSVP), *traffic-engineering tunnels* can be built in an MPLS network. Along with RSVP (using available bandwidth as the reservation criteria), MPLS helps to provide *call admission control* (CAC) for IP traffic. Traffic-engineering tunnels are built only when sufficient bandwidth is available on all the links from the source to the destination. Using traffic engineering, service providers can do capacity planning for bandwidth in the core network in a better and controlled manner. (More details about MPLS and traffic engineering can be found in Davie and Rekhter 2000.)

---

2. "Controlled manner" refers to the ability to determine the links traversed by the tunnel. The choice of the links can be static (fixed path from source to destination) or dynamic, based on criteria like availability of the link and other QoS requirements, such as bandwidth.

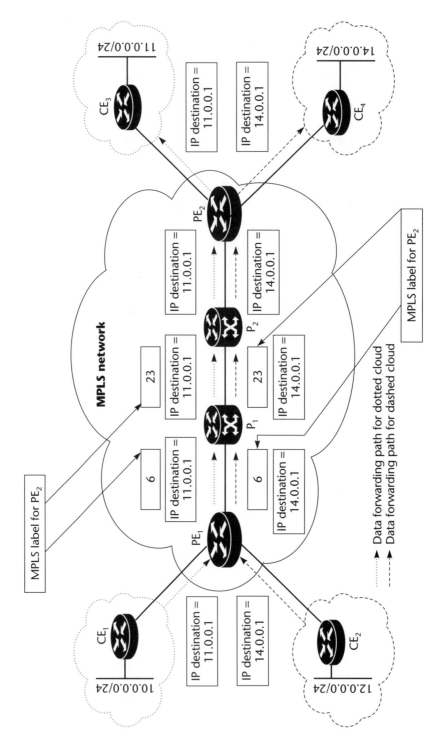

Figure 5.7 Example of hierarchical networks using MPLS.

QoS

MPLS also helps to provide additional features that are not available in an IP network: namely, end-to-end guaranteed bandwidth and end-to-end delay for IP traffic. (*End-to-end* refers to the path of IP traffic from the source to the destination.) Traffic engineering, together with some policing and traffic-shaping mechanisms at the IP layer, helps to provide guaranteed bandwidth.[3] This is the starting point for providing QoS in an IP network.

Intelligent queuing mechanisms on the MPLS switches help to implement traffic-engineering tunnels that guarantee minimal end-to-end delay and minimal jitter. QoS and traffic engineering (and IP routing) have a relationship in providing end-to-end QoS.

5.3.2 Virtual Private Networks

Another application of MPLS is in *virtual private networks (VPNs)*. A VPN by definition is a private network that is geographically dispersed. It is also private in the sense that the routing and the address plan within the network are completely independent of the routing and address plans of other networks. Informally, a VPN is a set of customer sites that can communicate with each other.

Traditionally, VPNs are built using overlay models (Davie and Rekhter 2000). Point-to-point links are built between the sites, and an IP network is built on top of these point-to-point links for the VPN. This means that a separate IP network is required for every VPN, to provide interconnectivity. For a service provider, this is a costly solution and does not provide the facilities to share the core IP network with several VPNs.

MPLS helps to build several VPNs using a single core IP network. Similar to the hierarchical model described in Section 5.3.1, the MPLS core makes use of the stack of labels to build several VPNs using the same core. The edge routers provide the facility to distinguish between several VPNs. IP addresses from the VPNs are mapped to MPLS labels, and IP packets from the VPN traverse as the MPLS packets. They carry two labels: one is the VPN label (provided by the edge router), and the other (the top label) is the MPLS label used for forwarding the packet in the MPLS core.

How Does It Work?

Provider (P) and provider edge (PE) routers share a common routing protocol within the core. These routers use this information to build label-switched paths between PE routers and use two levels of labels to forward packets.

---

3. IP can also depend on the policing and traffic-shaping support provided by Layer 2 protocols like ATM or frame relay to enforce the QoS policies.

Virtual routing and forwarding (VRF) instances are defined on the PE—each VRF instance represents the end point of a VPN, a separate RIB, a set of interfaces to which VPNs are attached. To make VPN routes unique on a PE, the VRF needs to define a *route distinguisher* (RD) that is preappended to each VPN route to make a VPN IPv4 route. For example, in Figure 5.8, the routing table of the dotted cloud VRF contains a route 10.0.0.0/24 and the dotted cloud VRF has an RD of 1:1. This route is passed via a *multiprotocol border gateway protocol* (MP-BGP) to peer PEs as 1:1:10.0.0.0/24. The routing table of the dashed cloud VRF contains a route 10.0.0.0/24 and the dashed cloud VRF has an RD of 1:2—this route is passed via MP-BGP to peer PEs as 1:2:10.0.0.0/24.

VPNs are built using an extended BGP community called *route target* (RT). RTs have 64 bits and have the format X:Y. A PE attaches RTs (export RT) to the routes learned from directly connected customer edge (CE) devices. This RT is sent to remote PEs as an extended BGP attribute of the route using MP-BGP. A set of VRFs on different PEs constitutes a VPN when they import routes that have the same RTs. For example, all routes from dotted cloud VRF VPN_1 have RT 1:1, and hence belong to the same VPN.

VPN routing tables are propagated between PEs using MP-BGP. MP-BGP is the extension to BGP that permits the exchange of additional information like labels, route distinguishers, and route targets (extended communities) between BGP peers. PEs that exchange extended community information use iBGP MP-BGP peering. MP-BGP carries the RD and the RTs associated with the VPN routes. The PE allocates labels to VPN routes learned from the CE, and this is propagated along with the MP-BGP updates to the remote PEs. The PE marks packets from CE routers with two labels: an inner label for the destination VPN route and a second, outside label to select the label-switched path to the remote PE (BGP next hop) that originated the destination VPN route. More details about MPLS-VPN architecture can be found in Rosen and Rekhter 1999 and at *www.rfc -editor.org/rfc/rfc2547.txt*.

Data Forwarding

The PE allocates labels to VPN routes learned from the CE, and this is propagated along with the MP-BGP updates to the remote PEs. At the ingress of the MPLS-VPN network, the PE adds two MPLS labels to the IP packets from CE routers: the first label (inner label) is for the destination VPN route, and the second, outer label selects the label-switched path to the remote PE (BGP next hop), which originated the destination VPN route.

The P routers do not use the VPN label and forward packets only based on the outer MPLS label. Any changes or instability in the VPN network does not affect the LFIB of the P routers. This data-forwarding paradigm makes the architecture scalable and stable.

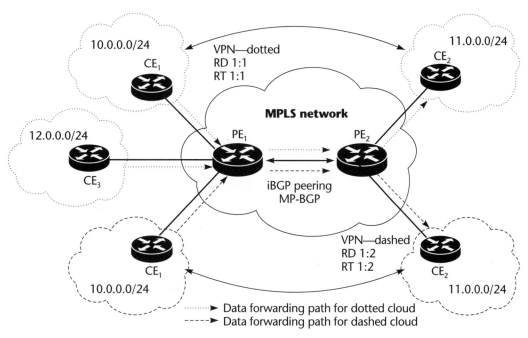

Figure 5.8 MPLS-VPN network.

Figure 5.9 gives an overview of how VPN traffic is forwarded in an MPLS-VPN network. At the ingress, PE_1 receives a packet whose destination is 11.0.0.1 (dotted VRF). The VPN label for 11.0.0.0/24 is 1. The BGP next hop for 11.0.0.0 (dotted VRF) PE_2 and the MPLS label for PE_2 is 6. P_1 and P_2 forward the data packet based on the MPLS label. P_2 is the penultimate hop in the data path, and it pops on the MPLS label (23) and forwards the packet to PE_2. PE_2 looks at VPN label 1 and forwards the packet out of the dotted VRF interface.

5.3.3 Multicast

At one end of the IP communication spectrum is unicast communication, in which a source sends a packet to a specific destination. At the other end of the communication spectrum is broadcast communication, in which a source sends a packet for all hosts. (The term *all hosts* here refers to all the hosts in the network to which the source belongs.) *Multicast communication* lies in between these two communication models. In multicast communication, a source sends packets to a selected group of hosts, identified by a multicast IP address. All hosts that are members of this group receive the packets destined for that multicast address.

Figure 5.10 shows an IP network that has a multicast source and a few multicast receivers. Traffic from the multicast source is forwarded from

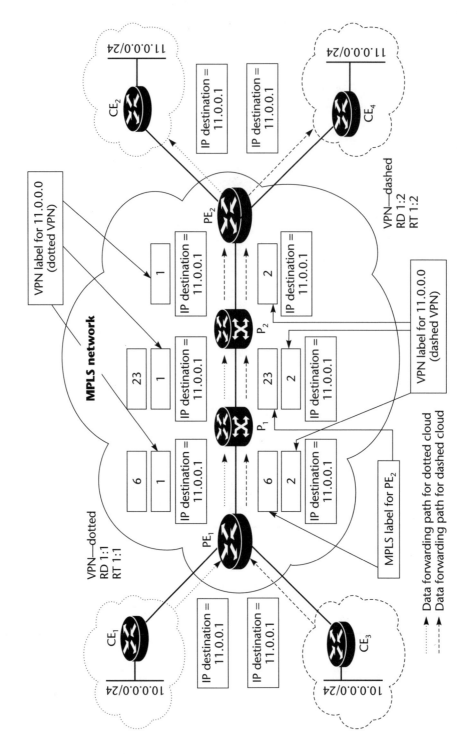

Figure 5.9 Data forwarding in an MPLS-VPN network.

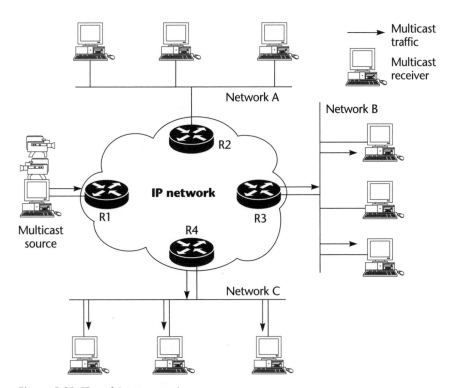

Figure 5.10 IP multicast scenario.

the multicast source to Networks B and C. No multicast traffic from the multicast source is forwarded to Network A. For each packet from the multicast source, routers R3 and R4 receive only one packet and forward only one packet to Network B and Network C, respectively.

Multicast Applications

Multicast applications are gaining popularity today. Since these applications are unidirectional (source to destination), most of them make use of UDP.

- *Multimedia conferencing* is a common application that comes to mind when one thinks about multicasting. In addition to audio and video, it permits users to share resources like files, whiteboards, and so on, during a conference. This helps remote users to have a virtual conference and also to share data and information at the same time. One typical use would be a group of people writing a report together, using the same file.
- *Data distribution* is another IP multicast application that is rapidly becoming popular. For an example, say information from a central database is distributed to remote databases on a daily basis. Instead

of sending the data multiple times from the central site to the remote sites, it can be multicast to all the sites.

- *Software upgrades* for multiple field devices is another application. If the same software has to be sent to hundreds of remote devices, a multicast transfer is a good solution.
- *Real-time data multicast* is another popular application. Financial institutions rely on information to do their business—a good example is the delivery of stock information to all of the workstations on a trading floor.

How Does It Work?

The following are necessary for multicast forwarding to work:

- *Multicast address:* Certain IP addresses are reserved for multicast applications.
- *Group membership:* Hosts need to register or become members of a multicast group.
- *Multicast routing:* The location of all the hosts belonging to a multicast group and the multicast source must be made available to all the devices (hosts and routers) in the network.
- *Multicast forwarding:* Multicast packets have to be forwarded to all the hosts of the multicast group.

Multicast Address

Unlike unicast IP addresses, which uniquely identify a single IP host, a multicast IP address specifies a group of IP hosts that have joined the group and wish to receive traffic sent to this group. IP multicast addresses have been assigned an address space by the Internet-assigned number authority (IANA). They have the binary prefix 1110 in the first four bits of the first octet of the IP address and range from 224.0.0.0 to 239.255.255.255. Some of the IP multicast addresses in this range are reserved for multicast applications by IANA.

Multicast Forwarding

In the unicast model, packets are forwarded based on the destination IP address. Each router along the path forwards the packet based on this address. Since the address is unique, this forwarding paradigm does not create any problems. Unlike a unicast IP address, a multicast IP address represents all of the hosts that are members of that address and want to receive packets sent there. These hosts can be scattered all over the network. Each router in the network has to maintain information about the location of all the multicast receivers for each multicast address.

An inefficient way of forwarding multicast packets is to forward them on all the interfaces except on the one on which the packets were received. This results in multiple packets arriving at the destination (if there are multiple paths from the multicast source to the destination). In order to conserve resources, avoid duplicate packets, and avoid loops, a tree can be built for each multicast address, with the multicast receivers as leaves of the tree. Depending on the root of the tree, the tree can be a *source tree*, or *shortest path tree* (SPT), with the multicast source as the root (see Figure 5.11), or a *shared tree*, with a node other than the multicast source acting as the root; this node can be the root for multiple shared trees (see Figure 5.12).

Multicast packets are forwarded only along the branches of the tree. The multicast forwarding table is maintained for each (S, G), where S is the multicast source and G is the multicast IP address. The forwarding table maintains (based on the tree) the list of outgoing interfaces on which the multicast packet (S, G) has to be forwarded.

In addition to the destination address, multicast forwarding also uses the source address to verify if the packet was received on the correct interface. A multicast packet (S, G) is received on the correct interface int_c on a router R, if the reverse path to the source S from the router R is via interface int_c. This verification is called a *reverse path forwarding* (RPF) *check*. When a multicast packet is received, the router forwards the packet only when the RPF check is successful.

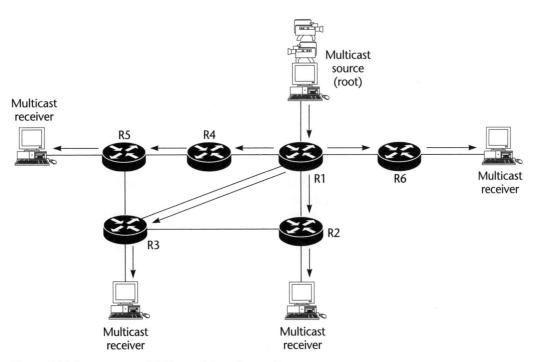

Figure 5.11 Source tree or SPT for multicast forwarding.

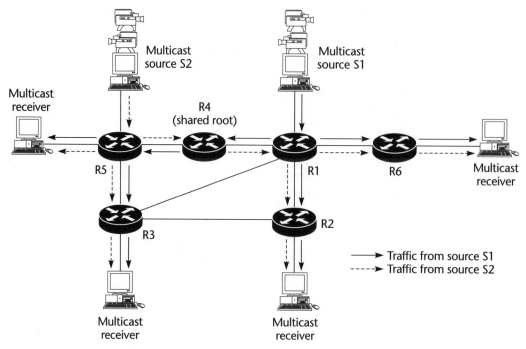

Figure 5.12 Shared tree for multicast forwarding.

The RPF check to verify that the source is in the reverse path depends on the multicast routing protocol. In some cases, the multicast routing protocol maintains a separate multicast routing table and uses it to perform the RPF check. In other cases, the unicast routing table is used to perform the RPF check.

Group Membership

Hosts have to announce themselves to be members of a multicast group so that they can receive multicast packets. In order to avoid a flood of messages and to reduce the complexity for themselves, hosts register with the nearest router running multicast routing. The router then uses a protocol to announce the existence of receivers for the multicast group. *Internet group management protocol* (IGMP) is used between the router and the hosts for this registration.

Multicast Routing

Multicast routing protocols can be classified into four categories:

- *Dense-mode protocols*, like *distance vector multicast routing protocol* (DVMRP) and *protocol-independent multicast—dense mode* (PIM-DM).

- *Sparse-mode protocols,* like *protocol-independent multicast—spare mode* (PIM-SM) and *core-based trees* (CBTs)
- *Link-state protocols,* like *multicast open shortest path first* (MOSPF)
- *Interdomain protocols,* like *multicast border gateway protocol* (MBGP) and *multicast source-discovery protocol* (MSDP)

Dense-mode protocols are based on the *flood-and-prune principle.* They use SPTs to deliver multicast packets using the *push principle.* The push principle assumes that every router has at least one multicast receiver for any multicast group and pushes or floods multicast packets to all the routers. Pruning is used to limit the traffic to only those branches that have routers with multicast receivers. When new receivers join at a later stage, *grafting* is used to include new branches to the SPT.

Sparse-mode protocols make use of shared trees to distribute multicast traffic based on the *pull principle,* which assumes that multicast traffic is not wanted unless it is requested specifically (pull the multicast traffic), using a *join mechanism* to join the shared tree.

Link-state protocols use the SPT to determine the reachability of the destination. However, the SPT is built using the multicast information that identifies the location of multicast receivers. This is distributed using MOSPF.

Interdomain routing protocols like MSDP and MBGP (MBGP can also be used within a domain) are used to route multicast traffic between domains. MBGP is used to forward information about multicast sources and uses the MBGP table for the RPF check.

Advantages and Disadvantages

Multicast communication has both advantages and disadvantages. It helps to reduce the amount of traffic in the backbone and to make better use of the link bandwidth, but this is not for free. It requires additional forwarding mechanisms (multicast forwarding) and routing protocols to forward multicast traffic in an efficient manner.

Multicast communication at the IP level is not reliable. Upper-layer protocols have to take care of reliability in case of packet loss or corruption. Unlike unicast forwarding, reliability for multicasting can be complicated. Consider the situation when out of 100 multicast receivers, one receiver does not receive the packet. Should the multicast source resend the packet as a unicast to this particular receiver, or should it send it as a multicast? Resending multicast packets to unicast addresses can be inefficient when several receivers do not receive the packet. Resending the multicast packet to the multicast address can cause confusion for those receivers that correctly received the packets in the first attempt. Multicast is also not scalable because multicast group addresses cannot be aggregated.

5.4 Transport Technology Overview

Several transport technologies are available today that can be used to build IP networks. This section gives an overview of some of those technologies and how they can be used to build IP networks: POS, ring topology, Ethernet, frame relay, ATM, ISDN, DSL, and cable.

5.4.1 Packet-over-SONET

Packet-over-SONET (POS) technology allows for efficient transport of data over SONET/SDH. It has certainly been a major player in accommodating the explosive growth of the Internet. POS is a point-to-point technology. Request for Comments (RFC) 2615 (Malis and Simpson 1999) is the Internet Engineering Task Force (IETF) specification that describes how to implement POS. POS uses a *point-to-point protocol* (PPP) in *high-level datalink control* (HDLC)–like framing encapsulation over SONET. Figure 5.13 shows the format of a POS packet.

POS Implementations

Figure 5.14 shows the implementation of POS using the PPP in HDLC-like framing. Router POS interfaces are frequently connected to *add-drop multiplexers* (ADMs), terminating point-to-point SONET/SDH links (see Figure 5.14(a)). Direct connections over dark fiber (see Figure 5.14(c)) or via *dense wavelength-division multiplexing* (DWDM) systems (see Figure 5.14(b)) are becoming increasingly popular.

POS provides the following features:

1. High bandwidth utilization (99% for a packet size of 4470 bytes)
2. Secure and reliable data transfer by using the features provided by SONET and also by using a self-synchronous payload scrambler
3. Fast restoration (less than 50 milliseconds) when using SONET (*automatic protection switching,* or *APS*), SDH (*multiple switching protection,* or *MSP*), or DWDM *(optical protection mechanism)*
4. Maximum bandwidth dependent on the physical layer. Today, POS can go up to 10 Gb/sec (OC-192 or STM-64)

8	8	8		16/32	8
Flag	Address	Control	PPP data	Frame check sequence (FCS)	Flag

Figure 5.13 POS packet format.

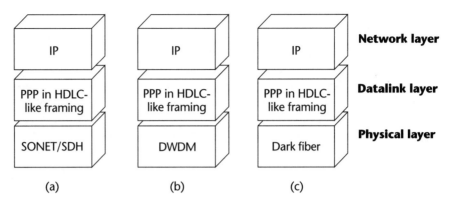

Figure 5.14 POS implementations.

Applications

POS provides a flexible solution that can be used in a variety of transport applications. Well-known applications include use in network backbone infrastructures and data aggregation or distribution on the network edge and in a metropolitan area. The use of POS for network connectivity can be broken down into the following three main application categories:

Core

Edge

Metro

The *core application* refers to the backbone infrastructure for interconnecting PoPs in a large network. Data transport between customer premises and PoPs as well as intra-PoP connectivity can be classified as *edge applications*. *Metro application* normally refers to interbuilding connections, such as in a small city downtown area or university campus.

Core Application of POS

A very common application of POS is wide area network (WAN) connectivity over SONET/SDH networks. This application was the primary motivation for the development of POS interfaces on routers. This section looks at three primary methods for connecting routers with POS interfaces:

Connectivity to SONET/SDH networks

Connectivity over DWDM systems

Router-to-router connectivity over dark fiber

POS on the Network Edge

The edge of the network is associated with traffic aggregation or distribution. It is also the point of convergence of regional traffic housed in
the PoP. A key component of the network edge is intra-PoP connections
between aggregation routers. Until recently, technologies like Ethernet
and ATM were used for intra-PoP connectivity in service provider networks, fast Ethernet, and fiber distributed data interface (FDDI), and had
bandwidth capability pegged at 100 Mb/sec. The huge bandwidth requirements for server-farm deployments and corresponding applications frequently required service providers to use multiple parallel 100 Mb/sec
connections. To keep up with the huge bandwidth available in the wide
area, most service providers have adopted POS as an alternative for high-
speed intra-PoP connectivity (see Figure 5.15). Using POS for intra-PoP
connectivity provides numerous benefits, the most significant being

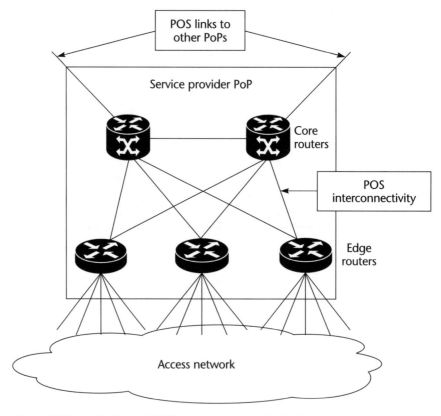

Figure 5.15 Applications of POS in a service provider PoP.

flexible design using mixed-bandwidth links from OC-3/STM-1 to OC-48/STM-16 (available today) and OC-192/STM-64 (in the near future).

Metro Application of POS

Unidirectional SONET/SDH rings are popular for high-speed connectivity between office buildings in metro areas. This type of ring is normally part of a carrier infrastructure and features ADMs for bandwidth drop-off to routers equipped with POS interfaces. DWDM or dark fiber can be used with POS in a similar fashion. Using POS rather than gigabit Ethernet to provide framing and data transport between connecting routers allows the use of rich management and other capabilities of SONET/SDH. It is worth mentioning at this point that gigabit Ethernet is cheaper than POS.

POS in Access Networks

Another application of POS is to build high-speed and reliable access networks. The high speed, failure protection mechanisms, and reliable data transfer make POS a good candidate to build access networks. However, it has its limitations, and compared to other access technologies, does not have many advantages. Some of the limitations of POS are

No aggregation capability

Lack of control on restricting bandwidth at the datalink layer

More expensive compared to gigabit Ethernet

5.4.2 Ring Topology

Ring topology is another access technology in the access network. Some of the traditional technologies based on ring topologies include Token Ring and FDDI. Unlike point-to-point technologies like POS or ATM, ring topologies help to reduce the number of fiber links required to make a full mesh. FDDI technology is very often used in metropolitan and campus networks. Token Ring and FDDI have not grown in terms of the link speed to keep up with the demand in the core and edge networks.

The *spatial reuse protocol* (SRP) has been developed by Cisco Systems for use with ring-based media and does not have the speed limitations of FDDI and Token Ring. It derives its name from the spatial reuse properties of the packet-handling procedure (Tsiang and Suwala 2000). SRP is a new generation of transport technology optimized for packet-based optical transport. This optical transport technology combines the bandwidth-efficient and service-rich capabilities of IP routing with the bandwidth-rich, self-healing capabilities of fiber rings to deliver fundamental cost and functionality advantages over existing solutions.

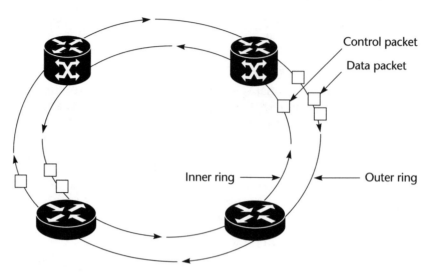

Figure 5.16 SRP ring implementation.

Implementation

SRP uses a bidirectional, dual-counter, rotating-ring topology. The rings are referred to as *inner* and *outer* rings, as seen in Figure 5.16. Both rings are concurrently utilized for transporting data and SRP control packets. SRP control packets handle tasks such as topology discovery, protection switching, and bandwidth control. Control packets propagate in the opposite direction from the corresponding data packets. For data packets being transported by the outer ring, the corresponding control packets use the inner ring as depicted in Figure 5.16.

SRP is a media-independent, *media access control*–layer (MAC-layer) protocol. Figure 5.17 shows the SRP as a MAC protocol. Like POS, SRP can be implemented over SONET/SDH, DWDM, or *dark fiber*. Figure 5.18 shows the format of an SRP packet. SRP allows for up to 32 nodes in a ring; the IP addresses of all the nodes belong to the same IP network.

SRP Features

SRP offers a lot of features that make it increasingly suitable for use in the metro networks and in service provider PoPs. Some of these features include

1. High-speed rings (up to OC-48 link speed).
2. Fast protection (≤ 50 ms) against a single link or node failure in the ring. The ring wrap feature helps to protect against link or node failure in a transparent manner to the upper layers.

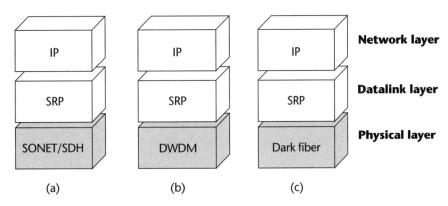

Figure 5.17 SRP implementation.

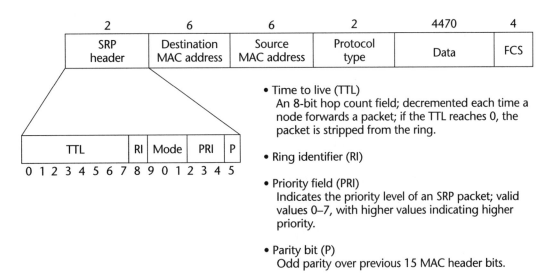

Figure 5.18 SRP packet format.

3. A distributed fairness algorithm that ensures that every node gets a fair share of its bandwidth. This algorithm makes SRP better than gigabit Ethernet: everyone can be assured a minimum bandwidth on the ring, unlike in a gigabit Ethernet medium.

4. A priority field that helps to implement QoS. The IP precedence bit can be copied to the priority field to provide QoS in a transparent manner.

5. Direct multicast support for IP.

6. A ring topology that requires fewer fiber connections to interconnect several devices in full mesh.

Applications

SRP can be used in the following areas:

Core networks with less than 32 nodes

Intra-PoP connectivity (connectivity between the edge and core routers in a service provider PoP)

Hierarchical rings (to aggregate traffic from several aggregation devices to the edge device located in a PoP in a metropolitan city)

Interconnectivity in a campus environment

5.4.3 Ethernet

Ethernet is a LAN implementation that includes four principal categories based on the supported bandwidth:

- *Ethernet and IEEE 802.3:* LAN specification that operates at 10 Mb/sec over coaxial cable or twisted pair or fiber
- *100 Mb/sec Ethernet:* Also known as *fast Ethernet;* runs over twisted-pair cable and fiber
- *1000 Mb/sec Ethernet:* Also known as *gigabit Ethernet;* operates at 1000 Mb/sec over fiber and twisted pair
- *10 Gb Ethernet:* An emerging technology

Transmission Technology

Typically, Ethernet is used as a shared media, so several devices can connect to the same media and share the bandwidth. An algorithm known as *Carrier Sense Multiple Access with Collision Detection (CSMA/CD)* helps all of the devices to share the same physical media. Ethernet can also be used as a point-to-point technology, in which case it can operate at full-duplex mode. Ethernet technology allows the device to make full use of the available bandwidth—it does not have the mechanism to restrict the bandwidth used by devices. When used in the shared mode, effective utilization starts to degrade (due to excessive collisions) when the utilization is high.

Today, Ethernet can be used up to a distance of 40 kilometers (25 miles) over fiber. This makes it possible to use it in the access network. Also, Ethernet is cheaper compared to other technologies, such as POS, ATM, and SRP.

Ethernet

8	6	6	2	46–1500	4
Preamble	Destination address	Source address	Type	Data	FCS

IEEE 802.3

8	6	6	2	46–1500	4
Preamble	Destination address	Source address	Length	802.2 header and data	FCS

Figure 5.19 Ethernet frame formats.

Data Encapsulation

The maximum packet size of a standard Ethernet frame is 1526.[4] Ethernet uses two frame formats to transmit data over the physical media, namely, *Ethernet format* and *IEEE 802.3 format* (see Figure 5.19). The type of data carried by Ethernet is indicated in the Type field for an Ethernet frame and in the 802.2 header for an IEEE 802.3 frame.

Each frame has a source and a destination address. Each device has a unique Ethernet address. Techniques must be made available to map the higher-layer address to the Ethernet address. In the case of IP, a protocol known as *address resolution protocol* (ARP) is used to map the IP address to the Ethernet address.

Broadcast and multicast addresses are available for Ethernet technology, making it efficient for services like videoconferencing, video-streaming, and so on.

Aggregation

Today, Ethernet can be used up to a distance of 10 kilometers using fiber. This makes it a good technology for the access network. Aggregation devices called *Ethernet switches* are available for Ethernet; these are intelligent devices that provide several functionalities: They permit several devices with Ethernet connection to communicate with each other. They provide dedicated ports for each device connected to the switch and provide point-to-point connection between any two devices connected to the switch. Ethernet switches also help to create multiple LANs that can be geographically spread over an entire campus. This concept is called *virtual*

---

4. This is valid for the standard Ethernet and IEEE 802.3 frames. However, proprietary encapsulations permit one to overcome this limitation.

LAN (VLAN). In a campus, several groups can share the same physical Ethernet network, but can be logically separate and isolated from one another (see Figure 5.20).

Ethernet switches also help to aggregate connections from multiple devices and terminate them on a single device in the service provider PoP. Encapsulation techniques using 802.1Q help to have several IP sessions (over Ethernet) on a single Ethernet interface on the edge device of the service provider PoP (see Figure 5.21).

5.4.4 Frame Relay

Frame relay is an access technology that operates at the physical and datalink layer of the OSI model. It is a packet-switched technology and permits packets of variable size to be switched through the network. Packets are switched through the frame relay network until they reach the destination.

Devices

A frame relay network consists of two types of devices: *data terminal equipment* (DTE) and *data circuit-terminating equipment* (DCE). DTE devices are located on customer sites, and DCE devices are the Internetworking devices located in the frame relay network. Some of the typical DTE devices are routers.

Switching

A basic principle of frame relay is a *virtual circuit*. A virtual circuit starts on a DTE device, traverses the frame relay network, and terminates on a DTE device. It is bidirectional and each virtual circuit has a unique identifier known as a *datalink connection identifier* (DLCI). Frame relay virtual circuits fall into two categories:

- *Switched virtual circuits* (SVCs): Temporary circuits that are built between a pair of DTE devices on a need-only basis and are torn down when no data is transferred using the virtual circuit. SVCs are not used very often because it requires a signaling protocol to establish them.
- *Permanent virtual circuits* (PVCs): Permanently established connections between DTE devices used for frequent and consistent data transfers.

Frame relay is connection oriented, in the sense that the virtual circuits have to be established end to end before data can be transferred. DCE devices switch the frame relay packets using the DLCI value in the packets. A single frame relay virtual circuit can be assigned a different DLCI on each end of a virtual circuit. Multiple virtual circuits can be terminated on a single DTE device on the same physical interface.

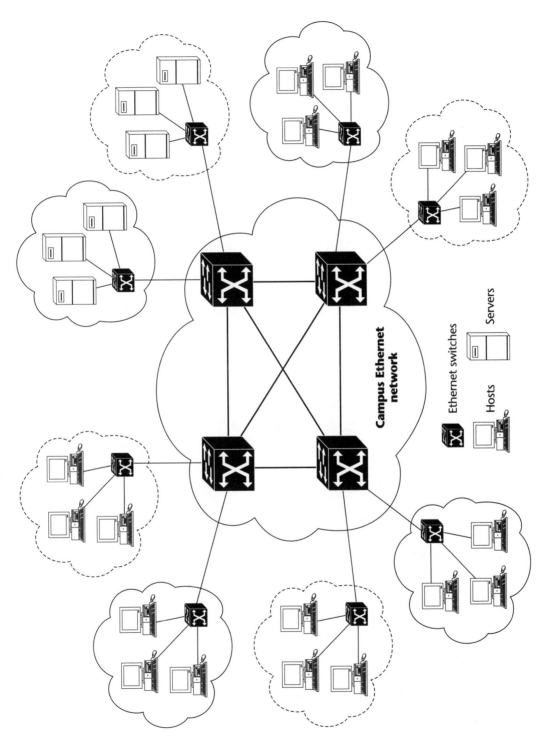

Figure 5.20 VLANs using Ethernet technology.

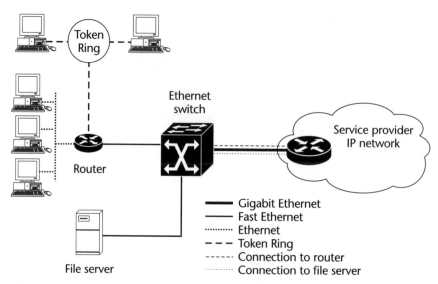

Figure 5.21 Aggregation using Ethernet.

Figure 5.22 shows a frame relay network with DTE and DCE devices. The DTE devices are mostly routers. DCE devices are frame relay switches with multiple interfaces. Hosts are connected to the routers, and PVCs are established between routers. Each PVC has a unique DLCI value. The frame relay network in the figure provides connectivity between a file server and two hosts located in different sites, using two PVCs.

Service Features

Frame relay provides the following features:

1. Unique identifier for each virtual circuit using DLCI
2. Point-to-point and point-to-multipoint virtual circuits
3. Congestion control mechanism using forward explicit congestion notification (FECN) and backward explicit congestion notification (BECN)
4. Bandwidth allocation and control per virtual circuit using the *committed information rate* (CIR); QoS support
5. Multiple PVCs on a single physical interface—ability to concentrate connections from multiple DTE devices to a single DTE device
6. Maximum speed of 45 Mb/sec

Aggregation

Frame relay provides the capability to aggregate several connections onto a single physical interface on the edge device located in the PoP of the

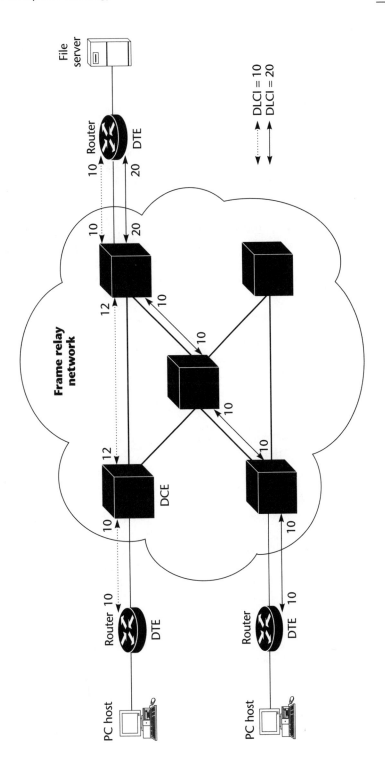

Figure 5.22 Frame relay network.

service provider. The frame relay switch can do this in a transparent manner and also ensure that the QoS assured to the individual frame relay connections is still guaranteed (see Figure 5.22).

5.4.5   ATM

ATM is a packet-switching and multiplexing technology that combines the benefits of circuit switching (guaranteed capacity and continuous transmission) with those of packet switching (flexibility and efficiency for intermittent traffic). The packets are called *cells* and they have a fixed size (53 bytes). Because ATM is asynchronous, it is more efficient than synchronous technologies such as TDM. In ATM, time slots are available on demand, and cells are switched based on the identification information contained in each cell. ATM can be operated over several physical media like fiber and copper. Links can traverse very long distances (hundreds of kilometers) and provide up to 155 Mb/sec.[5]

Cell

Figure 5.23 shows the details of an ATM cell. Each cell has 53 bytes, of which 48 bytes are the payload and 5 bytes are the header. The header contains the identification and other information that is used for local management and congestion management. The following description summarizes the ATM cell header:

- *Generic flow control* (GFC): Provides local function and is used on UNI interfaces.
- *Virtual path identifier* (VPI): In conjunction with the VCI, identifies the next destination of a cell.
- *Virtual channel identifier* (VCI): In conjunction with the VPI, identifies the next destination of the cell.
- *Payload type indicator* (PTI): Indicates in the first bit whether the cell carries user data or control data. If the cell contains user data, then the second bit indicates congestion and the third bit indicates whether the cell is the last in the series of the *ATM adaptation layer 5* (AAL5) frame.
- *Congestion loss priority* (CLP): Marked by ATM traffic management to mark cells in case of congestion. If the CLP bit is one, the cell should be discarded in preference to cells whose CLP bit is zero.
- *Header error check* (HEC): Checksum for only the cell header, used to verify that the ATM cell header is not corrupted.

---

5. The capacity of ATM links keeps increasing: today, using STM-4 or STM-16, ATM links can deliver up to 622 Mb/sec and 2.4 Gb/sec, respectively.

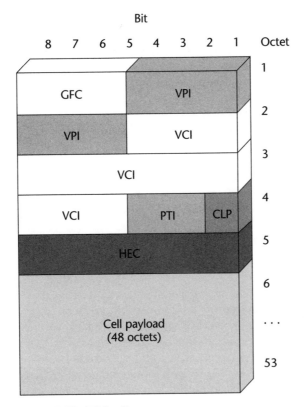

Figure 5.23 ATM cell.

ATM Adaptation

The ATM adaptation layer is responsible for adapting the higher-layer data to be transported as cells in an ATM network. This layer performs the segmentation and reassembly. There are five ATM adaptations defined, known as *ATM adaptation layers,* or AAL1 to AAL5.

- *AAL1:* This layer is designed for transport of higher-level services that have very strict constraints on data loss, delay, and jitter. It is normally used to transport CBR traffic and is also used for real-time *variable bit rate* (VBR) traffic like voice. It provides for clock recovery in the cell header and maintains 64 Kb/sec channel structure in the payload.
- *AAL2:* This layer is more suited for VBR and low-speed connections.
- *AAL3 and AAL4:* These layers are designed for switched multi-megabit data service/connectionless broadband data service (SMDS/CBDS) services and are seldom used.

- *AAL5:* Data traffic is transported via AAL5, and this layer does not provide for any clock recovery. Service categories that are supported by this layer include the *unspecified bit rate* (UBR) and the *available bit rate* (ABR). In the UBR, the network provides minimum QoS guarantees on a first come, first served basis. UBR with *early packet discard* or *intelligent packet discard* (EPD/IPD) helps to achieve "goodput"[6] at higher layers like IP and TCP. In the ABR, the network guarantees a minimum bandwidth that can be increased based on availability of bandwidth. This is done on feedback received from the flow control mechanism. IP traffic is transported using AAL5. (RFC 1483 provides a good description of how to transport IP over an ATM network using subnetwork attachment point (SNAP) encapsulation.)

ATM Switching

An ATM network consists of a set of switches connected by a set of point-to-point interfaces. ATM supports two types of interfaces: user-to-network interface (UNI) and network-to-network interface (NNI). The UNI connects ATM end systems (such as hosts and routers) to an ATM switch, and the NNI connects two ATM switches. A data path from one end system to another is called a *virtual circuit*. There are two types of virtual circuits, a permanent virtual circuit (PVC) and a switched virtual circuit (SVC). A PVC allows direct connectivity between end systems, guarantees the availability of the connection, and does not require call setup procedures between switches. However, the virtual circuit has to be set up manually. An SVC is created and released dynamically and remains in use as long as data is being transferred.

ATM is connection oriented, which means that a virtual circuit must be established before data can be transferred. Each virtual circuit has two identifiers, a virtual path identifier (VPI) and a virtual channel identifier (VCI). A virtual path is a bundle of virtual channels, and a bundle of virtual paths form the transmission path between two ATM switches. Each ATM switch forwards cells based on the VPI/VCI information in each cell. Figure 5.24 shows an ATM network with two virtual circuits. The first virtual circuit is from router 1 to router 3. The second is from router 2 to router 3.

ATM switches forward traffic based on the VPI/VCI information of each virtual circuit, so the circuit has to be established before traffic can be forwarded. For example, traffic from router 2 to router 3 starts with VPI/VCI = 0/40. In the last ATM switch, this virtual circuit has VPI/VCI = 0/50.

---

6. "Goodput" at the IP or TCP layer refers to the throughput achieved at this layer. During congestion, the throughput achieved at the ATM layer may result in a zero throughput at the higher layer. This can happen if cells are not discarded in an intelligent manner.

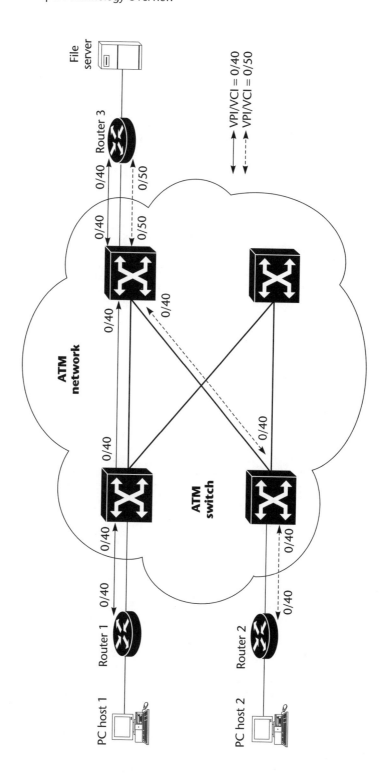

Figure 5.24 Switching in an ATM network.

Traffic Management

The most complex area of ATM is its traffic management capabilities. Traffic management ensures that the QoS guaranteed by ATM to the higher layers is carried across the ATM network. This is achieved by implementing intelligent policing and queuing mechanisms in the switches. Proper traffic management also has an impact on the data traffic carried by the ATM network. For example, TCP expects the network to react in a certain way in order to preserve the throughput at the TCP layer, and this requires that the ATM switches discard the cells in an intelligent manner so that at least some of the TCP packets arrive at the destination when there is congestion in the network.

ATM Service Classes

ATM defines a number of service categories related to the AALs. Table 5.1 lists the most common service classes, their traffic and QoS parameters, and their common usage.

Aggregation

Similar to frame relay, ATM also provides the means to aggregate several ATM connections onto an interface in the edge device of the service

Table 5.1   ATM service classes and their traffic and QoS parameters.

Traffic Class	Traffic Parameters	QoS Parameters	AAL	Usage
CBR	PCR, CDVT	CDV, CTD, CLR, CER	1	Voice, video
VBR-rt	PCR, SCR, CDVT, BT	CDV, CTD, CLR, CER	2, 5	Voice, video
VBR-nrt	PCR, SCR, CDVT, BT	CTD, CLR, CER	2, 5	Voice, video
ABR	PCR, MCR, CDVT	CLR	5	Data
UBR	CDVT	None	5	Data

ABR	available bit rate	CTD	maximum cell transfer delay
BT	burst tolerance	MCR	minimum cell rate
CBR	constant bit rate	PCR	peak cell rate
CDV	cell delay variation	SCR	sustained cell rate
CDVT	cell delay variation tolerance	UBR	unspecified bit rate
CER	cell error ratio	VBR-nrt	variable bit rate, non-real time
CLR	cell loss ratio	VBR-rt	variable bit rate, real time

provider network using ATM switches (see Figure 5.24). The ATM switch ensures that the QoS guaranteed to each ATM connection is also guaranteed when the connections are aggregated to a single edge device.

5.4.6 ISDN

ISDN comprises digital technology and data transport services offered by regional telephone carriers. It involves the digitization of the existing telephone network, which permits voice, data, video, and other sources to be transmitted over it. ISDN can be used to transport IP packets and can be used as an access technology to deliver IP packets from the customer site to the service provider PoP. It is typically used to provide connectivity to small and medium enterprises. Large enterprise offices also use ISDN, as a backup link; they typically have other access technologies as their main link. When the main link fails, ISDN serves as the backup (see Figure 5.25).

ISDN Components

ISDN components include terminals, terminal adaptors, *network termination* (NT) devices, and ISDN switches. ISDN terminals are of two types: specialized ISDN terminals, called *terminal equipment type 1* (TE1), and non-ISDN terminals like analog telephones, called *terminal equipment type 2* (TE2). TE2 requires a *terminal adaptor* (TA) to connect to the ISDN network. Beyond TE1 and TE2 are two NT devices, NT1 and NT2. NT1 connects to the ISDN switch; NT2 is more complicated and does the Layer 2

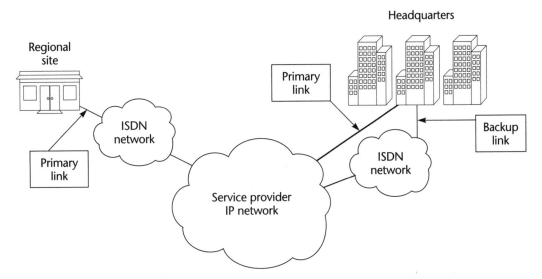

Figure 5.25 ISDN as access network.

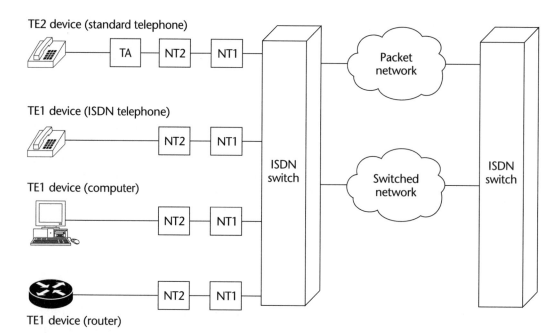

Figure 5.26 ISDN components.

and Layer 3 functions. Figure 5.26 shows the components of the ISDN network.

ISDN Interfaces

ISDN offers two types of interfaces: *basic rate interface* (BRI) and *primary rate interface* (PRI). The BRI offers two B channels and one D channel. The B channel service operates at 64 Kb/sec and is used to carry user data. The D channel service operates at 16 Kb/sec and is used to carry control and signaling information. The PRI service offers 23 B channels and 1 D channel in North America and Japan, yielding a total bit rate of 1.544 Mb/sec. In Europe, the PRI service offers 30 B channels and 1 D channel, yielding a total of 2.048 Mb/sec.

Data Encapsulation and Traffic Management

In order to carry IP traffic, most of the ISDN devices (e.g., routers) use PPP encapsulation. PPP also provides the security mechanism in terms of authentication and allocating IP addresses. ISDN is a dedicated link and hence guarantees the entire bandwidth for the user. With respect to IP traffic, all traffic is treated equally. Any additional features, such as differentiated services, have to be implemented in the higher layers (e.g., IP or TCP).

5.4.7 DSL

Digital subscriber line technology is a modem technology that uses existing twisted-pair telephone lines to transport high-bandwidth data. DSL services are dedicated, point-to-point, with public network access over the twisted-pair copper wire on the local loop (last mile) between the service provider's central office and the customer site. It can also be built on private local loops or on local loops created either intra-building or intra-campus. DSL has several variations, namely, asymmetric digital subscriber line (ADSL), high bit-rate digital subscriber line (HDSL), symmetric digital subscriber line (SDSL), very high speed subscriber line (VDSL), and so on. The most common among these is *asymmetric digital subscriber line* (ADSL) technology.

ADSL Technology

ADSL is asymmetric because the maximum upstream bandwidth is different from the maximum downstream bandwidth: downstream bandwidth (from the provider's central office to the customer site) is greater than upstream. ADSL can be used up to six kilometers (3.75 miles). The maximum bandwidth delivered by ADSL depends on the distance and the quality of the physical media. The asymmetry combined with an always-on feature makes it ideal for Internet surfing and video-on-demand, during which users typically download much more information than they upload.

An ADSL circuit connects an ADSL modem on each end of a twisted pair, creating three information channels: a high-speed downstream channel, a medium-stream full-duplex channel, and a basic-speed telephone channel. The high-speed channel typically ranges from 1.5 to 6.1 Mb/sec. The medium-speed channel ranges from 16 to 640 Kb/sec.

ADSL depends on advanced digital signal processing and on creative algorithms to squeeze maximum information through a twisted pair. Two encoding techniques—*carrierless amplitude and phase* (CAP) and *discrete multitone* (DMT)—are used to implement ADSL. Splitters are installed in the service provider's central office to separate the ADSL circuit from telephone circuits (see Figure 5.27). ADSL can coexist with the telephone connection when the local loop carries both analog and ISDN telephone connections.

Transport Mechanism

Above the ADSL encoding techniques, there are two possible ways of transporting data, namely, ATM (fixed-length cells) and frame (variable-

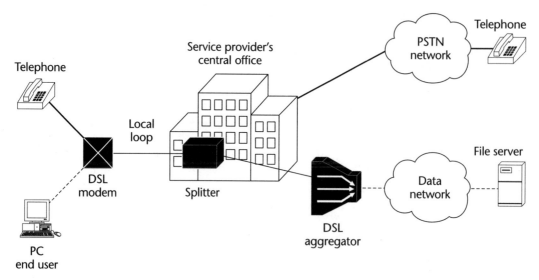

Figure 5.27 Coexistence of ADSL circuits and telephone connections.

length packets). The most popular is ATM, which makes it easy to aggregate several ADSL connections using an ATM uplink. The aggregating device terminates the ADSL circuit and transmits it over an ATM network to the service provider PoP. Figure 5.28 shows how this is typically done. All of the ADSL circuits are terminated on the DSL aggregator, and from there on the data is transported as ATM to the service provider PoP. The default VPI/VCI used for carrying data is VPI = 1, VCI = 32. VPI = 1, VCI = 33 is sometimes used to carry traffic in order to manage the ADSL modem.

Data Encapsulation

ATM only provides the transport mechanism for higher-layer services like voice, video, and data that make use of ADSL. A number of methods to transport data across an ATM network have been defined. Most common among them are *bridging,* using RFC 1483 and classic IP based on RFC 1577. In the case of RFC 1483, the ADSL modem has an Ethernet interface toward the end user, and in the case of RFC 1577, the ADSL modem has an ATM interface toward the end user (see Figure 5.29).

5.4.8 Cable Modem

Cable modems use the *cable television (CATV)* network to deliver data from the customer's premises to the nearest service provider PoP. With near-ubiquitous coverage, coaxial cable connections provide a potentially powerful platform for providing residences and small businesses with high-speed data access. Cable systems were originally designed to deliver

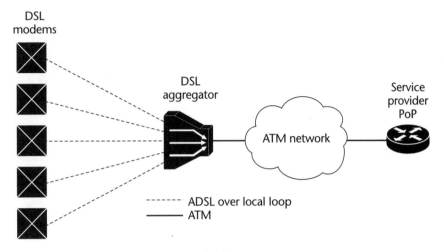

Figure 5.28 ADSL aggregation using ATM.

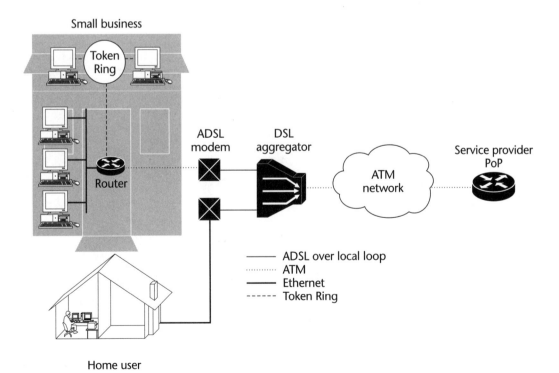

Figure 5.29 Data encapsulation techniques using ADSL.

broadcast television signals efficiently to subscribers' homes. To ensure that consumers could obtain cable service with the same TV sets they use to receive air-broadcast TV signals, cable operators re-create a portion of the air radio frequency spectrum within a sealed coaxial cable line.

Traditional coaxial cable systems typically operate with 330 or 450 MHz of capacity, whereas modern *hybrid fiber/coax* (HFC) systems are expanded to 750 MHz or more. Logically, downstream video programming signals begin around 50 MHz, the equivalent of channel 2 for air-broadcast television signals. The 5 to 42 MHz portion of the spectrum is usually reserved for upstream communications from subscriber homes.

Each standard television channel occupies 6 MHz of the radio frequency spectrum. Thus, a traditional cable system with 400 MHz of downstream bandwidth can carry the equivalent of 60 analog TV channels, and a modern HFC system with 700 MHz of downstream bandwidth has the capacity for some 110 channels.

Technology

Figure 5.30 shows the components of a cable access network. The HFC network is common to both the television and data networks. A *cable modem* provides connectivity between the data devices and the service provider network. A *splitter* is required to separate the frequencies used by the television (low frequency) and the cable modem. The *head-end device* (typically a router) is used to terminate all of the cable modem connections.

To deliver data services over a cable network, one television channel (in the 50 to 750 MHz range) is typically allocated for downstream traffic to homes, and another channel (in the 5 to 42 MHz band) is used to

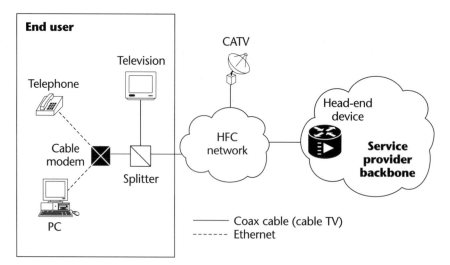

Figure 5.30 Components of a cable modem access network.

carry upstream signals. A cable modem head-end system communicates through these channels, with cable modems located in subscriber homes to create a VLAN connection. Most cable modems are external devices that connect to a PC through a standard 10 Base-T Ethernet card and twisted-pair wiring.

The cable modem access network operates at Layer 1 (physical) and Layer 2 (media access control/logical link control) of the OSI reference model. Thus, Layer 3 (network) protocols, such as IP traffic, can be seamlessly delivered over the cable modem platform to end users.

A single downstream 6 MHz television channel may support up to 27 Mb/sec of downstream data throughput from the cable head-end using the 64 *quadrature amplitude modulation* (QAM) transmission technology. Speeds can be boosted to 36 Mb/sec using 256 QAM. Upstream channels may deliver 500 Kb/sec to 10 Mb/sec from homes using 16 QAM or *quadrature phase shift key* (QPSK) modulation techniques, depending on the amount of the spectrum allocated for service. This upstream and downstream bandwidth is shared by the active data subscribers connected to a given cable network segment, typically 500 to 5000 homes on a modern HFC network.

Transport Technology

The media access control (MAC) mechanism is normally implemented in hardware or in a combination of hardware and software. The primary purpose of the MAC is to share the media in a reasonable way. Both the head-end device and the cable modem implement protocols to do the following:

- Range to compensate for different cable losses. It is essential that all upstream bursts from all cable modems be received in the head-end at the same level. If two cable modems transmit at the same time, but one is much weaker than the other, the head-end device will hear only the strong signal and assume everything is OK. If the two signals have the same strength, the signals will garble and the head-end device will know a collision has occurred.
- Range to compensate for different cable delays. The size of a CATV network calls for a fairly large delay in the millisecond range.
- Assign frequencies and so on to the cable modems. A cable modem first listens to the downstream to collect information about where and how to answer. It signs on to the system using the assigned upstream frequency, and so on.
- Allocate time slots for the upstream.

Data-over-cable service interface (DOCSIS) is the Layer 2 standard used between the cable modem and the head-end device. Figure 5.31 shows the format of a DOCSIS frame. The *frame control* (FC) field identifies the type of MAC header, 1 byte. Four common types are

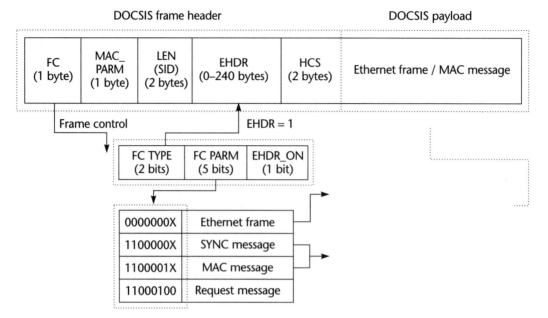

Figure 5.31 DOCSIS frame format.

0000 000X—data packet

1100 000X—timing header

1100 001X—MAC management header

1100 010X—request header

MAC_PARM is a multipurpose field, 2 bytes.

EHDR field length: if EHDR_ON = 1.

MAC frame count: for concatenated frames

Number of minislots: for bandwidth requests.

LEN (SID) is the length of the MAC frame, defined to be the sum of the number of bytes in the extended header (if present) and the number of bytes following the HCS field. (For a REQ header, this field is the service ID instead.) EHDR is the variable-size extended MAC header (where present), 0 to 240 bytes. HCS is the MAC header check sequence, 2 bytes.

Data over Cable Modem

Figure 5.32 shows a typical cable modem network. The HFC network is used to provide connectivity to the nearest service provider PoP. The head-end device is located in the service provider PoP. Multimedia

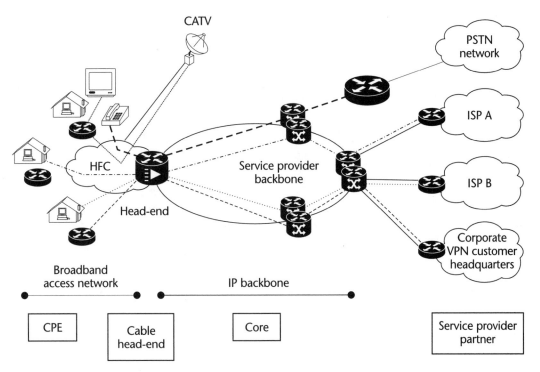

Figure 5.32 Cable modem network.

services (e.g., voice, data, and video) can be offered using a single cable modem for each customer.

An individual cable modem subscriber may experience access speeds from 500 Kb/sec to 1 Mb/sec or more, depending on the network architecture and traffic load. This provides more bandwidth than ADSL or dial-up alternatives. In addition to speed, cable modems offer another key benefit: constant connectivity. Because cable modems use connectionless technology, much like in an office LAN, a subscriber's PC is always online with the network. That means there's no need to dial in to begin a session, so users do not have to worry about receiving busy signals. Additionally, going online does not tie up their telephone line.

5.4.9 Summary

Now we will summarize the features of all of the transport technologies (see Table 5.2). The summary will be based on the following factors:

- *Link capacity:* Maximum capacity of each link
- *Application:* Whether it can be used as a transport layer in the access or core

Table 5.2   Summary of transport technology features.

Technology	Capacity	Application	Aggregation	QoS Features	QoS Transparency
POS	2.4 Gb/sec	Core, access	No	—	—
Ring topology	2.4 Gb/sec	Core, PoP	—	Bandwidth multicast	No
Frame relay	34 Mb/sec	Access	Yes	Bandwidth	Yes
ATM	2.4 Gb/sec	Core, access	Yes	Bandwidth, delay, delay variation	Yes*
ADSL	640 Kb/sec—upstream 6 Mb/sec—downstream	Access	Yes (when using ATM as the transport technology)	Bandwidth	Similar to ATM
Ethernet	10 Mb/sec 100 Mb/sec 1000 Mb/sec	Access, core	Yes	Bandwidth,† broadcast, multicast	—
ISDN	128 Mb/sec	Access	Yes‡	Bandwidth	Yes

* In order to guarantee bandwidth, this requires EPD/IPD.
† Ethernet does not provide any support to restrict bandwidth for each user when several users share the same physical connection.
‡ In the case of ISDN, the aggregation requires that the uplink be a different technology. The technology beween the aggregating device and the edge device will not be ISDN.

- *Aggregation:* Ability to aggregate several connections onto a single physical link
- *QoS features:* Controlling bandwidth for each user, guaranteed bandwidth when several connections are carried on the same physical link, delay and delay variation, broadcast, multicast support
- *QoS transparency:* QoS available at the transport layer is also applicable to QoS at higher layers like IP—for example, in an ATM network, in the case of bandwidth as a QoS parameter, cell discard due to congestion can result in zero throughput at the IP layer even when the throughput at the ATM still meets the QoS requirements

5.5 Service Creation

This section focuses on the ability of each technology to help the service provider create services and deliver multiservices using the same technology. Services can be provided in several flavors. The goal of the service provider is to create and provide new services for their customers in such a way that they are useful and interesting for the customers and, more importantly, that they are also profitable for the service provider. The services have to be created and delivered using the existing infrastructure or by minimum additions to the existing infrastructure in terms of hardware, software, and staffing requirements.

5.5.1 Role of MPLS

As seen from the discussion in Section 5.3.1, MPLS is a core technology. It helps service providers to build core networks that are stable and scalable. The core of the service provider network is mainly responsible for providing connectivity between the PoPs (edge devices) and must be capable of transporting traffic related to several services. In addition to these features, MPLS also helps to provide some value-added services, such as traffic engineering, and to meet the QoS requirements of the services that make use of the core network for transport.

Scalable Core

The growth in the number of services offered by the service provider should not necessitate the installation of new devices to support the additional services. The service provider will thus be able to reduce their cost in building and maintaining the core networks. The growth in core infrastructure required to support additional services should be at a minimum. Since all IP packets are transported as MPLS within the core, the same core can be used to transport IP packets from multiservices. As long as there is enough bandwidth in the core to meet the bandwidth requirement of all the services, new services can make use of the same core infrastructure to transport data from one PoP location to another. Thus, MPLS helps the service provider in reducing the cost of building and maintaining the core network.

Stable Core

"Stability" here refers to the separation of the *forwarding information base* (FIB) of the core network from the customer networks. Since the core network will be used to support multiservices and multiple customers, the RIB related to the customers must not have any impact on the RIB of the core network. Otherwise, instability in the RIB of a customer network will affect the core network and in turn can affect other customers.

MPLS helps to achieve this goal. The stack of labels supported by MPLS helps to distinguish between the RIB of the core network and the RIB of customer networks. The edge devices (PE) must have the necessary intelligence to introduce additional labels and switch the packets based on these labels. The RIB of the core devices contains information only about the core and edge devices; the RIB of edge devices contains information about the customer networks that are connected to the edge devices.

Figure 5.33 shows an example of how MPLS helps to achieve this stability. Here the MPLS network helps to transport IP packets from two different services (dotted cloud and dashed cloud). The P routers are the core routers, and the PE routers are the edge routers. The RIB of the edge routers includes the network 10.0.0.0/24, 11.0.0.0/24, 12.0.0.0/24, and 14.0.0.0/24. The RIB of the P routers contains information only about the edge routers. The P routers forward packets based on the labels for the PE devices.

Consider the normal IP traffic flowing from CE_1 to CE_3. Packets are switched from CE_1 to PE_1 based on the address 11.0.0.1. PE_1 encapsulates the IP packet in an MPLS header and attaches the label 6 (label for PE_2). P_1 and P_2 switch the MPLS packet based on the MPLS label for PE_2. PE_2 switches the packet based on the IP address 11.0.0.1. The addition of new customer networks has no impact on the RIB of the core devices. Withdrawal of the network 11.0.0.0 from the RIB of PE_1, PE_2, and CE_3 has no impact on the RIB of the P_1 and P_2 routers.

Traffic Engineering

As seen in Section 5.3.1, another feature supported by MPLS is traffic engineering, which helps the service provider to do constraint-based routing in a simple manner. Constraint-based routing is more complicated in a classic IP network because IP routing is not source-based. Each hop in the path from the source to the destination will determine how to route the traffic. Critics might point out that this can also be done in an IP network by building generic routing encapsulation (GRE) tunnels. However, this solution is not scalable because it is difficult to manage the routing through the GRE tunnels when the number of tunnels is large. Traffic engineering helps the service provider in several ways.

Bandwidth Management

When links between core devices become congested, traffic can be diverted through less-congested links. For example, in Figure 5.34, there are two paths from PE_1 to PE_2. Traffic from CE_1 to CE_3 requires 60% of the link capacity between core devices P_1 and P_2. Traffic from CE_2 to CE_4 is now forced from PE_1 to PE_2 via core devices P_3 and P_4 by creating a new traffic-engineering tunnel between PE_1 and PE_2.

Guaranteed Bandwidth

In conjunction with queuing and policing mechanisms, traffic-engineering tunnels can be used to implement guaranteed bandwidth tunnels. This helps to create new services that require guaranteed

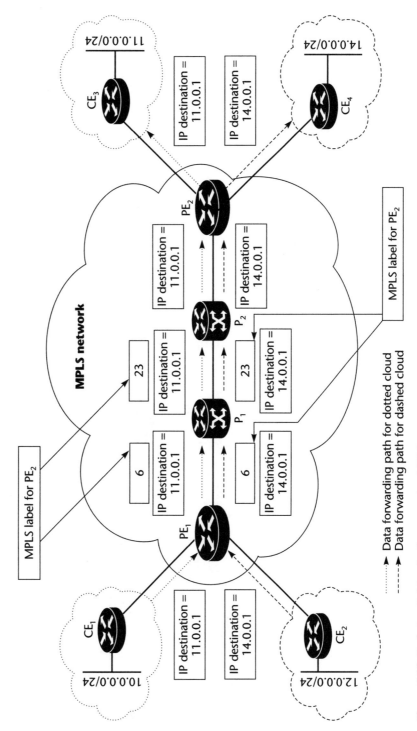

Figure 5.33 Packet switching in the core using MPLS.

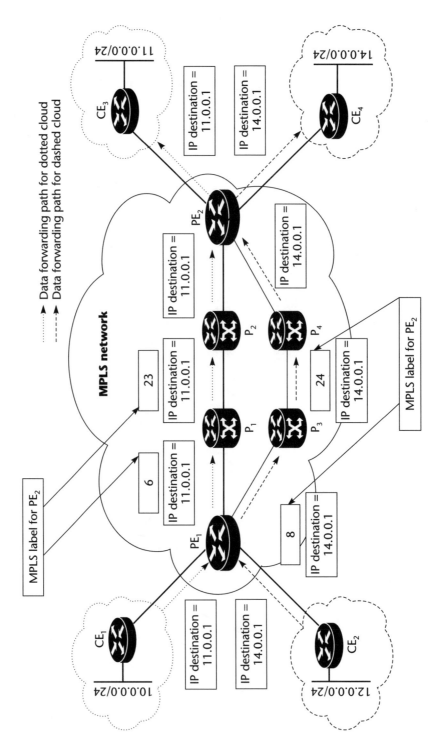

Figure 5.34 Traffic-engineering tunnel for each traffic flow.

bandwidth across the core network. This is possible because of the traffic-engineering capabilities of MPLS.

Consider the following scenario shown in Figure 5.35. Two traffic-engineering tunnels are built between PE_1 and PE_2. The dotted tunnel carries traffic from CE_1 to CE_3. The dashed tunnel carries traffic from CE_2 to CE_4. The end-to-end link capacity is 155 Mb/sec. Each tunnel has a bandwidth requirement of 100 Mb/sec, of which only the dashed tunnel has guaranteed bandwidth. Clearly, it is not possible to meet the requirements of both tunnels. However, by using good policing mechanisms, it is possible to restrict the bandwidth allocated to traffic-engineering tunnel 1 to 50 Mb/sec, thereby ensuring that traffic-engineering tunnel 2 gets 100 Mb/sec bandwidth.

QoS

MPLS is used to transport IP traffic across the core network. In order to support end-to-end QoS, MPLS must be capable of supporting the QoS guaranteed by IP. QoS in an IP network refers to the following aspects:

Bandwidth

Minimal delay, delay variation

Priority to certain classes of traffic over others

Implementing effective policing and traffic-shaping mechanisms can satisfy bandwidth requirements. Delay and priority requirements can be satisfied by differentiating packets belonging to different services and by implementing queuing mechanisms in the routers that will help deliver the QoS guaranteed to the different services.

In a multiservice environment, it is necessary to distinguish between the different services. To allow traffic to have different policies applied to it, some method of differentiation of packets is required. Within the IP header is an 8-bit field known as *type of service* (ToS), within which 3 bits were used as precedence, allowing for eight classes to be used. Figure 5.36 shows the details of the ToS field of the IP header.

In order for the MPLS to deliver the QoS guaranteed by IP, it is necessary to queue the packets using the same field, such as IP. MPLS, however, has 3 bits in the experimental field in the MPLS header, which the IP precedence is copied to, as an IP packet has a label appended to it. More details about QoS can be found in Chapter 7.

5.5.2 Role of MPLS-VPN

MPLS-VPN brings several benefits to the service provider and helps to create new services. VPNs provide data security and ensure that the network is isolated from other networks. Communication with other networks (e.g., the Internet) is done in a controlled manner. Traditionally, VPNs

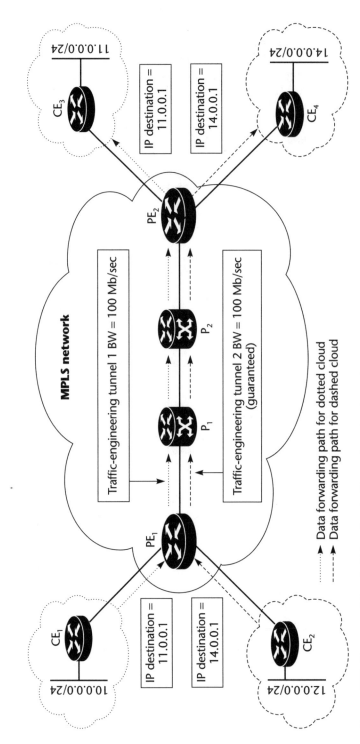

Figure 5.35 Guaranteed bandwidth using traffic-engineering tunnels.

IP packet

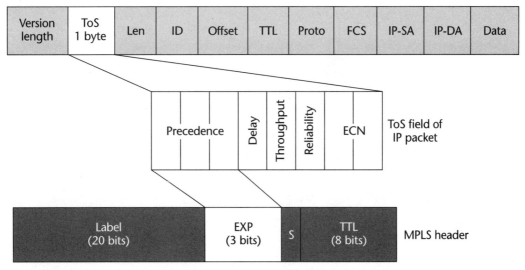

Figure 5.36 Mapping of precedence bits to experimental (EXP) bits.

implement these features by using separate Layer 2 networks. This does not make it scalable for the service provider because the core network can no longer be shared among several services.

Scalable Core Network

MPLS-VPN helps the service provider to implement multiple VPNs using the same core network by ensuring that the traffic from the different VPNs is isolated, even though all of these VPNs are implemented using the same core network. Moreover, the RIB of the VPN is independent from the RIB of the core. This also makes the core network scalable.

The intelligence is implemented in the PE routers. They maintain a separate RIB for each VPN. This helps to implement VPNs that have overlapping address space and still make use of the same core network. Figure 5.37 shows an example of how MPLS-VPN helps to implement VPNs that can share the same core network and how these VPNs can have overlapping address space. The dotted VPN and the dashed VPN use the same address space. The PE routers PE_1 and PE_2 maintain separate FIBs for each VPN and ensure the isolation between the VPNs. The core routers P_1 and P_2 do not have any information about the VPNs in their FIBs. The core routers forward the VPN traffic based on the core label, and the VPN label is transparent to the core routers. The PE router inserts two labels to the IP packet before forwarding it to the core router. The inner label is the VPN label and is used by the PE routers; the outer label is the

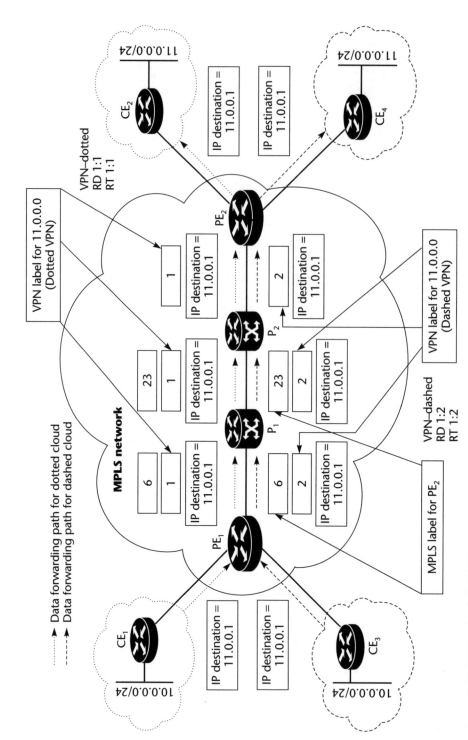

Figure 5.37 VPNs using MPLS-VPN.

MPLS label that is used by the core routers to switch the packets to the PE router.

For example, for the traffic flowing from CE_1 to CE_2 (dotted VPN), P_1 forwards this traffic based on the label for router PE_2. For the traffic flowing from CE_3 to CE_4 (dashed VPN), P_1 also forwards this traffic based on the label for router PE_2. The inner label (VPN label) is transparent to the routers P_1 and P_2 and is used only by PE_2. Irrespective of the number of routes connected to dotted VPN or dashed VPN or the number of VPNs connected to the PE routers, P_1 and P_2 forward traffic based on the labels for the PE routers. This makes the core routers stable and also scalable.

Security

Isolation of traffic between VPNs is implemented in the PE router. Only the PE routers have knowledge about the VPNs; they maintain a separate RIB for each VPN. The VPN labels are used to distinguish between packets from different VPNs. Unique labels are used to distinguish IP packets from different VPNs. This ensures that IP packets are delivered to the correct VPNs. For example, in Figure 5.37, the networks 11.0.0.0/24 belonging to the dotted VPN and the dashed VPN are connected to the router PE_2. PE_2 advertises the following labels to other PEs:

VPN label 1, for network 11.0.0.0/24 belonging to the dotted VPN

VPN label 2, for network 11.0.0.0/24 belonging to the dashed VPN

When PE_1 receives a packet from CE_3 that is destined for 11.0.0.1, it knows that traffic coming from CE_3 belongs to the dashed VPN. It imposes the VPN label 2 and MPLS label 6 onto the IP packet and forwards it to P_1. P_1 and P_2 forward the packets based on the MPLS label. When the packet arrives at PE_2, it sees the VPN label 2 and knows that this label is for the dashed VPN and forwards the packet to CE_4.

Extranets and Intranets

Other services that can be easily implemented using MPLS-VPN are extranets, intranets, and selective connectivity between intranets. Traditionally, extranets are implemented using policy routing, but it makes the life of the network administrator a nightmare to maintain all of the policies. Using MPLS-VPN, this can be done in a simple and easy manner. By selectively allowing certain routes to be leaked from a VPN to another VPN, it is possible to create extranets and connectivity between intranets. Firewalls can be implemented between intranets.

A typical application of extranets in the context of a large company would be in the data center where all of the servers are located. Some of the servers are dedicated to each department, and some of the common servers can be accessed by a group of departments. This can be easily

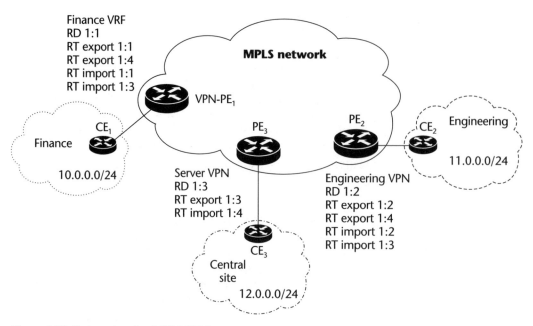

Figure 5.38 Extranets using MPLS-VPN.

implemented by creating a VPN for each department. The common servers are placed on a separate VPN (server VPN). The department VPNs cannot directly communicate with each other, but have access to the server
VPN. Figure 5.38 shows the implementation of extranets.

5.5.3 Role of ADSL Technology

ADSL technology helps a service provider to create new IP services. The
use of the local loop to transmit data and voice simultaneously also helps
to reduce costs. One of the advantages of ADSL is that the same local loop
can be used to carry voice and data traffic. This helps the service provider
to deliver multiservices (voice, data, and video) using the same physical
medium. This is a big selling point with residential customers, who can
now surf the Internet and at the same time use their telephone for voice
conversations (see Figure 5.39).

5.5.4 Role of Cable Technology

Cable technology also helps a service provider to create new IP services. As
with ADSL, the advantage of cable is that the same coax cable can be used
to carry voice and data traffic. The service provider cannot only offer voice
and data but also can offer video services using the same physical connection. Residential customers can now surf the Internet, carry on telephone
conversations, and watch TV all at the same time (see Figure 5.40). A

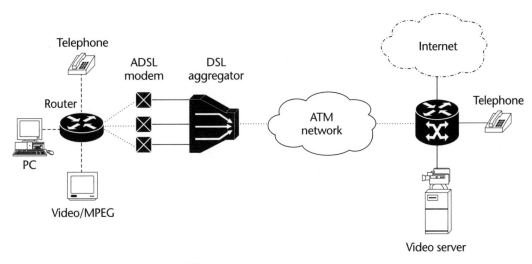

Figure 5.39 Multiservices using ADSL.

single point of contact and a single bill provide the customer with all three services.

5.5.5 Role of ATM

ATM as an access technology helps the service provider in several ways to create new services. In the access network, ATM is one of the most versatile technologies, and in combination with ADSL makes an excellent choice for offering several services to end customers.

Multiservices

As shown in Figure 5.41, ATM can also be used to deliver multiservices. Intelligent CPE devices can help aggregate traffic from several sources and deliver it to the service provider PoP using the ATM network. The QoS guaranteed by the ATM network helps to easily aggregate different classes of traffic onto a single ATM link and still guarantee the QoS requirements of all applications.

Aggregation

ATM is an excellent technology for aggregation. Aggregation helps the service provider to reduce link costs. Another advantage of aggregation is oversubscription. Assuming that all the customers do not send traffic at the same time, the access network can be oversubscribed. What this means is that the sum of all the link capacity of the incoming links on the aggregator exceeds the uplink capacity of the aggregator.

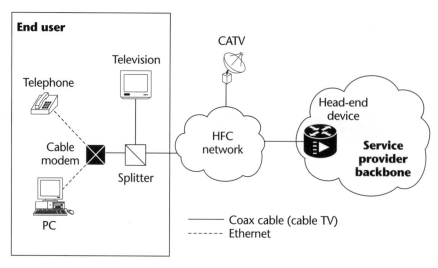

Figure 5.40 Multiservices using cable.

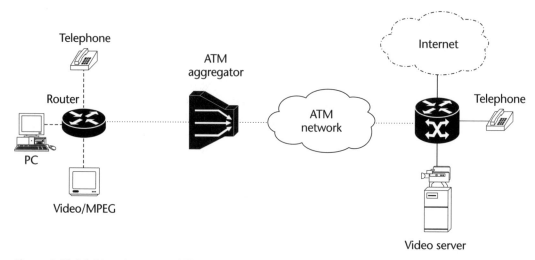

Figure 5.41 Multiservices using ATM.

QoS

The ATM layer helps to guarantee certain QoS to end customers. QoS here includes guaranteed bandwidth (for data transfer applications) and also guaranteed end-to-end delay for voice and video applications. For the service provider, the ATM layer helps to oversubscribe and to distinguish between different classes of customers. Customers who require premium services get better QoS than customers who require only best-effort services.

This helps the service provider to oversubscribe and thus accommodate more customers (and hence gain more revenue).

The QoS transparency between the IP layer and the ATM layer provides an excellent means for implementing IP networks using ATM technology. This reduces the burden on the IP layer to implement and enforce QoS requirements. The processing power on the router can be devoted to other activities related to IP services.

5.5.6 Role of Multicast

IP multicast also helps a service provider to create new services. As seen in Section 5.3.3, there are several applications that require multicast support. Some of these applications are also time-critical in nature. By using multicast to deliver data from these applications, the service provider can reduce the volume of traffic in the backbone. Customers can also get more value out of their link capacity.

Consider a company that has a central office and several remote offices. Each remote office has a copy of the company database. The remote database is updated every morning with a copy from the central office. If this must be done simultaneously, then a very fast link (equal to the sum of the link capacities of all the remote sites) is required from the central office. However, if multicast is used to update the database, then the link capacity of the central site need not be very large. Assuming that the service provider backbone supports multicast, the provider can easily offer this service to the customer and help them reduce their costs.

5.6 Chapter Review

This chapter provided an overview of the architecture of the IP network of a service provider, followed by a discussion on the various technologies that enable a service provider to build stable and scalable IP networks. Building a scalable and stable core network is very important for service providers because it will help them to support several services at once, thereby reducing maintenance costs. This topic was followed by a discussion on the various access technologies that help transport IP packets from the customer site to the nearest service provider PoP. Some of the features that must be supported by these access technologies to make them scalable were also discussed, such as aggregation and transparency in QoS between the access network and the IP network.

The latter part of the chapter focused on how the various technologies help to create new IP-based services for the service provider. The next chapter focuses on implementing IP-based services and the role of network management in developing and deploying those services.

IP-Based Service Implementation and Network Management

The previous chapter discussed IP and the technologies that help a service provider to develop IP-based services. This chapter discusses the implementation and delivery of those services. While technology plays an important role in developing services, it is also important that the services be provisioned and delivered in an easy and profitable manner. "Easy and profitable" here refers to the scalability of the solution in terms of the staffing and skills required to implement the solution for a mass market. Technical implementation in the lab is an academic exercise to show the feasibility of a solution. This solution may not be profitable for a service provider if provisioning the service for a large number of customers is too expensive or time-consuming.

It is important that the provisioning of the service be (1) simple, meaning that it can be done easily and does not require skilled staff, and (2) scalable, meaning that a significant number of customers can be provisioned in a reasonable period of time. The terms *significant number* and *reasonable period of time* have to be defined by the service provider with reference to profitability. The choice of network devices and provisioning tools plays an important role in making the service provision simple and scalable.

Another significant factor in provisioning services is *service upgrades*. A service upgrade may require changes in the configuration of existing devices or a software/hardware upgrade of the network devices. The ease and speed at which a service upgrade can be done for a large number of customers also play an important role in making a service profitable for the service provider.

Another important aspect of delivering IP-based services is network management. It is not enough if the service is implemented correctly. It must also be monitored on a regular basis to ensure that it is functioning properly. This requires an investment in equipment, staffing, and intelligence in the network devices. There is a trade-off between the cost of monitoring and the benefits provided by monitoring. Proactive monitoring is useful and helps to prevent service outages and network downtime. The cost of repairing a fault after its manifestation can be much higher than the cost of monitoring the network and preventing the occurrence of the fault in the first place.

Consider the situation in which a network device starts malfunctioning as the memory usage and load on it reaches a certain threshold. This device is in a remote location, so it takes a few hours for the maintenance crew to physically reach it. The load and memory usage are directly proportional to the number of customer connections terminating on the device. When the load reaches the threshold, the device stops functioning and must be reset. The maintenance crew must go to the site where it is located in order to reset it. Proactive monitoring of the load and memory usage of the device can help to prevent this situation. In order to keep a good balance between the cost and benefits of monitoring, it is necessary to have a good network management infrastructure.

This chapter focuses on the implementation of IP-based services, monitoring the network to ensure correct delivery of the services, and reporting the status of the devices to customers as part of the *service-level agreement* (SLA). As SNMP plays an important role in implementing IP-based services, a brief discussion on SNMP is presented in the beginning of the chapter.

Several aspects related to the implementation of IP-based services are presented in this chapter, such as security and management. The *operations support system* (OSS) is the system responsible for implementing the IP-based services. A discussion on the importance of OSS, its architecture, and its requirements is also presented here. (Chapter 8 presents several case studies that show the importance of the OSS in implementing IP-based services.)

6.1 Simple Network Management Protocol

The *simple network management protocol* (SNMP) is an application-layer protocol that facilitates the exchange of management information between network devices. It is part of the *transmission control protocol/Internet Protocol* (TCP/IP) suite. SNMP enables network administrators to manage network performance, find and solve network problems, and plan for network growth. Three versions of SNMP exist: SNMP version 1 (SNMPv1), SNMP version 2 (SNMPv2), and SNMP version 3 (SNMPv3). All three versions have a number of features in common, but SNMPv2 offers enhancements, such as additional protocol operations, and SNMPv3 offers security features.

SNMP plays an important role in managing networks. It helps provide a uniform interface to access and manage all network devices. More detailed information about SNMP can be found in Stallings 1998. This section makes use of information presented in Downes et al. 1998.

6.1.1 Description

SNMP defines a client/server relationship. The client program (called the *network management system,* or NMS) makes virtual connections to a server program (called the *SNMP agent*) that executes on a remote network device, and serves information to the NMS regarding the device's status. The database, controlled by the SNMP agent, is referred to as the SNMP *management information base* (MIB) and is a standard set of statistical and control values. SNMP additionally allows the extension of these standard values with values specific to a particular agent through the use of private MIBs.

Directives, issued by the NMS client to an SNMP agent, consist of the identifiers of SNMP variables (referred to as *MIB object identifiers* or *MIB variables*) along with instructions to either get the value for the identifier or set the identifier to a new value. Through the use of private MIB variables, SNMP agents can be tailored for a myriad of specific devices, such as network bridges, gateways, and routers. The definitions of MIB variables supported by a particular agent are incorporated in descriptor files, written in *Abstract Syntax Notation* (ASN.1)[ASN.1-1, ASN.1-2, ASN.1-3, ASN.1-4] format, made available to network management client programs so that they can become aware of MIB variables and their usage.

6.1.2 Components

As shown in Figure 6.1, an SNMP managed network consists of four key components: managed devices, agents, MIBs, and an NMS.

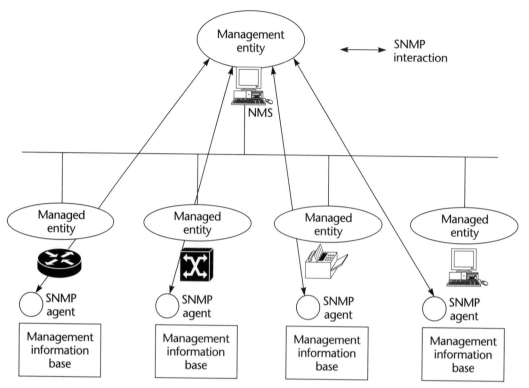

Figure 6.1 SNMP components.

- *Managed device:* A network node that contains an SNMP agent and resides on a managed network. Managed devices collect and store management information and make this information available to the NMS using SNMP. Managed devices, sometimes called *network elements,* can be routers and access servers, switches and bridges, hubs, computer hosts, and printers.
- *Agent:* A network management software module that resides in a managed device. An agent has local knowledge of management information and translates that information into a form compatible with SNMP.
- *MIB:* Consists of the management information that resides in the managed device. The agent provides a standard access to the MIB.
- *NMS:* Executes applications that monitor and control managed devices. The NMS provides the bulk of the processing and memory resources required for network management. One or more NMSs must exist on any managed network.

6.1.3 Operations

Managed devices are monitored and controlled using four basic SNMP commands: *read, write, trap,* and *traversal operations.*

- *Read command:* Used by an NMS to monitor managed devices. The NMS examines different variables that are maintained by managed devices.
- *Write command:* Used by an NMS to control managed devices. The NMS changes the values of variables stored within managed devices.
- *Trap command:* Used by managed devices to asynchronously report events to the NMS. When certain types of events occur, a managed device sends a trap to the NMS.
- *Traversal operations:* Used by the NMS to determine which variables a managed device supports and to sequentially gather information in variable tables, such as a routing table.

6.1.4 Management Information Base

A management information base (MIB) is a collection of information that is organized hierarchically. MIBs are accessed using a network management protocol such as SNMP. They are composed of managed objects and are identified by object identifiers. A managed object (sometimes called an *MIB object,* an *object,* or a *MIB*) is one of any number of specific characteristics of a managed device. Managed objects are composed of one or more object instances, which are essentially variables. Two types of managed objects exist: *scalar* and *tabular.* Scalar objects define a single object instance. Tabular objects define multiple related object instances that are grouped together in MIB tables.

Figure 6.2 shows a sample MIB tree and shows examples of scalar and tabular managed objects. An example of a scalar managed object is `ifNumber`, which is a scalar object that contains a single object instance, the integer value that indicates the total number of interfaces in the router. An example of a tabular managed object is `ifTable`, which is a tabular object that contains a multiple object instance. Each instance contains detailed information about the interfaces in the router. The top-level MIB object IDs belong to different standards organizations, while lower-level object IDs are allocated by associated organizations. Vendors can define private branches that include managed objects for their own products. MIBs that have not been standardized typically are positioned in the experimental branch. The managed object `ifNumber` can be uniquely identified either by the object name—*iso.org.dod.internet.mgmt.mib-2.interfaces.ifNumber*—or by the equivalent object descriptor—1.3.6.1.2.1.2.1.

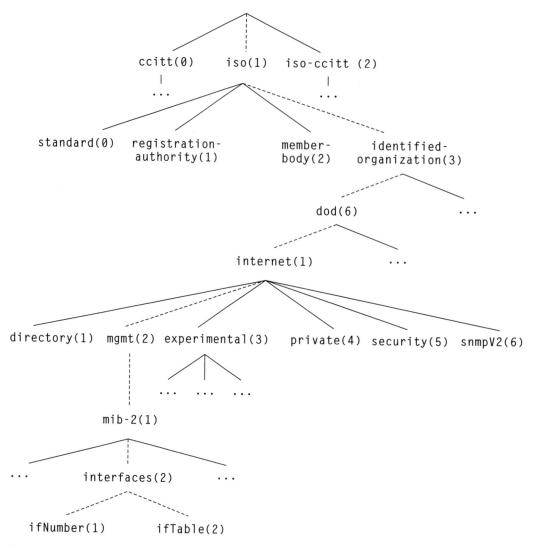

Figure 6.2 Sample MIB tree.

6.1.5   SNMP Version 1

SNMP Version 1 (SNMPv1) is the initial implementation of the SNMP protocol. It is described in RFC 1157 (Case et al. 1990) and functions within the specifications of the *structure of management information* (SMI). SNMPv1 operates over protocols such as the *user datagram protocol* (UDP), Internet Protocol (IP), OSI *Connectionless Network Service* (CLNS), AppleTalk's *Datagram-Delivery Protocol* (DDP), and Novell's *Internet Packet*

Exchange (IPX). SNMPv1 is widely used and is the de facto network management protocol in the Internet community.

SNMPv1 and Structure of Management Information

The structure of management information (SMI) defines the rules for describing management information, using ASN.1. The SNMPv1 SMI is defined in RFC 1155 (Rose and McCloghrie 1990). It makes three key specifications: ASN.1 data types, SMI-specific data types, and SNMP MIB tables.

SNMPv1 and ASN.1 Data Types

The SNMPv1 SMI specifies that all managed objects have a certain subset of ASN.1 data types associated with them. Three ASN.1 data types are required: name, syntax, and encoding. The name serves as the object identifier (object ID). The syntax defines the data type of the object (e.g., integer or string). The SMI uses a subset of the ASN.1 syntax definitions. The encoding data describes how information associated with a managed object is formatted as a series of data items for transmission over the network.

SNMPv1 and SMI-Specific Data Types

The SNMPv1 SMI specifies the use of a number of SMI-specific data types, which are divided into two categories: simple data types and application-wide data types. Three simple data types are defined in the SNMPv1 SMI, all of which are unique values: integers, octet strings, and object IDs.

- *Integer data type:* A signed integer in the range of $-2,147,483,648$ to $2,147,483,647$.
- *Octet strings:* Ordered sequences of 0 to 65,535 octets.
- *Object IDs:* Come from the set of all object identifiers allocated according to the rules specified in ASN.1.

Seven application-wide data types exist in the SNMPv1 SMI: network addresses, counters, gauges, time ticks, opaques, integers, and unsigned integers.

- *Network addresses:* Represent an address from a particular protocol family. SNMPv1 supports only 32-bit IP addresses.
- *Counters:* Nonnegative integers that increase until they reach a maximum value and then return to zero. In SNMPv1, a 32-bit counter size is specified.
- *Gauges:* Nonnegative integers that can increase or decrease but retain the maximum value reached.
- *Time tick:* Represents a hundredth of a second since some event.

- *Opaque:* Represents an arbitrary encoding that is used to pass arbitrary information strings that do not conform to the strict data typing used by the SMI.
- *Integer:* Represents signed integer-valued information. This data type redefines the integer data type, which has arbitrary precision in ASN.1 but bounded precision in the SMI.
- *Unsigned integer:* Represents unsigned integer-valued information and is useful when values are always nonnegative. This data type redefines the integer data type, which has arbitrary precision in ASN.1 but bounded precision in the SMI.

SNMP MIB Tables

The SNMPv1 SMI defines highly structured tables that are used to group the instances of a tabular object (i.e., an object that contains multiple variables). Tables are composed of zero or more rows, which are indexed in a way that allows SNMP to retrieve or alter an entire row with one Get, GetNext, or Set command.

SNMPv1 Protocol Operations

SNMP is a simple request-response protocol. The network management system issues a request, and managed devices return responses. This behavior is implemented by using one of four protocol operations: Get, GetNext, Set, and Trap.

- *Get operation:* Used by the NMS to retrieve the value of one or more object instances from an agent. If the agent responding to the Get operation cannot provide values for all the object instances in a list, it does not provide any values.
- *GetNext operation:* Used by the NMS to retrieve the value of the next object instance in a table or list within an agent.
- *Set operation:* Used by the NMS to set the values of object instances within an agent.
- *Trap operation:* Used by agents to asynchronously inform the NMS of a significant event.

6.1.6 SNMP Version 2

SNMP version 2 (SNMPv2) is an evolution of the initial version, SNMPv1. Originally, SNMPv2 was published as a set of proposed Internet standards in 1993. Currently, it is a draft standard. As with SNMPv1, SNMPv2 functions within the specifications of the SMI. In theory, SNMPv2 offers a number of improvements to SNMPv1, including additional protocol operations.

SNMPv2 and Structure of Management Information

The structure of management information (SMI) defines the rules for describing management information, using ASN.1. The SNMPv2 SMI is described in RFC 1902. It makes certain additions and enhancements to the SNMPv1 SMI-specific data types, such as including bit strings, network addresses, and counters.

- *Bit strings:* Defined only in SNMPv2 and comprise zero or more named bits that specify a value.
- *Network addresses:* Represent an address from a particular protocol family. SNMPv1 supports only 32-bit IP addresses, but SNMPv2 can support other types of addresses as well.
- *Counters:* Nonnegative integers that increase until they reach a maximum value and then return to zero. In SNMPv1, a 32-bit counter size is specified. In SNMPv2, 32-bit and 64-bit counters are defined.

SMI Information Modules

The SNMPv2 SMI also specifies information modules, which specify a group of related definitions. Three types of SMI information modules exist: MIB modules, compliance statements, and capability statements.

- *MIB modules:* Contain definitions of interrelated managed objects.
- *Compliance statements:* Provide a systematic way to describe a group of managed objects that must be implemented for conformance to a standard.
- *Capability statements:* Used to indicate the precise level of support that an agent claims with respect to a MIB group. An NMS can adjust its behavior toward agents according to the capability statements associated with each agent.

SNMPv2 Protocol Operations

The Get, GetNext, and Set operations used in SNMPv1 are also used in SNMPv2. SNMPv2 adds and enhances some protocol operations. The SNMPv2 trap operation, for example, serves the same function as that used in SNMPv1, but it uses a different message format and is designed to replace the SNMPv1 trap. SNMPv2 also defines two new protocol operations: GetBulk and Inform.

- *GetBulk operation:* Used by the NMS to efficiently retrieve large blocks of data, such as multiple rows in a table. GetBulk fills a response message with as much of the requested data as will fit.
- *Inform operation:* Allows one NMS to send trap information to another NMS and receive a response. In SNMPv2, if the agent responding to the GetBulk operation cannot provide values for all of the variables in a list, it will provide partial results.

6.1.7 Security Issues

SNMP lacks any authentication capabilities, which results in vulnerability to a variety of security threats. These include masquerading, modification of information, message sequence and timing modifications, and disclosure.

- *Masquerading:* Consists of an unauthorized entity attempting to perform management operations by assuming the identity of an authorized management entity.
- *Modification of information:* Involves an unauthorized entity attempting to alter a message generated by an authorized entity so that the message results in unauthorized accounting management or configuration management operations.
- *Message sequence and timing modifications:* These occur when an unauthorized entity reorders, delays, or copies and later replays a message generated by an authorized entity.
- *Disclosure:* Results when an unauthorized entity extracts values stored in managed objects, or learns of notified events by monitoring exchanges between managers and agents.

The security issues related to SNMP are addressed in a newer version of SNMP known as SNMP version 3 (SNMPv3).

6.1.8 SNMP Version 3

SNMP version 3 (SNMPv3) is the latest version of SNMP (Case et al. 1990; Wijnen et al. 1999). It uses the framework provided by SNMPv2 and provides some additional features. The new features of SNMPv3 (in addition to those of SNMPv2 listed above) include

- Security features:
  Authentication
  Privacy
  Authorization and access control
- Administrative framework features:
  Naming of entities
  People and policies
  Usernames and key management
  Notification destinations
  Proxy relationships
  Remotely configurable via SNMP operations

SNMPv3 includes three important services: authentication, privacy, and access control. To deliver these services in a flexible and efficient manner, SNMPv3 introduces the concept of a *principal,* which is the entity on whose behalf services are provided or processing takes place. A principal can be an individual acting in a particular role. It can also be a set of individuals with every individual acting in a particular role. In essence, a principal operates from a management station and issues SNMP commands to agent systems. The identity of the principal and the target agent together determine the security features that will be invoked, including authentication, privacy, and access control. The use of principals allows security policies to be tailored to the specific principal, agent, and information exchange, and gives human security managers considerable flexibility in assigning network authorization to users. SNMPv3 security options are shown in Figure 6.3. (More details about SNMPv3 security issues can be found in Stallings 1998.)

6.2 IP-Based Service Implementation—OSS

IP-based service implementation plays an important role in delivering services to customers. It is also critical for service providers, because it helps them to roll out their services in a timely manner, ensure that the services are implemented correctly, win the confidence of the customers, and thereby gain and maintain a large share of the customer base. A good service implementation model is the key to implementing services. The

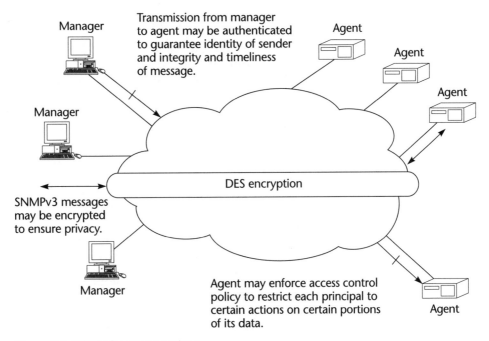

Figure 6.3 SNMPv3 security options.

term *implementation* as regards an IP-based service for a customer refers to several aspects of the service. It starts when the customer is sold the idea of the service, and the end result is when the customer can make use of the service.

To begin with, the customer is sold the idea of the service by the service provider. Once the service is sold, it has to be realized before the customer can actually use it. In some cases, the customer has to provide essential details for implementing the service—for example, information about the IP addressing plan of the customer network, the number of customer sites that require the service, the network infrastructure available at each site, and so on. Once all of the information is available, new network devices have to be installed as required on the customer sites and connected to the nearest PoP. The service provider's network devices have to be configured to provision all of the new connections; after the configurations are complete, the service is ready to be made available to the customer.

The devices have to be integrated into the network monitoring system of the service provider. SLA reporting for the customer (if relevant for the service) has to be activated so that reports can be generated and made available. The billing department has to be informed about the new service so that the customer can be charged for it.

Several key departments are involved in implementing IP-based services, including

- *Business marketing department:* Responsible for defining the business aspect of the services like pricing, service options, time to market, and so on
- *Sales department:* Responsible for selling the IP-based services to the customer, maintaining the customer contact, and also for getting the requirements and information from the customer that are required for implementing the IP-based services
- *Engineering department:* Responsible for developing and testing the technical solution for implementing the IP-based services
- *NMS department:* Responsible for developing the NMS tools required for mass deployment of the services, service upgrades, billing, and SLA reports
- *NOC:* Responsible for deploying the services, monitoring the network, and ensuring that SLAs are reported to the customer
- *Billing department:* Responsible for billing the customer for their IP-based services

Each department has information that is critical for the correct implementation of the services to each individual customer. Oftentimes, the information provided by one department is crucial input for another department in order to implement the service. For example, the NOC is responsible for deploying the services. The billing department needs to know when the services have been implemented in order to start billing the customer. If the customer is charged based on the bandwidth of each link from the customer site to the nearest PoP, then the NOC must also inform the billing department about the bandwidth of each installed link.

It is essential that information flow properly, accurately, and promptly from one department to another. The service implementation model must meet the requirements of all the departments and must also ensure that the services can be correctly implemented. This system responsible for the integration of all the requirements is often referred to as the *operations support system* (OSS). (More details about the OSS are presented in Section 6.5.)

6.3 Provisioning—What Are the Issues?

This section presents the issues related to provisioning the services for the customer. Details about the various tasks are also sketched out, giving you an insight into the complexity of provisioning.

6.3.1 What Is Provisioning?

First of all, it is important to define the term *provisioning* before discussing anything about the issues related to this subject. When an IP-based service is offered to a customer, it has to be implemented for that customer. This implementation can involve the following tasks:

1. Installing new devices (customer-premises equipment) at customer sites
2. Connecting the CPE device to the service provider network
3. Configuring the CPE devices for the new service
4. Updating the configuration of the relevant network devices in the service provider network to activate the service
5. Updating the network management systems with the information about the new customer and the network devices that have been installed
6. Activating the service
7. Activating the monitoring of the devices that are relevant for service delivery

All of these tasks may not be necessary for every new customer. The term *provisioning* loosely refers to all of the tasks mentioned above. The following section discusses these activities in detail.

Installation and Configuration of CPE Devices

Most services require a CPE device to be installed at the customer site. After the installation, they must be physically connected to the service provider network. The next step is the logical connection between the CPE device and the service provider network: CPE devices have to be configured, or programmed, to deliver the correct service for the customer. It is important that the configuration be correct in order for the service to be delivered correctly. In most cases, the configuration on the CPE device has several parts: a part that is responsible for the normal operation of the CPE device and other parts that are responsible for specialized functions specific to the service in question.

For example, consider a router that is responsible for providing Internet connectivity to a corporation. A part of the router is responsible for sending and receiving IP packets. This can be considered as a basic configuration on the router. Another part of the router is responsible for ensuring that the IP address space of the corporation is correctly advertised to the Internet using a routing protocol like BGP. This is the specialized configuration that is responsible for implementing the service (Internet access).

Another aspect of the configuration on the CPE devices is the parameters necessary to generate the configuration. Some of these parameters may be the same for all devices, while others are variable and depend on the service being offered or on the customer location. For example, consider the same router providing Internet access. The IP address on the router interface connected to the customer network is related to the IP addressing plan of the customer. The link capacity to the Internet also depends on the customer requirements. All of this information must be correctly configured on all of the CPE devices in order for the service to function properly.

Configuration of Network Devices

Before the CPE devices can communicate with the service provider network, the devices in the service provider network have to programmed, or configured. It may be necessary to program a single device or several devices before establishing communication between the CPE device and the service provider network. It is necessary that the configuration on all the intermediate devices be correct before the communication can be established.

For example, when ATM is used as the access technology, the VPI/VCI must be configured correctly on all of the ATM switches between the CPE and the PE in the access network. In addition, if bandwidth guarantee (QoS) is a requirement, then the ATM *class of service* (CoS) must also match on all of the ATM switches between the CPE and PE devices in order for the ATM network to meet the bandwidth requirements of the CPE device.

It is also important that the configurations of the CPE device and the service provider network match in order for them to communicate. Mismatch in configurations can result in no communication or incorrect delivery of the service. For example, the IP address on the CPE device and the PE in the service provider PoP must be in the same network in order for them to be able to exchange IP packets and routing information. If the

IP addresses do not match, then there will be no communication between these devices. In the case of guaranteed bandwidth services using ATM technology, mismatch in the ATM CoS parameters can result in loss of packets and hence a degradation in the service.

Service Activation

When all of the relevant devices have been correctly configured, the next step is to activate the service. This step may involve several activities, such as

1. Activating the Layer 2 connectivity on the CPE device
2. Introducing all of the new CPE devices into the monitoring system
3. Activating the monitoring of all CPE devices

When all of these steps are completed, the service has been activated.

6.3.2 Device Configuration

Every IP-based service requires configuration of the CPE and service provider network devices. Some of this configuration is specific to a service and may not affect all the devices. Several solutions may be available to implement the same service, and each solution will have its advantages and disadvantages.

Consider the following scenario, in which a service provider wants to implement guaranteed bandwidth services in the access network. The access technology is ATM, and the service provider has an ATM access network. The service provider manages the CPE device. In order to implement guaranteed IP bandwidth service, it is enough to implement ATM traffic shaping on the CPE device. In order to ensure that traffic shaping functions properly on the CPE device (after all, this is done in software and it is practically impossible to write bug-free software), ATM traffic policing can be implemented on the first ATM switch (see Figure 6.4). Another possible variation is to implement traffic shaping on all of the outbound interfaces and traffic policing on the inbound interfaces (see Figure 6.5). The second solution requires more resources to configure all of the devices and also makes the configuration more complicated.

Another major issue in the configuration of network devices is the chance of misconfiguration. The potential risk of misconfiguration is always there and cannot be avoided. Modifications to the configuration of network devices to provision new service requests may not be done correctly and may disrupt service for other customers if the changes to the configurations are incorrect and are not implemented in the correct order. By keeping configuration changes to a minimum number of devices, the overall chance of misconfiguration can be reduced.

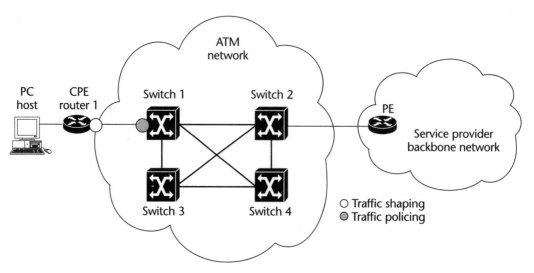

Figure 6.4 Implementing guaranteed bandwidth service—Solution 1.

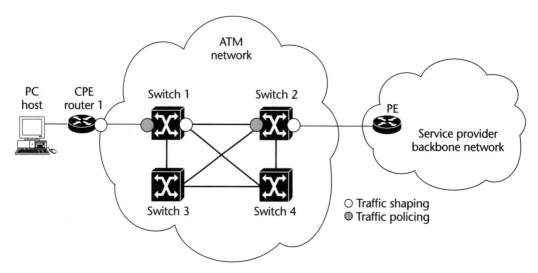

Figure 6.5 Implementing guaranteed bandwith service—Solution 2.

Consider again the scenario described in Figure 6.4. The link between the CPE device and the PE device is supposed to deliver 2 Mb/sec. In the case of Solution 2, due to a mismatch in configuration if the traffic policing on Switch 2 is set for 512 Kb/sec instead of 2 Mb/sec, then the effective bandwidth between the PC and the file server is only 512 Kb/sec. This problem could have been avoided if the policing were restricted to Switch 1.

To summarize, in order to keep a service simple and easy to implement, it is necessary to make the service-specific configuration as simple as possible and restrict it to a minimum number of devices. In doing so, one can reduce (1) the staffing and time required to provision a service request, (2) the risks of misconfiguration, and (3) disruption in service for other customers.

6.3.3 How to Configure the Devices

Most network devices have software installed on them that allows the configuration of the device in order to support several functions. Modification to relevant parameters in the device activates the corresponding functions on the device. Depending on the device and the manufacturer, several methods are available for modifying configurations of network devices. Some common methods include

- *Text-based command line interface* (CLI), to modify values of parameters or activate functions
- *Menu-based CLI,* to modify values of parameters or activate functions
- *Web-based CLI,* to modify values of parameters or activate functions
- *SNMP-based interface,* to set value of variables

Most of these methods provide the operator with an interface to modify the configuration. In order to prevent unauthorized access to the device, some form of authentication (username/password) is implemented on all, the devices. Operators are allowed to modify the configuration only when they have correctly identified themselves to the device.

Text-Based CLI

Text-based CLI provides the operator with the possibility of viewing and modifying the configuration of the device. This requires the operator to log onto the device. Devices normally have a console monitor that provides the interface to the device. The operator then has the possibility of typing the commands that are then executed by the device. A text-based interface requires the operator to have a good understanding of the syntax and semantics of CLI. The operator must also have a good knowledge about the semantics of the parameters that can be modified and also how to modify the value of parameters. The CLI, the syntax of the commands, and the semantics of the variables may all vary from device to device. Operators need to have a good understanding of all of these and must be well trained in order to reduce the risks of misconfiguration.

Menu-Driven CLI

Like the text-based CLI, menu-driven CLI helps the operator. Unlike the text-based CLI, however, the operator does not need to know the syntax of all the commands. The operator is prompted to choose from a list of commands—the menu-based CLI may have several choices—and is required to know the significance of each command. All of the commands may not be presented to the operator at the same time.

The menu-based CLI may be organized in a hierarchical manner, and the commands may be grouped based on functionality. In this case, the operator needs to have knowledge about the groups of commands and how to navigate through the set of menus before executing the necessary commands in order to make configuration changes.

Web-Based CLI

Today, Web-based interfaces are very popular in all domains. Most of the network devices from vendors also support Web-based interfaces. Web-based CLI helps provide a standard access method. Most workstations support some form of Web browsers and hence can be used to access the network device. Depending on the support available on the network device, the Web-based CLI may have either a menu-driven or a text-based CLI.

SNMP

The most popular method is the SNMP-based interface. SNMP is a standard protocol that is widely used in the industry. Its simplicity makes it a popular choice for configuring network devices. SNMP provides an operation known as *set,* with which it is possible to modify the value of parameters on the device. The MIB includes definitions for parameters, or variables, that are a part of the device configuration. By modifying the value of these parameters using SNMP, it is possible to change the configuration of a network device.

Each device has its own MIB. In order to provide a common interface independent of the network device and the manufacturer, standard MIB variables have been defined for IP networks. This standardization has helped to provide a common interface for accessing network devices independent of the manufacturer. The MIB also contains device-specific variables and vendor-specific features on each network device. These variables are defined as a private MIB specific to each device.

In order to use SNMP to configure a network device, the MIB on the network device must contain all of the variables that are required to modify the configuration. The SNMP agent residing in the network device must be capable of reading and modifying the value of these variables.

The use of SNMP helps to develop standard tools to configure devices, which in turn helps to automate the tasks of configuring new network devices and modifying the configuration of existing network devices in the service provider network. General-purpose tools reduce the staff required to configure network devices and help to fasten the process to provision new service requests. Automation also helps to reduce the chances of misconfiguration. Even if there is a misconfiguration due to software bugs in the configuration tools, it is easy to fix the bugs and ensure that all of the devices are correctly configured.

6.3.4 Service Modification

A typical service offered by a service provider will have several features. Over a period of time, the customer will want to modify the service to include additional features or to upgrade the quality of the service. This may require a change in the configuration of the devices or the installation of new devices. Consider the example shown in Figure 6.4. The customer is offered a guaranteed bandwidth service. Initially, the customer was offered a 512 Kb/sec ATM connection to the service provider network. Over a period of time, the volume of traffic from the customer has grown steadily, so the requirements have increased to 2 Mb/sec. This requires a change in the configuration of all of the ATM switches and the CPE device.

In the next phase, due to rapid expansion, the number of users in that customer site increased dramatically. The volume of traffic from this customer site has outgrown the maximum link capacity on the CPE interface. Now it is necessary to install new interfaces on the CPE device or install a new CPE device. This upgrade in service requires installation of new equipment and also modifications to the configuration of the new devices.

6.3.5 Database Information

Information about all of the devices in the network is necessary to manage the network. This information should be maintained in a database and must be accessible to all of the systems that require them. It must be correct and consistent. This is critical for the operation of the network, to guarantee the services to the customer, and to meet the SLA requirements of the customer. When new service requests are provisioned, it is necessary to update the database information as part of the provisioning process.

6.4 Network Management—What Are the Issues?

Network management is an integral part of any service offered by a service provider. It encompasses several issues and is important for the service provider to manage their network in order to ensure the correct operation of all of the devices and services that are offered using the network. A typical service provider network has a wide geographic spread, covering several cities. The network devices are installed in several locations and can be far apart. It is necessary to have a good infrastructure to access and manage these devices from a central location to reduce the cost of the network management infrastructure. Security is another important aspect that must also be taken into account when managing a network. The network management system and the network devices must be shielded from illegal access by intruders and hackers. Most service providers invest a lot of time and money in building a solid and secure network management infrastructure.

6.4.1 Network Management System

The *network management system* (NMS) is the crux of the network management of a service provider network, providing the necessary infrastructure to manage the network. It consists of both hardware and software that are necessary to perform the network management activities (see Section 6.4.2). Several off-the-shelf NMSs are available today that provide a framework to perform network management activities. The service provider must modify or adapt them to meet their requirements. Considering the fact that all service providers buy network devices and NMS solutions from vendors, the competitive edge lies in adapting the network devices and the NMS solutions to efficiently implement the services and deliver SLAs to customers. Since the NMS plays a crucial role, it is important that they have redundancy in case of failure. The design of the NMS infrastructure must take into account failure of components and must provide redundancy for critical components.

6.4.2 Network Management Activities

Managing a service provider network involves several activities, including

1. Verifying the status of all devices
2. Recording and analyzing the error messages from all devices, to monitor the health of all devices
3. Recording and analyzing statistical information, to monitor the health of the devices
4. Recording and analyzing statistical information for SLA reporting
5. Maintaining and periodically verifying all the configurations on all devices
6. Upgrading software and hardware to accommodate more customers or to remove bugs

Monitoring Devices

Network devices must be up and functioning correctly in order to deliver services to customers, so they must be monitored periodically. Monitoring can be a proactive or a reactive activity, depending on the nature of the devices. Proactive monitoring is important for critical devices. Reactive monitoring can be done for devices whose failure can be anticipated based on information received from other devices that do not affect the services offered to the customer.

Proactive monitoring is not free. It requires bandwidth to send requests and receive responses from devices, and it requires a good management system to handle the volume of traffic. The interval between each request to monitor the status of devices is also an important factor: If the interval is too high, then faulty devices may not be detected for a long time, and this increases the downtime of the device and the service offered by the device. Shorter intervals can help to overcome this problem, but they result in a lot of load on the device, the NMS system, and the network. A good balance has to be maintained between the two choices. The optimum interval for monitoring devices must be determined by the service provider when designing the monitoring system.

The monitoring system must be designed to take into account service windows during which devices may not be functioning (e.g., for software or hardware upgrades). It must be capable of selectively turning off the monitoring of devices that are being upgraded. The system must inform the operator when devices do not respond to monitoring requests. It must also be designed with the topology of the network and the physical and logical relationship between devices in mind. Sometimes, the failure of a single device may result in several other devices (connected to this device) not being reached by the monitoring system. In this case, the monitoring system must filter all of the alarms and forward a single alarm to the operator.

Error Logs

Most network devices are capable of detecting failure of hardware or software components. They can also anticipate such failures, depending on the situation. For example, temperature sensors can be used to detect high temperatures, and transmission errors on an interface can be used to detect loss of connectivity. Network devices can be configured to send this information (as alarms or error messages) to the NMS, which maintains it in a log. This log information is then used by other systems to detect the failure of components of devices or devices themselves, or even to anticipate failure and take corrective actions.

Error logs provide valuable information to the network operator in detecting and troubleshooting problems in the network. For example, increasing transmission errors on an ATM interface can be used to anticipate degradation in the QoS offered to the customer, and investigations can be initiated to determine the cause of this problem before complete loss of connectivity on that interface.

Network management systems must be properly designed to ensure that the network devices are configured to send critical error messages and to verify that these error messages are logged and analyzed. Similar to the problems associated with the monitoring interval, this must be designed properly to ensure that critical errors are logged and detected and also that the NMS is not flooded with too many alarms or error messages.

Statistical Information

Network statistics play an important role in managing a network, delivering IP-based services, and reporting SLA to customers. Most network devices collect and locally store statistical information in the device itself. This information can be retrieved by the NMS and stored in a database to be used at a later stage. (Section 6.4.3 provides more details about how the statistical information is collected from the network devices.) Statistical information can be used for several purposes, such as

1. Error detection and troubleshooting
2. SLA reporting
3. Capacity planning

Statistical information about errors observed by a network device can be useful in detecting and even anticipating faults. Errors can also provide useful information for troubleshooting. For example, the number of IP packets received on an interface can help to detect if the interface is properly receiving and forwarding IP packets. During troubleshooting, this information can be very useful in isolating faulty interfaces.

Statistical information is also useful in reporting link utilization to customers. It can be used to generate SLAs indicating the availability of the service—for example, the availability of a service may be computed in terms of the *uptime* of all the devices involved in delivering the service. (Uptime can be considered the time the device has been up, or active, since it was last reset.) Statistical information like link utilization or the number of interfaces on a device can be useful in capacity planning. When these values reach a certain threshold, it is time to install more interfaces for a new device with additional interfaces.

Hardware and Software Upgrades

Technology grows at a very rapid rate, so it is necessary to upgrade the hardware and software of network devices to keep up. Sometimes it is also necessary to upgrade the software on devices in order to fix problems. A hardware upgrade may be required to meet the growing demand for a service and to provision more customers.

Upgrading hardware and software is an important activity associated with network management. Procedures must be defined to do it so as to reduce the downtime associated with the services and the downtime for customers affected by the upgrade. Normally, an SLA has a provision for downtime specifying a fixed time. This is sometimes referred to as a *service window.* As far as possible, hardware and software upgrades must be done during the service window in order to minimize the service downtime.

6.4.3 How Is It Done?

As seen in this section, communication between the NMS and the network devices is critical for managing the network. Without this communication, it is almost impossible to configure and monitor the devices, generate SLAs for customers, or predict the growth of the network and do capacity planning. There are two aspects of the communication that are of interest: (1) the communication protocol and the access method between the NMS and the network device, and (2) the network that supports this communication.

Communication Protocols and Access Methods

For an IP-based network, it is logical to use a communication protocol based on IP for communication between the NMS and the network devices. Most of the network devices from vendors support some form of IP-based protocol to communicate with the network device. Depending on the communication protocol, the access method can also vary. Some of these methods have been standardized, and some of the most popular access methods and the communication protocols used by these methods are discussed in this section. Of course, there are also vendor-specific access methods and communication protocols. Each method has its advantages and disadvantages. Good NMS systems must incorporate all of these methods and help the operator in efficiently performing the tasks of network management.

SNMP

SNMP is the industry standard for communication between the NMS and network devices. The operations supported by SNMP make it practical for network monitoring and for the devices to report alarms to the NMS system.

- *snmptrap* is an operation supported by SNMP that makes it very useful for devices to report unusual activities to the NMS. The SNMP agent on the network device can be configured to report several types of alarms. *snmptrap* provides information about the severity of the trap, and additional information can be included in the trap to indicate the nature of the fault and the possible cause of the problem. Some of these traps have been standardized, and there are also device-specific and vendor-specific traps.
- *snmpget* is an SNMP operation that can be used to access and extract statistical information from a network device by the NMS.

- *snmpset* is an SNMP operation that can be used to modify the value of variables in the MIB of the network device. By using private MIB variables, this operation can be used to modify the configuration of the network device.

All of these operations make it possible to perform most of the activities of network management discussed in Section 6.4.2. SNMP requires IP connectivity between network devices and the NMS.

Text-Based CLI

Text-based CLI is another method to access network devices and get the required information to do some of the tasks associated with network management. It can be used to get the status of a device, to get statistical information, to modify the configuration of devices, and so on. It can use TCP-based protocols like *telnet* if the network device supports this protocol.

Text-based CLI is a popular method for getting small amounts of information—for example, interface status, configuration details, and so on for short-term activities like troubleshooting or quickly modifying the configuration of a device. An operator can use this method during troubleshooting to determine and isolate the cause of problems.

Text-based CLI may not scale for a network with a large number of devices to perform certain activities of network management like collecting statistical information. It can cause an unnecessary load on the devices when trying to extract information on a periodic basis. It also requires additional programs to process this information and save it in formats that can be used by other systems (e.g., SLA reporting). Most of the off-shelf NMSs use SNMP and provide some limited support for text-based CLI.

Depending on the vender and their implementation, text-based CLI may be able to provide more information than SNMP. Proprietary implementations of new technologies may not have the necessary MIBs to provide an SNMP interface. Under these circumstances, it may be necessary to develop tools that can help to automate network management activities. Tools that can process and extract information from text-based responses are required to enable an operator to efficiently perform tasks.

Other Methods

Several other methods are available for getting information status about network devices and also performing basic troubleshooting activities like device reachability. These tools use some IP-based protocols to achieve their tasks. For example, tools like *ping* use ICMP to determine the reachability of devices, and tools like *traceroute* use ICMP to trace the path to destination networks and network devices. These tools have to be adapted to meet the requirements of the network management activity.

Communication Network

A network is required for communication between the NMS and the network devices. It must support the protocol that is used for such communication. Two possible solutions are *in-band network management* and *out-band network management*.

In-Band Network Management

"In-band" refers to using the service provider network to communicate with all network devices. The links that forward customer traffic are used for communication between the NMS and the network devices. In-band network management is a simple solution (see Figure 6.6). All it requires is IP connectivity between the NMS and the service provider network. Once this is established, then IP communication between the NMS and network devices is very simple and straightforward.

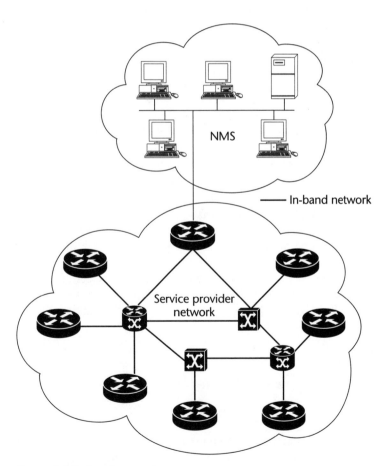

Figure 6.6 In-band network management.

The disadvantage of this approach is that failure in certain parts of the service provider network may result in loss of connectivity between the network device and the NMS. This may be critical at times when it is necessary to have direct access to network devices. Moreover, this approach requires additional bandwidth in the service provider network to accommodate the network management traffic.

Out-Band Network Management

Out-band network management implements a separate network to provide communication between the NMS and the network devices (see Figure 6.7). This network is implemented separately from the service provider network (which is used for transporting customer traffic) and is used only for communication between the NMS and the network devices. The advantage of this approach is that customer traffic will not affect the reachability between the NMS and the network device. Bandwidth need not be reserved in the service provider network for the purpose of network management.

6.4.4   Security Issues: Managing an IP Network

Security is an important issue that must be addressed when discussing the management of IP networks. Networks are prone to attack by hackers, so network devices and the NMS must be secured against intentional (or unintentional) intrusions. The NMS devices must be protected from external intrusion. This can be achieved by using firewalls between the service provider network and the NMS system.

6.5   OSS Architecture

The OSS architecture plays an important role in implementing IP-based services. Several key departments of both service providers and customers use this system in order to implement services. The OSS maintains information that is critical to service implementation and has the responsibility of ensuring that this information is made available promptly to the various departments.

6.5.1   OSS Components

Some of the key components of this system are as follows.

Database System

A good database system is the key to OSS architecture. The OSS has a lot of information that is relevant to service implementation and is also related to the customer. The OSS must be capable of maintaining all of this

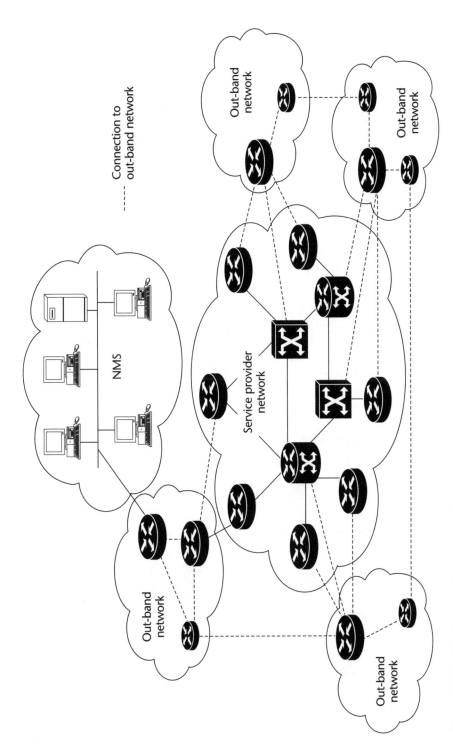

Figure 6.7 Out-band network management.

information and making it easily available to the different departments and to various other components of the OSS that are responsible for service implementation.

Network Provisioning and Monitoring Tools

Network provisioning and monitoring tools are also essential components of the OSS architecture. They can be vendor-specific, standard tools that are openly available, or even developed in-house. These tools interact with the network devices and are responsible for configuring the network devices, monitoring the status of these devices, and extracting information (e.g., link utilization) that is essential for SLA reporting and for billing. The OSS architecture must have the capability of seamlessly integrating all of these tools and ensuring that they can interact with other components in order to get the correct information that is essential for provisioning and monitoring the network devices.

SLA Reporting and Billing

SLA reporting and billing are important parts of service implementation. They use the information related to customer requirements, services requested by the customer, and the actual status of network elements responsible for delivering the services to the customer to generate periodic reports to the customer. It is essential that SLA reporting and the billing system have access to correct information.

6.5.2 Requirements of the OSS

Some of the requirements of the OSS architecture are that it be open, scalable, automated, and easy to interface between network operators in the NOC and customers.

Open Architecture

The OSS has several components that must communicate with one another in order to ease the task of service implementation. These components may be purchased from several different software vendors. It is essential that the OSS architecture allow the integration of all of these components into one system and ensure that the information required by a component for its proper functioning is readily made available to it.

Scalability

Scalability of the OSS refers to the ability to support a large number of services and customers, to implement service requests from multiple customers within a short period of time, and to maintain information related to several thousands of customers in order to implement the services. Service providers typically have a large customer base (hundreds of thousands of customers) and offer several services. It is essential that the OSS be capable of supporting the implementation of services for all of the customers.

When there is surge in demand for a new service, several customers may request this new service in a single day. This places a huge burden on the OSS to implement all of the service requests. Scalability in this context refers to the ability of the OSS to implement several service requests within a short period of time.

As the number of customers using a service offered by the provider increases, the OSS system must be capable of maintaining the information about all of the customers. The time required to access the customer information must not increase as the number of customers increases. This is essential when online SLA reports are made available to customers. SLA reporting must have access to customer information (e.g., number of links and the bandwidth for each customer link) and to the status of network devices (e.g., link utilization) in order to make reports available to the customer online.

Another aspect of scalability is related to the network provisioning and monitoring tools. These tools must be capable of managing several network devices. As the network grows, the number of network devices will increase. The time taken to manage the network devices must be independent of the number of devices managed by the OSS.

Automation

It is essential that the activities of implementing services are automated to the maximum possible extent and that the intervention by human operators is minimized as much as possible. This is a key requirement because it helps to minimize both the mistakes due to manual intervention and the time taken to implement the services.

As discussed in the beginning of Section 6.3, provisioning involves updating the configuration of various network devices before the service can be activated for a customer. Depending on the type of service and the SLA offered to the customer, the amount of information required to provision a service can be considerable. In order to ensure that all of this information is correctly configured on the relevant devices, it is better to have software tools that can automate this process. The software tools can extract this information from a database and consistently configure all relevant devices in the correct order. The advantage of software tools is that if they can correctly do a task once, they can do the same task correctly several times. This is what is required in order to provision several customer service requests in a short period of time and in a correct manner.

SNMP provides the basic means for communication between the NMS and the network devices. The operations provided for by SNMP help to extract information from network devices and allow the network devices to report problems or events to the NMS. Software tools based on SNMP can be used to automate the task of configuring network devices.

As seen in Section 6.4.2, network management involves many activities, most of which are repetitive tasks that have to be performed periodically. Some of these tasks involve correlating large volumes of data in order to verify the proper functioning of the network devices and also to generate reports. Software tools are best suited for such tasks, as they can do this much faster than human operators. Tools to periodically monitor the devices are a must when the number of devices in the network is large.

Intelligent systems based on rules or models (e.g., finite-state machines; Vijayananda 1996) can be easily built to scan through event logs from all of the devices. The rules or models can vary based on the service offered by the provider. Once these rules or models are defined, then they can be easily used to verify that the service offered to the customer is functioning properly.

SLA reporting is another activity that can be automated. The information required for generating the SLA reports must be made available to the reporting system in order to automate this task. Once this is done, the reports can be automatically generated, either periodically or on demand (e.g., upon customer request).

Using Web-Based Tools

Web-based interfaces to applications are becoming more and more popular. Web applications are based on HTML and use IP-based application-layer protocols like HTTP for communication with servers. Web-based tools can help standardize the interface to configure and manage network devices. With a few mouse clicks or keystrokes, an operator can easily modify the configuration of network devices and get information about their status. The tools also make it easy to present SLA reports to customers or provide customers with online information about the status of their service or other information (e.g., link utilization).

Web-based tools can help the service provider to allow online access to SLA reports. This will make it easy for customers to get information about their network. Information related to link utilization can help customers in doing capacity planning and ordering more bandwidth for sites that have very high link utilization.

6.6   Chapter Review

This chapter has stressed the need for simple and efficient provisioning and network management systems as a differentiator for the service provider. Good tools are required to simplify the task of provisioning new customers, to manage services, and to deliver the SLA reports promised to customers. A good OSS architecture is the key to rapid deployment of IP-based services and to making it scalable.

SNMP plays a key role in managing IP networks. The features provided by SNMP make the task of provisioning IP-based services and managing IP networks easier for service providers. However, SNMP only provides the basic means to communicate with the network device for the purpose of network management. SNMP-based tools must be developed by the service provider to perform network management activities in an efficient manner.

7

IP-Based Services: Advanced Topics

Chapters 5 and 6 presented several discussions on network technologies that help to create IP-based services and build IP networks by providing the basic infrastructure. While these technologies are very helpful in building basic IP-based services, they may not be able to meet the requirements of all customers who make use of the IP network. Some customers may have additional quality-of-service (QoS) requirements (other than just connectivity), such as guaranteed bandwidth, guaranteed minimized end-to-end delay and jitter, security, data privacy, and so on. With the rapid emergence of modern applications like B2B, e-commerce, video-on-demand, and voice-over-IP, the requirements listed above are important, so there is more demand on IP-based networks to deliver the requirements of these applications.

Applications like voice-over-IP and video are sensitive to delay and jitter. *Delay* is the amount of time taken by the IP network to deliver a packet from the source to the destination. *Jitter* is the variation in the delay. Unlike traditional IP-based applications that depended on best-effort services, voice-over-IP applications have strict delay and jitter requirements. Packets from these applications must be delivered to the destinations with a finite delay (about 150 milliseconds). Video applications like videoconferencing and video-on-demand also have bandwidth requirements in addition to delay and jitter requirements. They require *guaranteed end-to-end bandwidth*, meaning that at any given time, the IP network can guarantee a minimum throughput (measured in kilobits per second) from source to destination.

Privacy and security of data are of special concern to customers like banks and insurance companies. Privacy means that this data should not be accessible to others, and security means that even if the network is insecure and the IP packets transporting the data are accessible, contents of the packets must still be secure and not be compromised. These customers deal with sensitive data and are very concerned about the safety of that data. Since the traffic from these customers traverses the same IP backbone of the service provider (see Chapter 5 for an explanation of this subject), it is necessary to ensure that data privacy is maintained at any given time. The security concerns of these customers are addressed in Section 7.3.

There are also concerns about the address space limitations of IPv4. Theoretically, IPv4 address spaces can support up to four billion devices. Even though VPNs make it possible to reuse IP address space, there are some people who feel that IPv4 may not be able to meet the current growth in the number of IP devices. One of the main issues addressed in IPv6 is the address-space limitation of IPv4.

Optical networking is another advanced topic. With the rapid emergence of this technology and concepts like IP-over-optics, a discussion on this topic is a must. We offer some insight into how it can help create IP-based services.

This chapter provides details about these advanced topics, which can help service providers to enhance and add new IP-based services to their portfolios in order to meet the additional requirements of their customers. The demand for QoS in an IP network is increasing every day. With the rapid emergence of applications like voice-over-IP and video-on-demand, the expectations of customers are also increasing. QoS and applications like voice-over-IP are discussed in separate sections, followed by a discussion of IPv6. A discussion of the *local-to-multipoint distribution system* (LMDS) is also included in this chapter to show how this technology can be used by service providers to provide connectivity between customer sites and the service provider PoP without using the local loop. Optical networking is a quickly emerging technology; this chapter shows the synergy between IP and optical networking and discusses how optical networking can help service providers to create more services.

7.1 Quality of Service

The term *quality of service,* or *QoS,* can be used in a broad sense and, depending on context, can have several meanings. QoS is normally understood to indicate a set of service requirements that have to be met by a network. QoS functions are intended to deliver the service requirements that have been guaranteed by the network. This is achieved by giving the network operator control over the usage of network resources, including bandwidth, memory to store and forward packets, and CPUs. Some of the techniques that can be used to satisfy QoS requirements are the following:

- *Resource reservation* at each node in the network. Reservation is done according to policies implemented by the service provider based on customer requirements. The reservation mechanism depends on routing tables/routing protocols to find the path with sufficient resources. This gives the operator control over the resources that are allocated to customers.
- *Scheduling mechanisms* to effectively allocate resources based on demand. The scheduling mechanisms have to be implemented by the service provider based on customer requirements.
- *A combination of resource reservation and scheduling mechanisms* to manage the network resources and meet the QoS requirements of the customers.

Scheduling mechanisms are local to a network device. However, in order to ensure the end-to-end QoS requirements (meaning that QoS is guaranteed along all the links and nodes, from the source node to the destination node), it is important that all of the nodes in the network have a common agreement on how to implement the scheduling mechanisms. Resource reservation also requires cooperation among all of the nodes in a network. All of the nodes that are in the path from the source to the destination must implement the reservation policy. Resource reservation depends on routing to find out the path from the source to the destination and reserve resources on all of the nodes.

QoS in an IP network is not an afterthought. Founders of IP had envisioned the need for QoS and have provided for a field called *type of service* (ToS) in the IP header (see Figure 7.1) to facilitate QoS in IP networks.

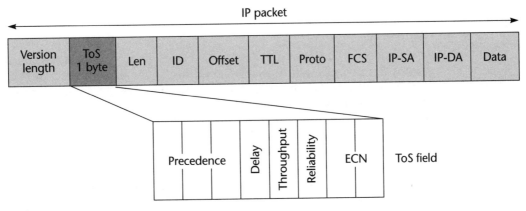

Figure 7.1 ToS field of an IP packet.

Traditionally, IP networks offered best-effort services, meaning that the only QoS offered was that packets might be eventually delivered to the destination. Since the Internet was mostly used by applications like telnet and file transfer, best-effort service was enough to meet the QoS requirements of these applications. The QoS requirements of the applications that use the Internet today are much higher.

Internet QoS development has undergone a lot of standardization to provide end-to-end QoS over the Internet. These standardization efforts are concentrated in two areas:

- *Integrated services:* Based on reserving the resources on all network devices for each *flow,* or *connection,* before data from the connection is transported across the network. This requires a reservation protocol like RSVP to be understood by all network devices. (Section 7.1.2 provides more details about this activity.)
- *Differentiated services:* Based on managing the resources on all network devices for each flow (based on some information, e.g., IP address, ToS field, or tags) as the data packets are transported through the network. This requires implementing QoS functions like packet classification, policing, traffic shaping, and the queuing mechanism on each network device. (More details about differentiated services can be found in Section 7.1.3.)

7.1.1   QoS Parameters

The QoS guarantees provided by the network are measured using the performance of the network. Bandwidth, packet delay and jitter, and packet loss are some common measures used to characterize a network's performance. The QoS requirements vary depending on the requirements of the applications: for voice-over-IP or IP telephony, delay, packet loss, and jitter are important; for applications that involve bulk data transfer, bandwidth is a QoS requirement.

Bandwidth

The term *bandwidth* is used to describe the throughput of a given medium, protocol, or connection. It describes the size of the pipe that is required for the application to communicate over the network. An application requiring guaranteed bandwidth wants the network to allocate a minimum bandwidth specifically for it on all the links through which the data is transferred through the network. Depending on the type of network, the bandwidth guarantee can be provided at either the IP layer or the datalink layer. Guaranteed bandwidth at the IP layer depends on the type of datalink network. Not all datalink network support guarantees bandwidth when several IP connections share the same network—for example, it is not possible to reserve bandwidth in an Ethernet network with several hosts.

Packet Delay and Jitter

Packet delay, or latency, at each hop consists of serialization or transmission delay, propagation delay, and switching delay.

- *Serialization or transmission delay:* The time it takes for a device to send the packet at the output rate. This depends on the size of the packet and the link bandwidth. A 64-byte packet on a 4 Mb/sec line takes 128 μs to be transmitted. The same 64-byte packet on a 128 Kb/sec line takes 4 ms to be transmitted.
- *Propagation delay:* The time taken for a bit to be transmitted by the transmitter and to be received by the receiver. This is a function of the media and the distance and is independent of bandwidth.
- *Switching delay:* The time taken for a device to start transmitting a packet after receiving it. This depends on the status of the network and the number of packets in transit at this hop.

End-to-end delay for a packet belonging to a flow is the sum of all of the above types of delays experienced at each hop. All packets in a flow need not experience the same delay—it depends on the transient delay in each hop in the network. If the network is congested, queues will be built at each hop, and this increases the end-to-end delay. This variation in the delay is called *jitter.* Queuing mechanisms at each node can be used to ensure that the delay of certain flows is minimized and also that the jitter has an upper bound. (This is described in Section 7.1.4.)

Packet Loss

Packet loss specifies the number of packets lost in the network during transmission. The loss can be due to corruption in the transmission media, or packets can be dropped at congestion points due to lack of buffer space in the incoming or outgoing interface. Packet loss due to drops should be rare for a well-designed network that is correctly subscribed or undersubscribed. Packet loss due to faulty transmission media can also be avoided by building good physical networks.

QoS at Layer 2

Depending on the QoS requirements, QoS functions are available at the datalink layer (Layer 2) and network layer (Layer 3) of the OSI model. Guaranteed bandwidth as a QoS requirement can be provided by several Layer 2 technologies, such as frame relay or ATM, when the physical medium is shared by several Layer 3 connections simultaneously. ATM can also meet other QoS requirements like minimizing delay and jitter.

(The discussion on access technologies in Chapter 5 provides more details about QoS functions available at the datalink layer.)

7.1.2   Integrated Services Model

The *integrated services* (IntServ) model is based on the concept of requesting resources along all the links in a network from the source to the destination. This reservation is done using protocols like the *resource reservation protocol* (RSVP), a network-control protocol that enables Internet applications to obtain special QoS for their data flows. RSVP is not a routing protocol; instead, it works in conjunction with routing protocols and installs the equivalent of dynamic access lists along the routes that routing protocols calculate. RSVP occupies the place of a transport protocol in the OSI-model seven-layer protocol stack.

Researchers at the University of Southern California Information Sciences Institute (ISI) and Xerox Palo Alto Research Center originally conceived RSVP. The Internet Engineering Task Force (IETF) is now working toward standardization through an RSVP working group (Braden et al. 1997; Wroclawski 1997). RSVP operational topics discussed later in this chapter include data flows, QoS, session start-up, reservation style, and soft-state implementation.

How Does It Work?

IntServ using RSVP works in the following manner:

1. Applications signal their QoS requirements via RSVP to the network.
2. Every network node along the path must check to see if the reservation request can be met.
3. Resources are reserved if the service constraints can be met.
4. An error message is sent back to the receiver if the constraints cannot be met.
5. Network nodes make sure there are no violations of the traffic contract.
6. Nonconforming packets are either marked down or dropped.

Some of the main drawbacks of the IntServ model are

- It is an "all-or-nothing" model, meaning that it cannot be partially deployed—every node in the network must implement it in order for it to work.
- The network needs to maintain each reservation for each flow.
- It is oriented for real-time traffic.
- Scalability: The number of RSVP reservations is directly proportional to the number of IP streams that require resource reservation. This issue is addressed by aggregating multiple RSVP reservations into one

reservation. Work is currently ongoing to provide aggregated RSVP (Baker et al. 2001).

An example of an application that uses the IntServ model is voice-over-IP, which makes use of RSVP to make path reservations before transporting voice traffic over a data network. For more details, see Section 7.2.3.

7.1.3 Differentiated Services Model

The *differentiated services* (DiffServ) approach to providing QoS in a network is based on employing a well-defined set of blocks with which one can build a variety of services. It is based on the *differentiated services code point* (DSCP) byte and ToS byte of the IP packet (Blake et al. 1998; Heinanen et al. 1999; Jacobsen et al. 1999; Nichols et al. 1998). The DiffServ architecture provides a framework within which service providers can offer a wide range of services to customers, each service being differentiated based on the DSCP field in the IP packet. This value specifies the *per-hop behavior* (PHB) of the packet as it traverses the service provider network.

Differentiated Services Code Point (DSCP)

To allow traffic to have different policies applied to it, some method of differentiation of packets is required. Within the IP header is an eight-bit field known as *type of service* (ToS), within which three bits are used as precedence, allowing for 8 classes to be used. This field has recently been redefined by the IETF as the differentiated services code point (DSCP) and uses six bits of the field, allowing for 64 different classes. Figure 7.2 shows the details of the DSCP field (and also the precedence field) of the IP header. In the case of DSCP, the currently unused bits are not used and are reserved for future implementation.

MPLS has only three bits in the experimental (EXP) field of the MPLS (shim) header. The IP precedence bits (3 left-most bits of the TOS field of the IP header) are copied to the EXP field of the MPLS header when the MPLS header is appended to the packet. This effectively means that full use of DSCP can only be made in links where MPLS is not enabled. All other links in the network run MPLS, but only the first three higher-order bits of DSCP can be used to classify traffic.

The limited number of bits in the MPLS header is not necessarily a drawback of MPLS. MPLS is used in the core network. The DSCP field of the IP header is used to classify the customer traffic. In the core network, traffic from several customers can be aggregated into a single class. Typically, there are up to four classes in the core network: voice, priority, guaranteed bandwidth, and best-effort. Since the MPLS packet encapsulates the IP packet with the MPLS header, the DSCP field in the IP is not

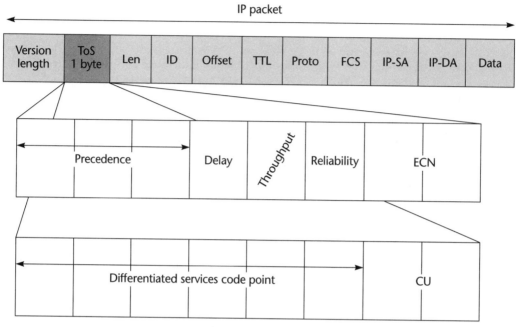

Figure 7.2 Description of the ToS field of the IP header.

lost and can be recovered at the edge of the network when the MPLS header is stripped and the IP packet is forwarded to the customer.

DiffServ Architecture

All the nodes that follow the DiffServ model are in a *DiffServ domain*. All the nodes on a Diffserv domain observe the PHB of a packet based on the DSCP value. Figure 7.3 shows the DiffServ architecture and the two functional building blocks, traffic conditioners and PHB.

- *Traffic conditioners* are used to classify the IP packets by marking the ToS or DSCP field of the IP packet or the EXP bit of the MPLS packet. Traffic conditioners are applied when the traffic enters the DiffServ domain. These functions are implemented on the edge nodes of the DiffServ domain. Packets are policed and marked based on the traffic profile. The DSCP field of the packets is also marked based on the traffic profile. The traffic conditioner used to police the packet may drop the packets if they do not match the profile or may shape the traffic when it does not meet the requirements of the profile.
- *PHB functions* must be implemented on all of the nodes in the DiffServ domain. They allocate resources for the packets to be scheduled and transmitted out of each node and implement the drop policy when there is congestion.

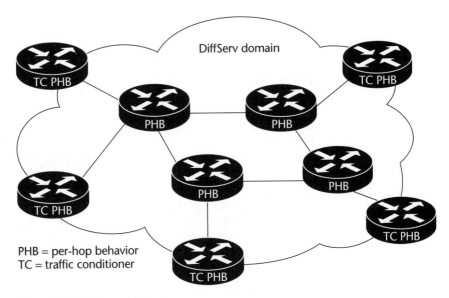

Figure 7.3 DiffServ architecture.

DiffServ versus IntServ

The DiffServ model is more scalable than the IntServ model and has fewer flows than the IntServ model. However, this model requires that the traffic conditioners and PHB be implemented in the DiffServ domain. Provisioning the services using the DiffServ model can be challenging because the traffic conditioners and PHB have to be correctly implemented on every interface of all the nodes in the DiffServ domain. It can be a tedious task to implement and verify the implementation on all of the nodes.

The IntServ model on top of the DiffServ model is an interesting concept that can be used to take advantage of both models. While the DiffServ model will make it scalable, the IntServ model will assure that resources are made available to each flow for which the IntServ model is used.

7.1.4 IP QoS Implementation

IP QoS implementation can be divided into the following categories:

- *Classification:* This involves marking the IP packet (setting DSCP or the IP precedence value) based on customer requirements. Once the packets are correctly classified, they can be properly handled by the other QoS mechanisms like congestion management and policing to implement end-to-end QoS requirements. Packet classification is typically done on the edge of the network. Sometimes the service provider reclassifies packets in the core network by re-marking certain fields in the packet. This reclassification is required when traffic is aggregated, however, the service provider must ensure that the original value of the IP precedence (DSCP) field in the IP packet is restored at the edge of the service provider network when the packet is delivered to the customer. This can be done in an MPLS network because two fields are available. The IP precedence field can be used to classify customer packets, and the MPLS EXP field can be used by the service provider to reclassify packets in the core network.

- *Congestion management:* This involves the creation of queues, assignment of packets to the proper queues, and scheduling of queues and the packets within the queues. The number of queues depends on the customer requirements and the number of CoSs offered by the service provider. Assignment of packets to queues and the scheduling policies are determined by the service provider depending on the type of QoS offered to the customer. For example, high-priority traffic like voice-over-IP requires preemptive queue mechanisms that will ensure that the packets are scheduled and transmitted before other packets.

- *Congestion avoidance techniques:* Congestion avoidance is a preemptive mechanism that monitors the network load and ensures that there is no congestion in the network. Congestion avoidance is achieved by dropping the packets; the packets that have to be dropped are determined based on the drop policy. This depends on the CoSs offered by the service provider. For example, during network congestion, traffic from the best-effort class should be dropped first. Traffic from the guaranteed bandwidth class should not be dropped before the minimum bandwidth has been guaranteed to that class.

- *Policing and shaping mechanisms:* These ensure that each CoS (based on the marked IP packet) adheres to the service contract. The service contract can include several issues, such as bandwidth, burst size, and delay.

- *QoS signaling:* This is used between nodes in the network to signal the QoS requirements of each class and to reserve resources. RSVP is a QoS signaling protocol that can be used to reserve resources like bandwidth. QoS signaling mechanisms also depend on routing protocols to determine the best path between the source and the destination.

Implementing QoS in an IP network is a challenging task. It requires a good understanding of queuing theory and the requirements of customers in order to determine the parameters for the queuing policies. One challenge is the communication between the signaling plane (QoS signaling protocols like RSVP) and the data-forwarding plane (congestion in the network) to ensure that the resource reservation for an application can be done in the correct manner. For example, RSVP uses bandwidth as the resource in order to do reservations. In addition to bandwidth, other network resources like queue buffers on the network devices are also important resources that are required to guarantee QoS. Congestion in the network device due to lack of queue buffers must be communicated to RSVP so that RSVP can use alternate paths (between the source and the destination) that have enough network resources (e.g., bandwidth, queue buffers) to meet the QoS requirements of the application making the RSVP request. More details about QoS implementations in an IP network can be found in Vegesna 2001.

7.1.5 Creating New Services Using QoS

Applications like voice-over-IP have strict QoS requirements regarding delay, jitter, and bandwidth. Real-time applications like video-on-demand also have QoS requirements that cannot be met by the best-effort services offered by a traditional IP network. By enabling QoS in the IP network (either by using the DiffServ model, the IntServ model, or both), service providers can offer differentiated services or guaranteed services (or both) to their customers. This will also enable them to offer new services like voice-over-IP and use the last mile, or local loop, to implement telephony services.

Differentiated services (offered using the DiffServ model) can help the service provider to distinguish between business customers (who pay more money for the services) and customers who are satisfied with best-effort services. By offering better QoS to the business customers—by allocating sufficient bandwidth and ensuring that the traffic from the business customer gets forwarded preferentially over the best-effort customer in case of congestion—the service provider can have oversubscription in their network and still meet the QoS requirements of all of their customers.

A QoS-enabled network will also help the service provider to offer additional services like guaranteed bandwidth to a customer. Applications like video-on-demand and videoconferencing have bandwidth requirements. By ensuring guaranteed bandwidth to customers, the service provider assures customers that their network is capable of meeting the bandwidth requirements of the customer's applications.

QoS implementation helps the service provider to offer bundled services, like voice, video, and data, on a single physical link. This requires QoS implementation on a link between the customer premises and the service provider PoP to differentiate between the voice, video, and data traffic. Cable, ADSL, frame relay, ATM, and Ethernet are examples of access technologies with which the service provider can offer bundled services.

7.2 Voice-over-IP

Of the key emerging technologies for data, voice, and video integration, voice-over-IP (VoIP) is arguably very important. The most QoS-sensitive of all traffic, voice is the true test of the engineering and quality of a network. Demand for voice-over-IP is leading the movement for QoS in IP environments, and will ultimately lead to use of the Internet for fax, voice telephony, and video telephony services. Voice-over-IP will ultimately be a key component of the migration of telephony to the LAN infrastructure.

7.2.1 Requirements

Voice traffic is sensitive to delay and delay variations. Communication between gateways must be reliable and be delivered on time. In an IP network, reliable packet delivery can be assured by using robust transport and session protocols. However, routers and specifically IP networks offer some unique challenges in controlling delay and delay variation (see Section 7.1.4 for more details).

Traditionally, IP traffic has been treated as best-effort, meaning that incoming IP traffic is transmitted on a first-come, first-served basis. Packets have been variable in nature, allowing large file transfers to take advantage of the efficiency associated with larger packet sizes. These characteristics have contributed to large delays and large delay variations in packet delivery. The second part of supporting delay-sensitive voice traffic is to provide a means of prioritizing the traffic within the router network in order to minimize the delay and delay variation. Section 7.1 provides details about assuring QoS in an IP network.

7.2.2 Components

In this section, we briefly introduce the components that are involved in delivering voice traffic over a data network:

- *Packet voice network:* Responsible for converting the voice traffic into data packets and delivering the voice traffic over a data network
- *Protocols like H.323 and session initiation* (SIP): Help to provide multimedia communication (voice, video, and data) over a data network and operate with the traditional voice networks

Packet Voice Network

All packet voice systems follow a common model, as shown in Figure 7.4. The packet voice transport network, which may be IP-based, frame relay, or ATM, forms the traditional cloud. At the edges of this network are devices, or components, called *voice agents* or *gateways*. It is the mission of these devices to change the voice information from its traditional

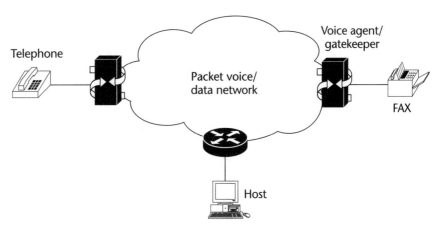

Figure 7.4 Packet voice network.

telephony form to a form suitable for packet transmission. The network then forwards the packet data to a gateway serving as the destination, or called party. This voice-agent connection model demonstrates the two issues in packet voice networking that must be explored to ensure that packet voice services meet user needs.

The first issue is voice coding: how voice information is transformed into packets and how the packets are used to re-create the voice. Voice has to be transformed into digital signals before it can be transported over a packet network. At the other end of the packet network, the digital signal has to be reconverted into voice signals. Special devices are used to convert voice to a digital signal and then back to voice. These devices are called coder-decoders (CODECs).

The second issue is the signaling associated with identifying the calling party and ascertaining where the called party is in the network. Two signaling protocols, H.323 and SIP, are discussed below.

Voice Coding

Analog communication is ideal for human communication. However, analog transmission is neither robust nor efficient at recovering from line noise. Analog signals have to be digitized before they can be transported over a packet voice network. Digital samples are composed of one and zero bits, and it is much easier for them to be separated from line noise. Therefore, when signals are regenerated, a clean sound can be maintained. When the benefits of this digital representation became evident, the telephony network migrated to *pulse code modulation* (PCM).

PCM converts analog sound into digital form by sampling the analog sound 8000 times per second and converting each sample into a numeric code. After the waveform is sampled, it is converted into a discrete digital form. This sample is represented by a code that indicates the amplitude of the waveform at the instant the sample was taken. The telephony form of PCM uses 8 bits for the code and a logarithm compression method that assigns more bits to lower-amplitude signals. The transmission rate is obtained by multiplying 8000 samples per second by 8 bits per sample, giving 64,000 bits per second, the standard transmission rate for one channel of telephone digital communications.

Two basic variations of 64 Kb/sec PCM are commonly used: MU-law and A-law. The methods are similar in that they both use logarithmic compression to achieve 12 to 13 bits of linear PCM quality in 8 bits, but are different in relatively minor compression details (e.g., MU-law has a slight advantage in low-level signal-to-noise ratio performance). Usage has historically been along country and regional boundaries, with North America using MU-law and Europe using A-law modulation. It is important to note that when making a long-distance call, any required MU-law to A-law conversion is the responsibility of the MU-law country.

Another compression method often used is *adaptive differential pulse code modulation* (ADPCM). A commonly used instance of ADPCM, ITU-T G.726 encodes using 4-bit samples, giving a transmission rate of 32 Kb/sec. Unlike PCM, the 4 bits in ADPCM do not directly encode the amplitude of speech but the differences in amplitude as well as the rate of change of that amplitude, employing some very rudimentary linear predictions.

The most popular voice-coding standards for telephony and packet voice include

- *G.711:* Describes the 64 Kb/sec PCM voice-coding technique outlined earlier. G.711-encoded voice is already in the correct format for digital voice delivery in a public phone network or through PBXs.
- *G.726:* Describes ADPCM coding at 40, 32, 24, and 16 Kb/sec; ADPCM voice may also be interchanged between packet voice and public phone or PBX networks, provided that the latter has ADPCM capability.
- *G.728:* Describes a 16 Kb/sec low-delay variation of *code-excited linear prediction* (CELP) voice compression. CELP voice coding must be transcoded to a public telephony format for delivery to or through telephone networks.
- *G.729:* Describes CELP compression that enables voice to be coded into 8 Kb/sec streams. Two variations of this standard (G.729 and G.729 Annex A) differ largely in computational complexity, and both generally provide speech quality as good as that of 32 Kb/sec ADPCM.
- *G.723.1:* Describes a technique that can be used for compressing speech or other audio signal components of multimedia service at a very low bit rate.

More details about voice-coding techniques and standards can be found in Davidson and Peters 2000.

H.323

H.323 is the standard that has been developed for multimedia communication over a LAN or network that does not provide guaranteed QoS. The accepted model for internal signaling for IP packet voice networks is the H.323 standard. While H.323 is popularly viewed as a packet video standard, it actually defines a set of multimedia communications standards between users. In fact, only voice services are required for H.323 participation; video and data support are optional.

H.323 defines a complete multimedia network, from devices to protocols. Linking all of the entities within H.323 is H.245, which is defined to negotiate facilities among participants and H.323 network elements. A scaled-down version of ISDN's Q.931 call protocol is used to provide for connection setup. Figure 7.5 shows the components of H.323. In H.323 terms, the voice agents are *terminals,* although the common usage of this concept suggests a single user. H.323 also defines a *gatekeeper* function that performs the address translation and also mapping between a telephone number and the IP address of the remote gateways. If the network in a packet voice application is actually made up of several different kinds of transport networks, H.323 defines a *gateway* function between networks that performs the packet data format translation and signaling translation

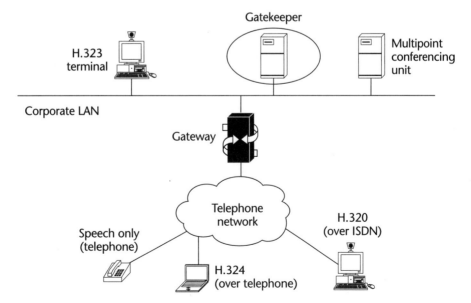

Figure 7.5 Components of H.323.

required for proper communications across the network boundary. The most common use of this gateway is the conversion of videoconferencing from H.320 to H.323 format, permitting packet video users to communicate with traditional room- or cart-based video systems that rely on the circuit-switched form of video. More details about H.323 can be found in Davidson and Peters 2000.

Session Initiation Protocol

The session initiation protocol (SIP) is an application-layer control protocol that can establish, modify, and terminate multimedia sessions or calls. These multimedia sessions include multimedia conferences, distance learning, Internet telephony, and similar applications. SIP is defined in RFC 2543.

SIP is a peer-to-peer protocol where end devices (*user agents,* or *UAs*) initiate sessions. The two components of an SIP system are UAs and network servers. Calling and called parties are identified by an SIP address. (Figure 7.6 shows the SIP components.) UAs are client end-system applications that contain both the *user-agent client* (UAC) and a *user-agent server* (UAS), otherwise known as a *client* and *server*. The client initiates the SIP request and acts as the calling party. The server receives the request and returns the response on behalf of the user and acts as the called party. Examples of UAs include SIP phones, gateways, PDAs, and robots.

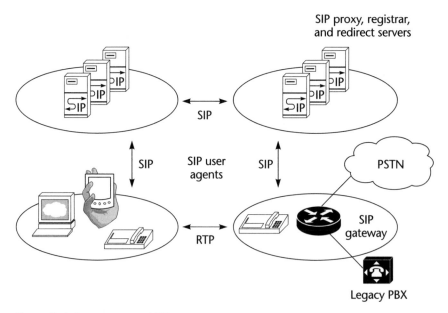

Figure 7.6 Components of SIP.

Network servers are optional components in the context of SIP. There are three types of servers: proxy server, redirect server, and location server.

- *Proxy server:* Acts on behalf of the UA and forwards the SIP messages to the other UAs after modifying the header. Rewriting the header identifies the proxy server as the initiator of the request and ensures that the response follows the same path back to the proxy server.
- *Redirect server:* Accepts SIP requests from the UA and sends a redirect response back to the UA with the address of the next server or the calling party. Redirect servers do not accept calls, nor do they forward or process SIP requests.
- *Location server:* Maintains the SIP address of UA devices. The redirect server and the proxy server use the location server to locate the called UA.

SIP addresses, also called SIP *universal resource locators* (URLs), exist in the form of *users@host*. The *user* portion can be a name or telephone number, and the *host* portion can be a domain name or network address. The following examples depict two possible SIP URLs:

sip:vijay@vijay.com

sip:0012012012222@10.10.10.10

Figure 7.7 shows a call setup using a proxy server. A UA can send an SIP request directly to the local proxy server or to the IP address and port corresponding to the called party (e.g., *vijay@10.10.10.10*). Sending it to a proxy server is relatively easy because the calling UA does not have to know the exact URL of the called UA.

7.2.3 How Does Voice-over-IP Work?

The general steps to connect a packet voice telephone call through a voice-over-IP router are described in the example below. This example is not a specific call flow, but it gives a high-level view of what happens when you make a phone call work over a packet voice network. The general flow of a two-party voice call is the same in all cases:

1. The user picks up the handset, signaling an off-hook condition to whatever the local loop is connected to (e.g., PBX, PSTN central office switch, signaling application in the router).
2. The session application issues a dial tone and waits for the user to dial a phone number.
3. The user dials the number, which is accumulated by the session application.

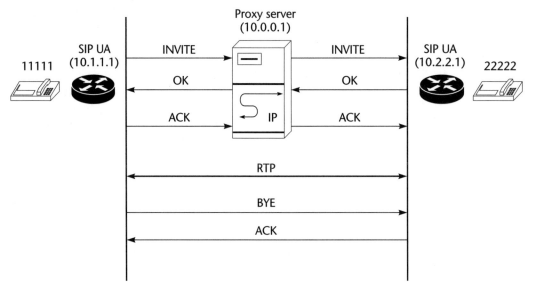

Figure 7.7 Call setup using an SIP proxy server.

4. The number is mapped via the dial plan mapper to an IP host (by sending a request to the gatekeeper), which talks either to the destination phone directly or to a PBX, which finishes completing the call.
5. The session applications run a session protocol (e.g., H.323) to establish a transmission and a reception channel for each direction over the IP network. Meanwhile, if there is a PBX involved at the called end, it finishes completing the call to the destination phone.
6. If using RSVP, the RSVP reservations are put in place to achieve the desired QoS over the IP network.
7. The voice CODECs/compressors/decompressors are turned on for both ends, and the conversation proceeds using IP as the protocol stack.
8. Any call progress indications and other signals that can be carried inband (e.g., remote phone ringing, line busy) are cut through the voice path as soon as an end-to-end audio channel is up.
9. When either end hangs up, the RSVP reservations are torn down (if RSVP is used), and the session ends, with each end going idle waiting for another off-hook.

When the dial plan mapper determines the necessary IP address to reach the destination telephone number, a session is invoked. H.323 is the current session application. Figure 7.8 shows a breakdown of the steps taken to form the H.323 session. The initial TCP connection is usually made on port 1720 to negotiate the H.225 portion of the H.323 session. During this portion, the TCP port number for the H.245 portion of the H.323 session is passed back to the calling unit.

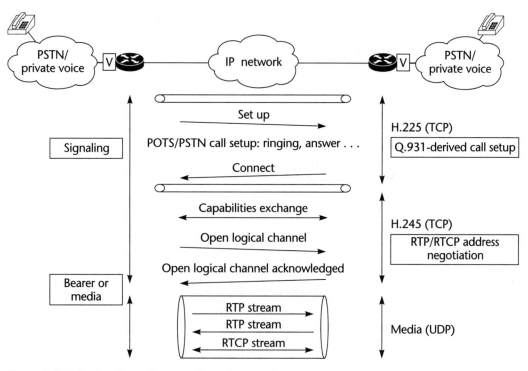

Figure 7.8 Call setup in a voice-over-IP environment.

During the H.245 portion of the H.323 session, the RTP and RTCP addresses are passed between the calling unit and the called unit. The RTP address used is in the range of 16,384 plus four times the amount of channels available on the calling device. After all portions of the H.225 and H.245 sessions are complete, the audio is then streamed over RTP/UDP/IP. (RTP stands for *real-time protocol*.)

7.2.4 Services Using Voice-over-IP

This section presents a discussion on how voice-over-IP can help a service provider in creating new services and reducing operational costs. By offering voice and data services over a single network, service providers can reduce the costs of managing two networks. Voice-over-IP can also help service providers to augment their portfolio with add-on services that will provide customers with single network connectivity for both voice and data services.

Merging Voice and Data Networks

Voice over a packet network uses less transmission bandwidth than conventional voice because the digitized signal is compressed before it is transmitted. This allows more traffic to be carried on a given connection in a packet network as compared to a conventional voice network. Where telephony requires as many as 64,000 bits per second, packet voice often needs fewer than 10,000. For many companies, there is sufficient reserve capacity on national and international data networks to transport considerable voice traffic, making voice essentially "free." A packet/data network can deliver voice traffic using less bandwidth. Given a certain amount of bandwidth, more voice traffic can be transported using an IP network compared to a voice network.

Voice-over-IP is an excellent solution that can help to carry both voice and data traffic using the same IP network (see Figure 7.9). An IP network connects two remote sites, Site A and Site B. Voice (telephone) and data applications are connected to the router at each site. The router is also the gateway for the voice-over-IP application. X1234 and X5678 are the telephone numbers of Site A and Site B, respectively. The IP network transports both voice and data packets. The same network connection between Site A and Site B is used to transport both voice and data traffic. Merging voice and data onto one network can help reduce the cost of maintaining two networks both in terms of infrastructure and the staffing required to maintain the networks. The challenge lies in ensuring that the IP network can guarantee the quality required for delivering voice traffic. (Section 7.1 provided details about how to overcome some of these challenges.)

Toll Bypass

Toll bypass will be the most common application that corporations will look toward for deploying voice-over-IP networks. It allows corporations to replace the tie lines that currently hook up their PBX-to-PBX networks and route voice calls across their existing data infrastructures (see Figure 7.10). Corporations will also use voice-over-IP to replace smaller key systems at remote offices while maintaining larger-density voice-over-IP

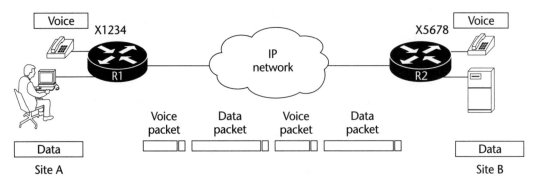

Figure 7.9 Merging voice and data networks using voice-over-IP.

Figure 7.10 Toll bypass using voice-over-IP.

equipment at the sites with larger voice needs. Another benefit to using voice-over-IP is that real-time fax relay can be used on an interoffice basis, an advantage since a large portion of long-distance minutes is fax traffic.

7.3 IP Security

IP security (known as *IPSec*) provides interoperable, high-quality, cryptographically based security for IPv4 and IPv6. The security services offered by IPSec include

Access controls (connectionless integrity ensuring data is transmitted without alteration)

Data origin authentication (knowing received data is the same as sent data and who sent the data)

Protection against replays and partial sequence integrity

Confidentiality (encryption)

Limited traffic flow confidentiality

One of the most common ways of breaching the security of a network is to capture some genuine data and then play it back to gain access. Therefore, IPSec provides a means of securing against this data capture and replay. While it is good to know whether data has been tampered with, a priority for most customers is that they do not want their data read by unwanted parties. The most common way of preventing the wrong people from reading data is encryption. This not only protects data but also provides limited traffic flow confidentiality, as it can hide the identities of the sender and receiver.

The IPSec protocol suite comprises a set of standards that are used to provide privacy and authentication services at the IP layer. The current IPSec standards include three algorithm-independent base specifications that are currently standards-track RFCs. These three RFCs, listed below, are in the process of being revised, and the revisions will account for numerous security issues with current specifications.

- *RFC 2401, the IP security architecture:* Defines the overall architecture and specifies elements common to both the IP authentication header and the IP encapsulating security payload.
- *RFC 2402, the IP authentication header* (AH): Defines an algorithm-independent mechanism for providing exportable cryptographic authentication without encryption to IPv4 and IPv6 packets.
- *RFC 2406, the IP encapsulated security payload* (ESP): Defines an algorithm-independent mechanism for providing encryption to IPv4 and IPv6 packets.
- *RFC 2408, the Internet security association and key management protocol* (ISAKMP): Defines the procedures for authenticating a communicating peer, creation and management of security associations, key-generation techniques, and threat mitigation (e.g., denial of service and replay attacks). All of these are necessary to establish and maintain secure communications (via IP Security Service or any other security protocol) in an Internet environment.
- *RFC 2409, the Internet key exchange* (IKE): Describes a protocol using part of the Oakley key-determination protocol and part of the secure key-exchange mechanism (SKEME) in conjunction with ISAKMP to obtain authenticated keying material for use with ISAKMP and for other security associations, such as AH and ESP.

7.3.1 Concepts and Terminologies

This section introduces the concepts and terminologies related to IPSec. The fundamental concepts are authentication, encryption, key management, and security association.

Authentication

Authentication, in IPSec terms, is knowing that we trust the "person" that has sent us the data, that the data has not been altered in transit, and also, but to a lesser extent, being able to prove that the data was sent. This can be achieved by using a hashing algorithm: The sender takes the data and a key (a password of sorts) and hashes these together. The answer, which is always the same length for that particular key and hashing algorithm, is known as a *message authentication code.* IPSec refers to the message authentication code as the *integrity check value* (ICV). The message authentication code and the data are sent to the receiver. The receiver takes the data, the key, and the hashing algorithm and performs the same calculation as the sender. The receiver compares his or her answer, that is, the message authentication code, with that sent by the user. If the answers match, the receiver knows that the data has not been altered (or the answer would be different) and knows who sent the data (the person who knows the same key).

Encryption

Encryption is the transformation of a clear text message into an unreadable form to hide its meaning. The opposite transformation, retrieving the clear text message, is decryption. The keys are often symmetric—that is, the same key is used for encryption and decryption. The most common encryption algorithm is the *data encryption standard* (DES). DES is a block encryption algorithm: it takes the data and encrypts it in blocks of bits. The blocks of data are 64 bits and the most common key lengths are 56 or 168 (*triple DES,* or *3DES*). With DES, the 56-bit key is often expressed as a 64-bit number, with every eighth bit used for parity. From the key, 16 subkeys are derived that are used in 16 rounds of the algorithm. The cipher text is always the same length as the clear text.

Key Exchange

Both authentication and encryption are based on the use of keys. A key is a bit pattern that is used to encrypt messages. The length of the key depends on the encryption technique. The key is used by the sender, who encrypts the message with it, and by the receiver, who decrypts the message with it. Therefore, the key has to be exchanged between the sender and the receiver.

The IPSec protocol suite also includes cryptographic techniques to support the key management requirements of the network-layer security. ISAKMP provides the framework for Internet key management and the specific protocol support for negotiation of security attributes. By itself, it does not establish session keys; however, it can be used with various session key establishment protocols, such as Oakley, to provide a complete solution to Internet key management.

The Oakley key-determination protocol provides the important security property of *perfect forward secrecy* and is based on cryptographic techniques that have survived substantial public scrutiny. Perfect forward secrecy ensures that if any single key is compromised, only the data encrypted with that particular key will be compromised; it will not compromise any data encrypted with subsequent session keys.

The ISAKMP and Oakley protocols have been combined into a hybrid protocol. The resolution of ISAKMP with Oakley uses the framework of ISAKMP to support a subset of Oakley key-exchange modes. This new key-exchange protocol provides optional perfect forward secrecy and full security association attribute negotiation, as well as authentication methods that provide both repudiation and nonrepudiation. Implementations of this protocol can be used, for example, to establish VPNs and also to allow users from remote sites (who may have a dynamically allocated IP address) access to a secure network.

Authentication Header

An authentication header (AH) provides an authentication and integrity mechanism for IP traffic. Figure 7.11 shows the fields of the AH. The preceding IP header will contain a protocol value of 51. The next header field identifies the type of the next payload. The value specified is one of the IP protocol numbers, as defined in the most recent assigned numbers (currently RFC 1700).

The payload length is the length of the header in 32-bit words minus 2. The reserved field is always set to zero. The security parameter index (SPI) is 32 bits long, and the value is determined when the *security association* (SA) is established. The sequence number is also 32 bits long and is always present, even if antireplay is not enabled. The sequence number is set to zero when the SA is established and will never cycle if antireplay is enabled. The size of the authentication data field contains the message authentication code—which in IPSec terminology is the ICV. It must be a multiple of 32 bits, and padding can be added if needed.

An extra header (AH) is inserted onto the IP header (see Figure 7.12). HMAC (keyed hashing for message authentication) algorithms like SHA (secure hash algorithm) or MDS is used to generate the AH. This header is generated using the entire IP packet and a secret key. Fields of the IP packet that get modified in transit (TTL, ToS, header checksum, flags) are not used in generating the AH. This header is used to verify that the content of the IP packet has not been modified.

Although IPSec is connectionless, it uses a sequence number to detect duplicate packets in order to provide protection against *denial-of-service* (DoS) attack. This mechanism is referred to as *antireplay* because it prevents packets from being duplicated and retransmitted by hackers as a part of DoS attack. The sequence number in the AH is used to detect

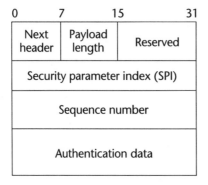

Figure 7.11 Fields of the authentication header.

Original IP datagram

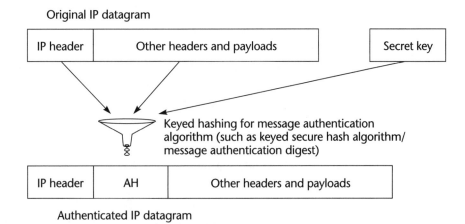

Figure 7.12 Generating an authentication header for an IP packet.

Original IP datagram

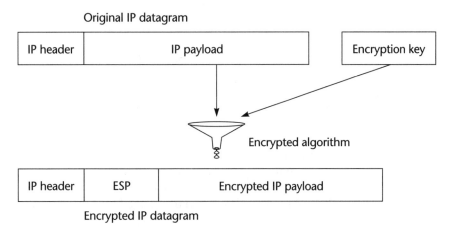

Figure 7.13 Encryption using ESP.

duplicate packets. AH does not ensure the confidentiality of the payload of the IP packet. This means that AH does not encrypt the payload.

Encapsulated Security Payload

The encapsulated security payload (ESP) encrypts the entire payload of the IP packet using DES or 3DES in order to provide confidentiality for the payload of the IP packet. As shown in Figure 7.13, the ESP header is inserted between the IP header and the encrypted payload to generate the encrypted IP packet. It also provides for an optional authentication/ integrity mechanism for the payload. ESP can be used by itself or in conjunction with AH. ESP is defined in RFC 2406.

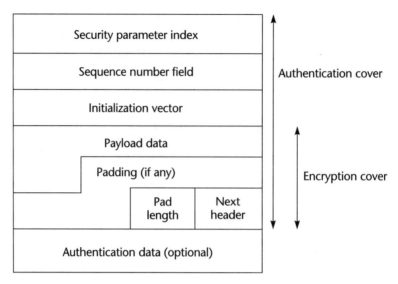

Figure 7.14 ESP header.

Figure 7.14 shows the details of the ESP header. The IP header contains a protocol value equal to 50 to indicate that the IP packet has an ESP header. (The SPI and sequence numbers have been discussed in the preceding section.)

There are three different reasons why padding may be added: The first is that the encryption algorithm may require the data to be multiples of numbers of bytes. The second is that the pad length and next header fields must be right-aligned within the 4-byte words. The last, and sometimes surprising reason, is to hide the size of the packet. The standard defines that a user may add between 0 and 255 bytes of padding. The pad length is the number of bytes of padding preceding this field. This field is always present, so if no padding is added, the field will be zero. The authentication data field is present if the security association demands authentication, and its length is dependent on the authentication algorithm used.

Security Association

The concept of security associations (SAs) is fundamental to IPSec. An SA is a connection that provides security to the traffic that it carries. The security is either AH or ESP, but not both. An SA applies in one direction only, so for security for both inbound and outbound traffic, two SAs will be established. If both AH and ESP are required for a particular connection, an SA bundle will be established. An SA is identified by three parameters: a destination IP address, the security protocol (AH or ESP), and the SPI. The SPI is a 32-bit number that is used to uniquely identify the particular SA. Numbers 1 to 255 are currently reserved by the IANA for future expansion.

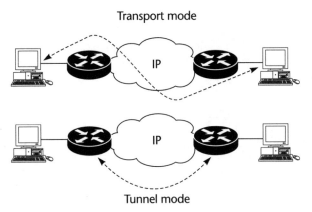

Figure 7.15 Two modes of SAs.

There are two main types of SAs: transport mode and tunnel mode (see Figure 7.15). In a transport mode SA, the source and destination of the IP packet also do the IPSec processing. In this case, each end station would have a stack that was IPSec capable and the traffic would be secured end to end. If one or more of the devices is a security gateway—for example, a router—the SA is in tunnel mode. In this scenario, the IPSec processing is not done by either the source or the destination of the IP packet. In Figure 7.15, the IP packets would only be secured between the two routers. Sometimes people refer to the routers as "acting as a proxy"—they are providing security for clients who are unable to provide security for themselves, or providing security in addition to that provided by the clients.

It is important to realize that a particular IP packet may experience both types of SAs in the path between source and destination. For example, the sending station may use ESP to encrypt the packet. The sending station would establish an SA in transport mode. The forwarding router may then apply AH security to that packet using an SA that is in tunnel mode.

So what is the difference between tunnel and transport mode, other than the device that performs the IPSec processing? The main difference is that in transport mode, the security is applied to upper protocol levels, whereas in tunnel mode, the security is applied to the entire IP packet. Figures 7.16 and 7.17 show the difference in the packets generated by tunnel mode and transport mode.

7.3.2 How Does IPSec Work?

The IPSec standard will enable interoperable, secure, and authenticated data flow at the IP level for interchangeable devices, including hosts, firewall products, and routers. The following example illustrates how IPSec is used to provide for authenticated, confidential data communication between the remote router and campus firewall, shown in Figure 7.18. All

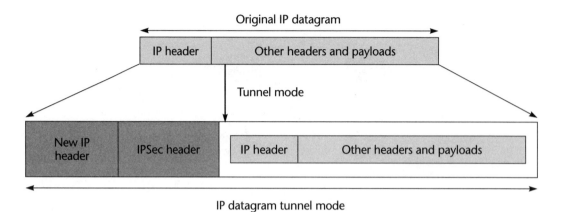

Figure 7.16 Tunnel mode packets.

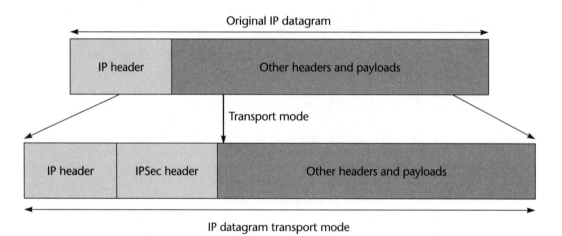

Figure 7.17 Transport mode packets.

traffic from the remote router destined to the campus firewall must be authenticated before passing traffic through. The router and firewall must first agree on a security association, which is an agreement between the two on a security policy. The SA includes

Encryption algorithm

Authentication algorithm

Shared session key

Key lifetime

An SA is unidirectional, so for two-way communication, two SAs must be established, one for each direction. Generally, the policy is the same,

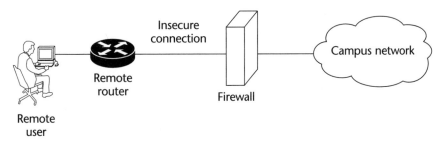

Figure 7.18 Router to firewall security.

but this leaves room for asymmetrical policies in either direction. These SAs are negotiated via ISAKMP, or they can be defined manually. After the SA is negotiated, it is then determined whether to use authentication, confidentiality, and integrity or simply authentication. If only authentication is desired, the current standard specifies the use of a hashing function. Specifically, implementations must use at least the MD5 algorithm with 128-bit keys. The packet header and data are run through the hashing function, and the results of the hash computation are inserted into the specified field in the AH.

Note that for IPv4, the following fields are set to zero:

Type of service (ToS)

Time to live (TTL)

Header checksum

Offset

Flags

The new packet, with the authentication header between the IP header and data, is now sent through the router to the campus destination. When the firewall receives the packet, it verifies the authenticity of the packet by recomputing the hash with the hashing function specified in the SA. The hashing function must be the same on both sides. As shown in Figure 7.18, the firewall then compares its computed hash with the parameter found in the field in the AH, and if they match, it is assured of authentication and integrity (i.e., that the packet came from the remote router and no bits have been modified). Note that since the original packet is expanded because of the insertion of the AH, fragmentation may be required. Fragmentation occurs after the AH for outgoing packets and before the AH for incoming packets.

If there is also a requirement for confidentiality, then the SA specifies that all traffic from the remote router destined to the campus firewall must be authenticated and encrypted before passing traffic through. The ESP provides authentication, integrity, and confidentiality. Note that since the original packet is expanded because of the insertion of the AH, fragmentation may be required. Fragmentation occurs after ESP for outgoing packets and before ESP for incoming packets.

7.3.3   Advantages

The advantages of IPSec network-layer security include the following:

- It can support completely unmodified end systems, though in this case, encryption is no longer strictly end to end.
- It is particularly suitable for building VPNs across nontrusted networks.
- It can support transport protocols other than TCP (e.g., UDP).
- It hides the transport-layer headers from eavesdropping, providing somewhat greater protection against traffic analysis.
- With AH and replay detection, it protects against certain DoS attacks based on swamping (e.g., TCP synchronization attacks).

7.3.4   IPSec versus MPLS-VPN

After reading this section on IPSec, some questions may arise:

1. How do the VPNs created using IPSec differ from the MPLS-VPNs?
2. Is there any need for MPLS-VPNs if VPNs can be created using IPSec?
3. What additional benefits does IPSec bring to the table?

The VPNs created by IPSec and MPLS-VPNs are quite different. MPLS-VPN creates VPNs at the network layer by using special routing protocols that help to distinguish between different networks and by using packet-forwarding mechanisms based on labels to forward packets only within the VPN. The mechanisms used by MPLS-VPNs are scalable and can be used to create and maintain several VPNs. The MPLS-VPN solution is scalable because there is no need to build and maintain point-to-point tunnels between the different sites of the VPN. The number of labels required to build a VPN is directly proportional to the number of sites (or the total number of network addresses within a VPN).

IPSec forms VPNs by creating associations between hosts and other network entities that belong to the same VPN and ensuring that communication is possible only between network elements that are part of the association. The solution provided by IPSec is not scalable for a large number of VPNs because one needs to form associations between the different entities belonging to a VPN and the complexity of the number of associations is $O(N^2)$, where N is the number of hosts belonging to a VPN. The advantage of IPSec lies in the additional security mechanisms. IPSec can supplement the security by means of authentication and encryption.

IPSec and MPLS-VPN are not two competing technologies, but they supplement each other so as to overcome the disadvantages of each other. IPSec on top of an MPLS-VPN provides a solution that is more secure (with the additional security provided by IPSec) and also scalable (by using MPLS-VPN). IPSec can be used to strengthen the security of the network and also to protect the integrity and confidentiality of the data that is transported across the IP network.

7.4 IPv6

The current version of IP is version 4, which uses 32 bits for its address. Therefore, theoretically, the IPv4 addressing scheme supports up to four billion hosts (2^{32} because the IPv4 address has 32 bits). Today, half of this address space has been used. Public IP addresses are distributed by agencies like the Internet Assigned Number Authority (IANA) and Réseaux IP Européens (RIPE). In order to overcome the address space limitation, concepts like *network address translation* (NAT) were developed in the early stages. This proved to be a practical solution. However, it has its limitations; some of the issues related to NAT are scalability and lack of transparency when it comes to developing differentiated services based on IP addresses. Given the ubiquity of IP and the rapid proliferation of devices with IP addresses (see Figure 7.19), there arose a need to redesign the addressing scheme of IP.

In the early 1990s, work started on the next-generation IP (IPng, currently known as IPv6) to address the issues related to the addressing limitations of IPv4. The primary motivation for IPv6 is the need to meet the

Figure 7.19 Explosion of new IP devices.

anticipated future demand for globally unique IP addresses. Applications such as mobile Internet-enabled devices (e.g., PDAs, telephones, and cars), *home area networks* (HANs), and wireless data services are driving this demand. IPv6 quadruples the number of network address bits from 32 bits (in IPv4) to 128 bits, which provides more than enough globally unique IP addresses for every networked device on the planet. By being globally unique, IPv6 addresses inherently enable global reachability and end-to-end security for networked devices, functionality that is crucial to the applications and services that are driving the demand for the addresses. Additionally, the flexibility of the IPv6 address space reduces the need for private addresses and the use of NAT; therefore, IPv6 enables new application protocols that do not require special processing by border routers at the edge of networks.

7.4.1 Features

This section presents some of the features and benefits of IPv6. Feature highlights are

1. Expanded address space (128 bits compared to 32 bits in IPv4)
2. Header format simplification (header has fixed length)
3. Autoconfiguration and multihoming (no need for DHCP)
4. Mobile IP without triangular routing
5. Class-of-service/multimedia support
6. Authentication and privacy capabilities
7. No more broadcast—multicast address

The following sections provide more details about the features and benefits of IPv6.

Addressing

IPv6 addresses are 128 bits long and are represented as a series of 16-bit hexadecimal fields separated by colons (:) in the format x:x:x:x:x:x:x:x. Following are examples of two IPv6 addresses that have different lengths:

FEDC:BA98:7654:3210:FEDC:BA98:7654:3210

1080:0:0:0:8:800:200C:417A

There are three types of IPv6 addresses: unicast, anycast, and multicast.

Unicast

A unicast address is for a single interface. A packet that is sent to a unicast address is delivered to the interface identified by that address. Figure 7.20 shows the fields of an IPv6 global unicast address. There are several types of unicast addresses:

FP	TLA ID	Reserved	NLA ID	SLA ID	Interface ID
3 bits	13 bits	8 bits	24 bits	16 bits	64 bits

FP = Format prefix (unicast (001), multicast, anycast)
TLA = Top-level aggregator (global ISP)
NLA = Next-level aggregator (ISP)
SLA = Site-level aggregator (customer)
Interface ID = Host

Figure 7.20 IPv6 global unicast address.

- *Aggregatable global address:* An IPv6 address from the aggregatable global unicast prefix, the structure of which enables strict aggregation of routing prefixes that limits the number of routing table entries in the global routing table. Aggregatable global addresses used on links are aggregated upward through organizations, then to intermediate-level ISPs, and eventually to top-level ISPs.
- *Site-local address:* An IPv6 unicast address that uses the prefix FEC0::/10 (1111 111011) and concatenates the subnet identifier (the 16-bit SLA field) with the interface identifier. Site-local addresses can be used to number a complete site while not having a globally unique prefix. They can be considered private addresses because they can be used to restrict communication to a limited domain. Figure 7.21(a) shows the structure of a site-local address. IPv6 routers must not forward packets that have site-local source or destination addresses outside of the site.
- *Link-local address:* An IPv6 unicast address that can be automatically assigned using the link-local prefix FE80::/10 (1111 111010) and the interface identifier. Nodes on a local link can use link-local addresses to communicate; they do not need site-local or globally unique addresses. Figure 7.21(b) shows the structure of a link-local address. IPv6 routers must not forward packets that have link-local source or destination addresses to other links.
- *IPv4-compatible IPv6 address:* An IPv6 unicast address that has zeros in the high-order 96 bits of the address and an IPv4 address in the low-order 32 bits of the address (see Figure 7.22). The format of an IPv4-compatible IPv6 address is 0:0:0:0:0:0:A.B.C.D.

Anycast

An anycast address is an address that is assigned to a set of interfaces that belong to different nodes. A packet sent to an anycast address is delivered to the closest interface (as defined by the routing protocols in use)

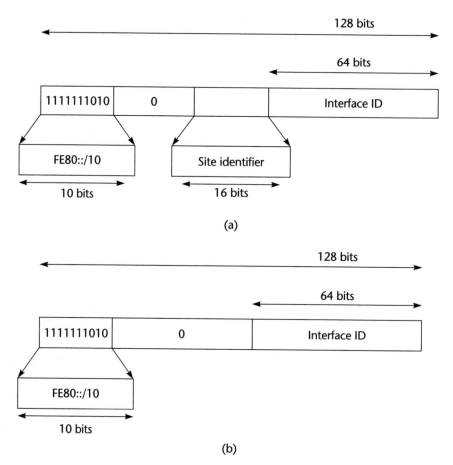

Figure 7.21 IPv6 site-local (a) and link-local (b) addresses.

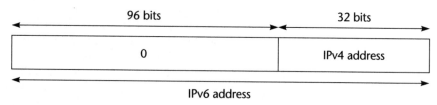

Figure 7.22 IPv4-compatible IPv6 address.

identified by the anycast address. Anycast addresses are syntactically indistinguishable from unicast addresses because they are allocated from the unicast address space. Assigning a unicast address to more than one interface makes a unicast address an anycast address. Nodes to which the anycast address is assigned must be explicitly configured to recognize that the address is anycast.

Multicast

An IPv6 multicast address has a prefix of FF00::/8 (1111 1111). It is an identifier for a set of interfaces that belong to different nodes. A packet sent to a multicast address is delivered to all interfaces identified by the multicast address. The second octet following the prefix defines the lifetime and scope of the multicast address. A permanent multicast address has a lifetime parameter equal to 0; a temporary multicast address has a lifetime parameter equal to 1. A multicast address that has the scope of a node, link, site, organization, or globe has a scope parameter of 1, 2, 5, 8, or E, respectively. For example, a multicast address with the prefix FF02::/16 is a permanent multicast address with a link scope. Figure 7.23 shows the format of the IPv6 multicast address.

Simplified IPv6 Header

The basic IPv4 packet header consists of 12 fields with a total size of 20 octets (160 bits) (see Figure 7.24). The 12 fields may be followed by an Options field, which is followed by a data portion that is usually the transport-layer packet. The variable length of the Options field adds to the total size of the IPv4 packet header. The shaded fields of the IPv4 packet header shown in Figure 7.24 are not included in the IPv6 packet header.

The basic IPv6 packet header consists of 8 fields with a total size of 40 octets (320 bits) (see Figure 7.24). Fields were removed from the IPv6 header because, in IPv6, routers do not handle fragmentation and checksums at the network layer. Instead, fragmentation in IPv6 is handled by the source of a packet, and checksums at the datalink layer and transport layer are used. (In IPv4, the UDP transport layer uses an optional checksum. In IPv6, use of the UDP checksum is required to check the integrity of the inner packet.) Additionally, the basic IPv6 packet header and Options field are aligned to 64 bits, which can facilitate the processing of

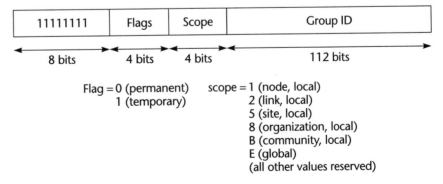

Figure 7.23 IPv6 multicast address.

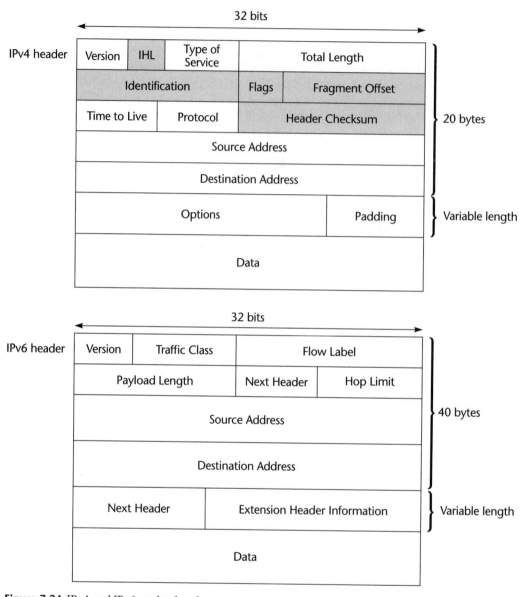

Figure 7.24 IPv4 and IPv6 packet headers.

IPv6 packets. Table 7.1 provides more details about the fields of the IPv6 header.

7.4.2 Advantages

IPv6 has advantages in addition to the larger address space compared to IPv4. These advantages are discussed in this section.

Table 7.1   Description of fields of the IPv6 header.

Field	Description
Version	Similar to the Version field in the IPv4 packet header, except that the field lists number 6 for IPv6 instead of number 4 for IPv4.
Traffic Class	Similar to the Type of Service field in the IPv4 packet header. The Traffic Class field tags packets with a traffic class that is used in differentiated services.
Flow Label	A new field in the IPv6 packet header. The Flow Label field tags packets with a specific flow that differentiates the packets at the network layer.
Payload Length	Similar to the Total Length field in the IPv4 packet header. The Payload Length field indicates the total length of the data portion of the packet.
Next Header	Similar to the Protocol field in the IPv4 packet header. The value of the Next Header field determines the type of information following the basic IPv6 header. The type of information following the basic IPv6 header can be a transport-layer packet—for example, a TCP or UDP packet, or an Extension Header, as shown Figure 7.24.
Hop Limit	Similar to the Time to Live field in the IPv4 packet header. The value of the Hop Limit field specifies the maximum number of routers that an IPv6 packet can pass through before the packet is considered invalid. Each router decrements the value by one. Because there is no checksum in the IPv6 header, the router can decrement the value without needing to recalculate the checksum, which saves processing resources.
Source Address	Similar to the Source Address field in the IPv4 packet header, except that the field contains a 128-bit source address for IPv6 instead of a 32-bit source address for IPv4.
Destination Address	Similar to the Destination Address field in the IPv4 packet header, except that the field contains a 128-bit source address for IPv6 instead of a 32-bit source address for IPv4.

Autoconfiguration

All interfaces on IPv6 nodes must have a link-local address, which is usually automatically configured from the identifier for an interface, and the link-local prefix FE80::0. A link-local address enables a node to communicate with other nodes on the link and can be used to further configure the node. Nodes can connect to a network and automatically generate site-local and global IPv6 addresses without the need for manual configuration or help of a server, such as a *dynamic host configuration protocol* (DHCP) server. With IPv6, a router on the link advertises in router advertisement messages any site-local and global prefixes and its willingness to function as a default router for the link. Router advertisement messages are sent periodically and in response to router solicitation messages, which are sent by hosts at system start-up. It is worth mentioning that other configuration parameters like a DNS server address still have to be configured on each node.

Prefix Aggregation

The aggregation nature of the IPv6 address space enables an IPv6 addressing hierarchy. For example, an enterprise can subdivide a single IPv6 prefix from a service provider into multiple, longer prefixes for use within its internal network. Conversely, a service provider can aggregate all of the prefixes from the customers and advertise only the aggregate address.

Multihomed Sites

Multiple IPv6 prefixes can be assigned to networks and hosts. Having multiple prefixes assigned to a network makes it easy for that network to connect to multiple ISPs without breaking the global routing table.

IP Mobility

In IPv6, Mobile IP is implemented using the routing extension header. This enables a mobile node to send IP packets directly to a destination node after the mobile node establishes an initial connection to the home agent. Direct routing in Mobile IP is the ability of a mobile node to bypass the home agent when sending IP packets to a destination node. Optional extensions make direct routing possible in Mobile IP for IPv4 (the extensions might not be implemented in all deployments of Mobile IP for IPv4), whereas direct routing is built into Mobile IP for IPv6.

Security

IPSec functionality is essentially identical in both IPv6 and IPv4; however, IPSec in IPv6 can be deployed from end to end—data may be encrypted along the entire path between the source node and destination node. (Typically, IPSec in IPv4 is deployed between border routers of separate networks.) In IPv6, IPSec is implemented using the authentication extension header and the ESP extension header. The authentication header provides integrity and authentication of the source. It also provides optional protection against replayed packets. The authentication header protects the integrity of most of the IP header fields and authenticates the source through a signature-based algorithm. The ESP header provides confidentiality, authentication of the source, connectionless integrity of the inner packet, antireplay, and limited traffic flow confidentiality.

Other Advantages

Other advantages of IPv6 include

Flow label for more efficient flow identification (avoids having to parse the transport-layer port numbers)

Neighbor unreachability detection protocol for hosts to detect and recover from first-hop router failure

More general header compression (handles more than just IP and TCP)

Drawbacks

It also may be worth pointing out that the IPv6 routing/addressing architecture is pretty much the same as IPv4. This means that all of the problems and issues with the scalability of IPv4 routing exist in IPv6 as well.

7.4.3 Migration Strategy

Integration and coexistence with IPv4 is a prerequisite to enable the smooth transition to IPv6. IPv6 has been designed from the beginning to be transition-rich. Following are some of the approaches available to facilitate the integration of IPv6 networks with IPv4 networks:

- Nodes that support both the IPv4 and IPv6 protocol stacks (see Figure 7.25(a))
- IPv6 tunnels over IPv4 core networks (see Figure 7.25(b))

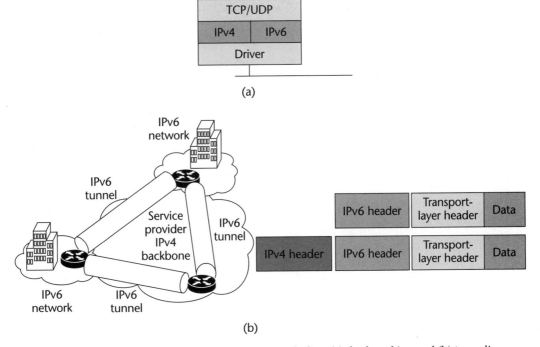

Figure 7.25 Migration strategies from IPv4 to IPv6, including (a) dual stacking and (b) tunneling.

- Translation gateways (e.g., *network address translation–protocol translation,* or *NAT-PT)*
- IPv6 services integration on MPLS backbones
- Dedicated IPv6 networks (which support both the IPv6 and IPv4 protocol stacks) over common Layer 2 infrastructures such as frame relay, ATM, and optical (e.g., *wave-division multiplexing,* or *WDM)*

7.4.4 Creating New Services

IPv6 helps to overcome the address space shortcomings of IPv4. With the proliferation of IP devices that connect to the public Internet, NAT is not a scalable solution. By making their network IPv6-compatible, service providers can be ready to offer IPv6 services to customers who require them. As seen in Section 7.4.3, IPv4 and IPv6 can coexist in the same network. By enabling IPv6, providers can offer additional IPv6 services to their customers.

7.5 Local Multipoint Distribution Service

LMDS is a broadband, wireless point-to-multipoint communication system operating above 20 GHz (depending on country of licensing) that can be used to provide digital two-way voice, data, Internet, and video services. The acronym LMDS is derived from the following:

- *Local:* Denotes that propagation characteristics of signals in this frequency range limit the potential coverage area of a single cell site; ongoing field trials conducted in metropolitan centers place the range of an LMDS transmitter at up to 8 kilometers (five miles).
- *Multipoint:* Indicates that signals are transmitted in a point-to-multipoint or broadcast method; the wireless return path, from subscriber to the base station, is a point-to-point transmission.
- *Distribution:* Refers to the distribution of signals, which may consist of simultaneous voice, data, Internet, and video traffic.
- *Service:* Implies the subscriber nature of the relationship between the operator and the customer; the services offered through an LMDS network are entirely dependent on the operator's choice of business.

LMDS can provide up to 1.25 Gb/sec of bandwidth in both directions. It is an access-layer technology and can help service providers to provide connectivity between a customer site and the nearest service provider PoP without using copper or fiber. This helps the service provider to avoid the problems related to local loops.

7.5.1 Components

The LMDS network architecture (see Figure 7.26) consists primarily of three parts:

Base station

Customer-premises equipment

Fiber-based infrastructure

Base Station

The base station is where the conversion from fibered infrastructure to wireless infrastructure occurs. Base station equipment includes the network interface for fiber termination; modulation and demodulation functions; and microwave transmission and reception equipment, typically located atop a roof or a pole. Key functionalities that may not be present in different designs include local switching. This function implies that billing, channel access management, registration, and authentication occur locally within the base station.

The alternative base station architecture simply provides connection to the fiber infrastructure. This forces all traffic to terminate in ATM switches somewhere in the fiber infrastructure. In this scenario, if two customers connected to the same base station wish to communicate with each other, they do so at a centralized location. Billing, authentication, registration, and traffic management functions are performed centrally.

CPE

Customer-premises configurations vary widely from vendor to vendor. Primarily, all configurations will include outdoor mounted microwave equipment and indoor digital equipment providing modulation, demodulation, control, and customer-premises interface functionality. The CPE may attach to the network using *time-division multiple access* (TDMA), *frequency-division multiple access* (FDMA), or *code-division multiple access*

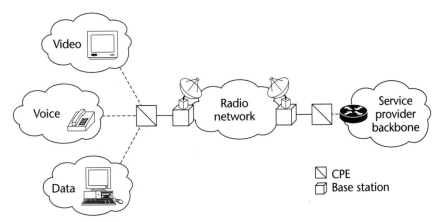

Figure 7.26 Components of an LMDS network.

(CDMA) methodologies. The customer-premises interfaces will run the full range, including *plain old telephone service* (POTS), Ethernet, unstructured DS1, structured DS1, frame relay, ATM-25, serial ATM over T1, DS3, STM-1 ATM, and POS. The customer-premises locations will range from large enterprises (e.g., office buildings, hospitals, and campuses), in which the microwave equipment is shared between many users, to mall locations and residences, in which single offices requiring 10BaseT and/or two POTS lines will be connected. Obviously, different customer-premises locations require different equipment configurations and different price points.

7.5.2 Advantages

Point-to-point fixed wireless networks have been commonly deployed to offer high-speed dedicated links between high-density nodes in a network. Moreover, since a large part of a wireless network's cost is not incurred until the CPE is installed, the network service operator can time capital expenditures to coincide with the signing of new customers. LMDS provides an effective last-mile solution for the incumbent service provider and can be used by competitive service providers to deliver services directly to end users. Benefits can be summarized as follows:

Lower entry and deployment costs

Ease and speed of deployment (systems can be deployed rapidly with minimal disruption to the community and the environment)

Fast realization of revenue (as a result of rapid deployment)

Demand-based build-out (scalable architecture employing open industry standards, ensuring services and coverage areas can be easily expanded as customer demand warrants)

Cost-effective network maintenance, management, and operating costs

High bandwidth (up to 1.25 Gb/sec in both directions)

7.6 Optical Networking

Optical networking provides the means to interconnect devices by using optical fiber and to transport data over that optical fiber. Light is used to convey information from one device to another. It is generated using *light-emitting diodes* (LEDs) or laser diodes. Optical fiber has a number of advantages over copper. It is lightweight, has enormous bandwidth potential, and is immune to electromagnetic interference. Optical fiber also has its disadvantages, such as loss or attenuation (weakening of signal over distance) and dispersion (equivalent to noise). The disadvantages can be overcome with improvements in technology, and the advantages provide an enormous potential to send more data using the same physical medium.

This section introduces the concept of optical networking and discusses how IP networks can be implemented on *optical transport networks* (OTNs), as well as the advantages and applications of optical networking technologies.

7.6.1 Technologies

Optical networking uses light to communicate information from one point to another. An optical network consists of optical nodes connected by fiber links. Depending on the transport technology, the optical nodes differ in their intelligence in terms of switching and providing failure mechanisms. The physical-layer technology includes SONET/SDH. Some of the transport technologies include POS, ATM, 10-gigabit, and resilient packet rings (also known as SRP). Another physical-layer technology that is rapidly emerging and replacing transport technology is dense wavelength-division multiplexing (DWDM).

SONET and SDH

SONET (synchronous optical network) and SDH (synchronous digital hierarchy) are recognized standards that make use of optical fiber to convey information. SONET defines optical signals and a synchronous frame structure for multiplexed digital traffic. It is a set of standards defining the rates and formats for optical networks specified in ANSI T1.105, ANSI T1.106, and ANSI T1.117. SDH, a similar standard, has been established in Europe by ITU-T. SONET equipment is generally used in North America, and SDH equipment is used everywhere else.

Both SONET and SDH use an *optical carrier* (OC). OC standards specify the physical properties of the optical signal (i.e., power, pulse shape, modulation techniques, spectral widths, etc.). OC speeds are currently specified from OC-1 (51.84 Mb/sec) to OC-192 (9953.28 Mb/sec). Both SONET and SDH are based on a structure that has a basic frame and speed. The frame format used by SONET is the *synchronous transport signal* (STS), with STS-1 being the base-level signal at 51.84 Mb/sec. An STS-1 frame can be carried in an OC-1 signal. The frame format used by SDH is the *synchronous transport module* (STM), with STM-1 being the base-level signal at 155.52 Mb/sec. An STM-1 frame can be carried in an OC-3 signal.

Both SONET and SDH have a hierarchy of signaling speeds. Multiple lower-level signals can be multiplexed together to form higher-level signals. For example, three STS-1 signals can be multiplexed together to form an STS-3 signal, and four STM-1 signals multiplexed together will form an STM-4 signal.

DWDM

Dense wavelength-division multiplexing (DWDM) is a technology that allows multiple information streams to be transmitted simultaneously over a single fiber at data rates as high as the fiber will allow (2.4 Gb/sec). The DWDM approach multiplies the simple 2.4 Gb/sec system by up to 16 times, giving an immense and immediate increase in capacity using embedded fiber. A 16-channel system (which is available today) supports 40 Gb/sec in each direction over a fiber pair, while a 40-channel system under development will support 100 Gb/sec, the equivalent of 10 STM-64/OC-192 transmitters. The benefits of DWDM over the first two options—adding fiber plant or deploying STM-64/OC-192 for increasing capacity—are clear.

Advantages of DWDM

To transmit 40 Gb/sec over 600 kilometers (373 miles) using a traditional system would require 16 separate fiber pairs with regenerators placed every 35 kilometers (22 miles) for a total of 272 regenerators. A 16-channel DWDM system, on the other hand, uses a single fiber pair and four amplifiers positioned every 120 kilometers (74.5 miles) for a total of 600 kilometers (373 miles).

Applications of DWDM

As occurs with many new technologies, the potential ways in which DWDM can be used are only beginning to be explored. Already, however, the technology has proven to be particularly well suited for several vital applications:

- DWDM is ready-made for long-distance telecommunications operators that use either point-to-point or ring topologies. The sudden availability of 16 new transmission channels where there used to be only 1 dramatically improves an operator's ability to expand capacity and simultaneously set aside backup bandwidth without installing new fiber.
- This large amount of capacity is critical to the development of self-healing rings, which characterize today's most sophisticated telecom networks. By deploying DWDM terminals, an operator can construct a 100% protected, 40 Gb/sec ring, with 16 separate communication signals using only two fibers.
- Operators that are building or expanding their networks will also find DWDM to be an economical way to incrementally increase capacity, rapidly provision new equipment for needed expansion, and future-proof their infrastructure against unforeseen bandwidth demands.
- Network wholesalers can take advantage of DWDM to lease capacity, rather than entire fibers, either to existing operators or to new

market entrants. DWDM will be especially attractive to companies that have low-fiber-count cables that were installed primarily for internal operations but that could now be used to generate telecommunications revenue.

7.6.2 IP and Optical Networking

Figure 7.27 shows the evolution of the optical networks and how IP can use them. The last part of the figure shows IP directly over the optical adaptation layer—optical technology is heading in this direction. Generalized multiprotocol label switching (GMPLS) is an example of such a technology. Running IP directly over an optical network (DWDM and using GMPLS) helps reduce the complexity of the protocol stack. It also helps to significantly reduce the complexity and time required to provision the networks, as well as the overheads of layers like ATM and POS, and provides additional bandwidth and enhanced protection mechanisms.

The optical network is no longer a group of point-to-point links; it has nodes and links. The nodes are *optical switches* (*optical cross-connects,* or *OXCs*) that switch light (based on wavelength) from one port to another. The network is resilient and provides protection mechanisms. Transforming the optical layer from a collection of point-to-point links to a resilient and manageable network is achieved by introducing devices called

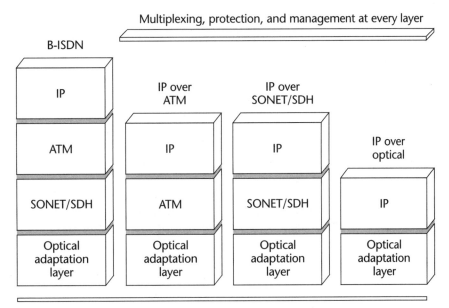

Figure 7.27 IP and optical networking.

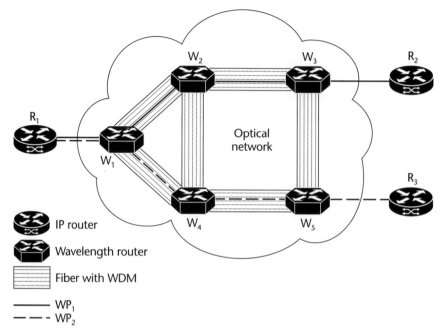

Figure 7.28 Optical network with IP routers.

wavelength routers (see Figure 7.28). These are huge optical switches, switching wavelengths through an optical network. The wavelength routing capacity implemented in the wavelength routers makes it possible to provision end-to-end wavelength paths between IP routers dynamically. The wavelength routers implement signaling mechanisms to provide protection in case of link and node failures.

Figure 7.28 shows three IP routers (R_1, R_2, and R_3) interconnected using an optical network. The optical network has five wavelength routers (W_1, W_2, W_3, W_4, and W_5). A wavelength path (WP_1) is established between W_1 and W_3 to provide IP connectivity between R_1 and R_2. Another wavelength path (WP_2) is established between W_1 and W_5 to provide IP connectivity between R_1 and R_3.

Similar to the IP network, the optical network also has two planes: the *control plane* and the *forwarding plane*. The control plane provides the intelligence and is responsible for establishing the wavelength-switching matrix in each wavelength router and also for providing the protecting mechanism for each wavelength path. The forwarding plane is responsible for switching the wavelength based on the wavelength-switching matrix.

Two architectures are common in implementing IP directly over optical networks:

- *Overlay model:* In this model, the optical network is opaque to the IP network—that is, the IP network is not aware of the topology of the optical network. The control planes of the optical network and IP network are independent.
- *Peer model:* In this model, the IP network is aware of the optical network, and the control planes of the IP and optical networks are integrated into one control plane.

Overlay Model

This overlay model is similar to the overlay model used in the IP-over-ATM and IP-over-frame relay architectures. The underlying optical network is visible as point-to-point links to the IP network. Figure 7.29 shows the overlay model. The topologies of the IP network and optical network are not the same, and the IP network does not have any knowledge of the

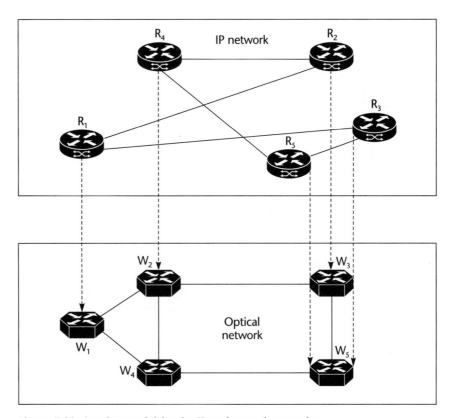

Figure 7.29 Overlay model for the IP and optical networks.

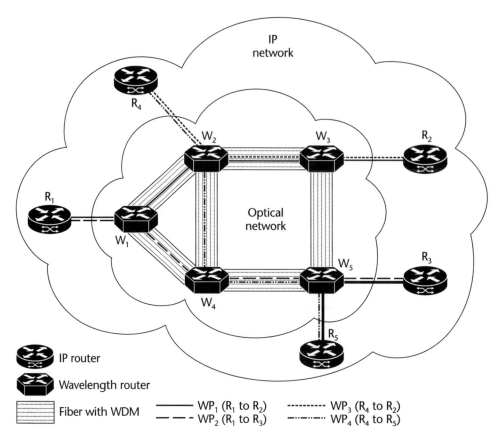

Figure 7.30 Overlay model—implementation.

topology of the optical network. The optical network is visible as a set of point-to-point links to the IP network.

Figure 7.30 shows the implementation of the overlay model for the IP and optical networks. The control plane for the optical network is independent of the control plane of the IP network. The optical network provides bandwidth and protection services to the IP network in a transparent manner. This model is typically used when one service provider owns the optical network and another owns the IP network. The IP service provider buys bandwidth from the optical service provider: the optical service provider is a bandwidth broker and provides bandwidth (on demand) to other service providers.

Peer Model

In a *peer model,* several service providers own both the optical network and the IP network. They look for ways in which to streamline and have a

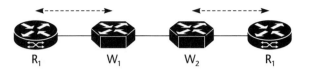

IP plus optical network

Figure 7.31 Integrated optical and IP peer model.

single control plane for both networks. The IP network (based on MPLS) uses labels to switch packets, and the optical network uses lambda (wavelength) to switch packets. The principles of the control plane are similar for both networks. One is used to assign labels and the other is used to assign lambdas. Integrating the two control planes into one will help service providers streamline their networking.

The peer model (also known as the *integrated optical and IP peer model*) uses a common control plane for both the optical and IP networks. Figure 7.31 shows the integrated optical and IP peer model. In this architecture, the IP routers and wavelength routers are peers and use the same control plane. The topology of the optical network is visible to the IP network. The same signaling mechanism is used in order to establish paths between IP routers and between wavelength routers. This concept is described in detail in the following section.

7.6.3 Generalized Multiprotocol Label Switching

Generalized multiprotocol label switching (GMPLS), also referred to as *multiprotocol lambda switching,* is a multipurpose control plane paradigm that supports not only devices that perform packet switching but also devices that perform switching in the time, wavelength, and space domains. Recent work has been done to extend and adapt the MPLS control plane, and specifically MPLS constraint-based routing, so that it can be used not just with routers and ATM switches but also with *optical cross-connects* (OXCs). This is a fundamental step in the evolution and integration of data and optical network architectures.

Some enhancements are clearly required to the existing MPLS routing and signaling protocol to address the peculiar characteristics of optical transport networks. The IETF, under the framework of GMPLS, is standardizing these protocol extensions. Figure 7.32 shows one type of GMPLS network that does lambda switching. The *lambda switching router* (LSR) in this network switches lambdas (wavelengths of light) from one port to another. MPLS is used at the signaling plane to establish the *lambda switch paths*. Once the lambda switch paths are established, then data is transmitted through this optical network with the help of the LSRs.

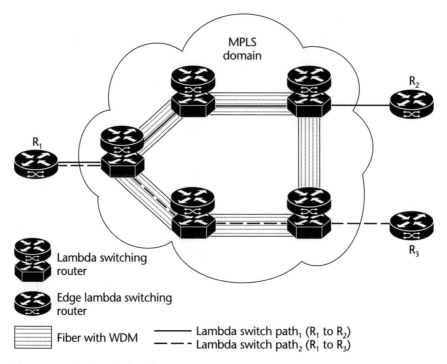

Figure 7.32 GMPLS network.

Several issues must be addressed in order to make this technology feasible. Signaling and routing enhancements and protection mechanisms are required to be built into the optical layer in order to make it robust. Several enhancements are currently being proposed in order to make GMPLS more scalable and robust. The concepts of generalized interfaces, label-switched path hierarchy, and link bundling make GMPLS scalable. The link management protocol can be used to make the underlying links more manageable. The signaling capabilities of GMPLS will allow service providers to quickly build out high-capacity agile infrastructures that support fast provisioning of connectivity between any two points in an IP network.

7.6.4 Applications of Optical Networks

Optical networks help the evolution of the service provider network in several areas. This includes the metro network and the core network. The evolution helps the service provider to reduce provisioning time as bandwidth requirements increase every day, to offer a more resilient network (using advanced protection mechanisms offered by the optical network), and to merge the control planes of the transport and IP networks.

Metro Network

The *metro network* provides coverage in a metropolitan area and is used to aggregate traffic from several metro locations. It also helps to overcome the last-mile problem by providing fiber connectivity directly to customer locations. Providing interconnectivity between the various metro locations means that there is a constant need to increase bandwidth, because the aggregated traffic will grow and more bandwidth is required to connect to the nearest PoP location. Providing fiber to a customer site means constantly provisioning new customers.

Optical technologies like gigabit, 10-gigabit, POS, resilient rings (SRP), and IP-over-DWDM meet these requirements of the metro network. Gigabit, 10-gigabit, and POS help to provide direct fiber connectivity to homes. SRP and IP-over-DWDM help to aggregate traffic from several metro locations to the nearest service provider PoP location.

Core Network

Today, legacy SONET/SDH protection ring architectures at STM-64/OC-192 provide connectivity between core nodes in a service provider network. The protection mechanism provided by SONET (APS) helps to provide seamless connectivity between core nodes. The limitations of this technology are wasted bandwidth to provide protection (backup links that are used only in case of failure) and an inability to increase bandwidth between core locations without installing new fibers.

The integrated optical and IP peer model helps to overcome both of these problems. Bandwidth can be increased on demand without installing new fibers. The optical network provides protection without wasting any bandwidth. The integration of the control plane for IP and the optical network helps in reducing the operation, administration, maintenance, and provisioning costs in the core network.

Bandwidth-on-Demand

The optical network helps to provide bandwidth-on-demand between two locations. This means that the bandwidth between any two locations can be increased without installation of additional fibers. The integrated optical and IP model helps to achieve this in a transparent manner between any two locations that require IP connectivity. The single control plane for the IP and optical network helps to provision new IP connections between any two points in the IP network in a transparent manner and reduces the complexity of provisioning new links between IP routers. This will help a service provider to provide bandwidth-on-demand to other service providers.

7.7 Chapter Review

This chapter has provided an overview on some advanced topics related to IP-based services. These topics supplement the features supported by IP and enhance the services that can be offered by the IP network. For readers who are interested in more details about the topics covered in this chapter, the bibliography at the end of the book provides suggestions for further reading.

Today, the requirements of applications using the IP network are more than just "best-effort." In order to meet requirements like guaranteed bandwidth; minimized delay, jitter, and packet loss; and security, it is necessary to implement the QoS functions in the network. Transporting voice over an IP network helps to merge the voice and data networks. This helps customers to reduce the cost of maintaining two networks and also to make effective use of the IP networks. Voice-over-IP has QoS requirements like minimizing delay and jitter and ensuring bandwidth. By enhancing the QoS functions of an IP network, it can support applications like voice-over-IP.

IPSec helps to enhance the security of the IP network. MPLS-VPNs provide secure networks by ensuring that VPNs are private and that data from one VPN does not get forwarded to a different VPN. However, MPLS-VPNs do not guarantee data confidentiality. If someone manages to break into the VPN, that person can then access the packets and the contents of the packets. IPSec provides data confidentiality by encrypting the data before transmitting it over the VPN.

The rapid growth in the number of devices with IP addresses has led to the evolution of IPv6. The addressing structure of IPv4 limits the number of devices to about 2^{32}. NAT helps overcome this problem to a certain extent, but it has its own limitations, such as loss of transparency and inability to provide end-to-end QoS. IPv6 overcomes this restriction by using 128 bits for an IP address.

Optical networking is a hot topic that is emerging rapidly. IP and optical networking will help the service provider to resolve the problems related to bandwidth, resiliency, and rapid provisioning in the core network. Bandwidth-on-demand is becoming increasing popular, and optical networks and IP together can provide a good solution to this requirement.

Case Studies

The previous chapters presented business and technical factors that drive IP-based service development and deployment. They offered perspectives from the service provider, the end customer, and the supplier in order to explain the motivation to develop IP-based services. Further examining the role of IP-based technology with advanced topics, such as optics, demonstrated why IP-based technology is tantamount to service development. Building the case for IP-based services has been our focus thus far. This final chapter presents how actual service providers, end customers, and suppliers use IP-based technology to solve business problems and what lessons can be learned from their experiences.

In this chapter, we outline two conceptual case studies as well as a real-world case study, which together demonstrate how IP-based services can be developed and deployed by service providers to generate revenue. The case studies emphasize the role of OSS architecture in implementing IP-based services. The two conceptual case studies are composites of real experiences of various service providers. The combination of these two conceptual studies with a real-world example demonstrates the full impact of IP in both business and technical aspects.

The conceptual case studies present scenarios for both Greenfield and incumbent service providers. The results of implementing IP-based technology to develop services are included since they derive from actual

221

examples and provide a good view of the business impact. The real-world example is based on the authors' experiences working with a European incumbent. The conceptual studies are based on the experiences of U.S. service providers, but are not restricted to the North American market—they are applicable to Europe, Latin America, Asia, the Pacific region, and emerging markets as well. The issues and challenges are similar, including assessing market potential for new services, implementing new services, and improving service provisioning.

The common thread in these case study examples, both conceptual and real, is defining the financial incentives to develop IP-based services. Further, the challenging task for service providers is to assure that there is no misalignment between their product strategies and the end customer's requirements. Specifically, there has to be an incentive for a customer to contract for IP-based services. Finally, these players analyze whether or not it is financially and technically feasible to develop an IP-based service architecture that will support the services in question. Identifying how these issues are addressed by service providers is in the scope of this chapter.

The technical aspects discussed in the first conceptual case study (λ-Networking, Inc.) are very detailed and lengthy (Section 8.1.9). The terms and concepts used in this section are reused later in the other two case studies. You are asked to refer to the first case study for technical details related to the other case studies.

8.1 Conceptual Case Study—Greenfield

The company in this conceptual case study is based in the United States. It is not an incumbent and is categorized as a competitive local exchange carrier (CLEC). The case study's focus is on how this company has used IP-based technology to construct its network infrastructure and present a bundled service offering with a single bill to its customer base. (Service bundles are defined in Chapter 1. The concepts of service pricing and packaging are discussed in Chapters 3 and 4.) The financial incentive of purchasing a service bundle for the customer is to have a discount for multiple services that are packaged together by a service provider. Another incentive for the customer is to have a single bill for the bundled services as opposed to separate billing, which can be complex. Customers may prefer to have their services delivered from a single vendor. Service bundles mean that the service provider manages the services. The financial incentive for the service provider in offering service bundles is that they ensure a flow of revenue. For service providers, bundling subsidizes lower-margin services with higher-margin services and results in a margin increase. In fact, offering bundled services makes it more difficult for a customer to switch to other providers, because the services are packaged together.

Thus, service providers use bundles to "lock" a relationship with the customer.

8.1.1 Background

The company, referred to as λ-Networking, Inc., is an East Coast–based CLEC that has constructed a national fiber backbone, operating at an OC-192/STM-64 speed, with metropolitan networks in over 60 cities. λ-Networking has invested in its fiber-based network infrastructure for the past seven years, and its stock is publicly traded in the U.S. stock market. The service differentiator for this company is that it can offer customers a single, simple invoice for value-added services such as voice-over-IP, Web hosting, corporate IP-VPN, and so on. Such billing is difficult, as most U.S. Greenfield service providers do not possess a national network.

λ-Networking has a total fiber installation that spans approximately 450,000 fiber miles (725,000 km). By constructing and owning its fiber infrastructure at both a metropolitan and a national level, the company is able to provision the "last mile," therein controlling its network end to end. (Associated regulatory issues are discussed in Chapter 1.)

The company offers broadband access services via LMDS technology. (LMDS is highlighted in Chapter 7.) The result of this service offering is that λ-Networking is able to provide direct access to end customers by using LMDS to bypass the regional Bell operating companies (RBOCs). Customers are able to connect to λ-Networking via either dial access, for speeds up to 56 Kb/sec; DSL, for speeds up to 2.3 Mb/sec; or dedicated leased lines, ranging from T-1 to full OC-3 access.

λ-Networking consists of approximately 5,500 employees in the United States. Its key services include Web hosting, local voice, long-distance voice, intranet-VPN, and Internet access. Its pivotal technology strategy is to provide a single-source, high-capacity, multiservice-capable, secure, and reliable network that will be used to deploy new services. The company's emphasis has been on constructing its high-speed IP network and developing the value-added service suites that will be deployed in this network.

The target customer segments are small to medium businesses, with partial coverage to large enterprises and the government sector. An emphasis on simple, unified (end-to-end) billing based on flat-rate pricing permits λ-Networking to quickly penetrate the desired market segments. (A usage- and content-based billing from the service start would have required a significant amount of time for OSS billing integration; content-based billing examines the application layer for billing and is often associated with Web hosting and e-commerce services.)

This case study represents a Greenfield service provider's approach to using IP for service development and deployment. (The approach is discussed in Chapter 3.) We will now explore the dynamics between the customer, λ-Networking, and the equipment vendors in order to understand the issues and pressures associated with defining IP-based services. Moreover, measuring the profitability of these services will also be examined.

8.1.2 Business Aspects

λ-Networking does not position itself as a regular CLEC—specifically, the company has advertised its intentions to expand internationally. Some CLECs have focused on the wholesale market, while others have targeted small and midsize businesses. λ-Networking targets small, midsize, and large businesses, as well as the federal and some local government sectors. The company focus in 2000 was to build metropolitan fiber networks with the intent to tackle the last mile in order to control the network end to end.

In 2000 the leadership team was also challenged by the competitive environment to rapidly develop a service portfolio that would be accepted by the target markets. In the background, λ-Networking continued the rollout of its high-speed IP network infrastructure based on DWDM architecture, believing that such an infrastructure would speed deployment of new services to corporate customers. The DWDM architecture is scalable, since the same fiber can be used for traffic from multiple sources (this architecture is discussed in Chapter 7.) DWDM is deployed in the core network, and LMDS is at the access network.

The infrastructure build-out was completed in 2001. From 2000 to 2001, the company evolved its business strategy by developing value-added services for its business and government customers. In a highly volatile environment where most new entrants have failed and gone out of business, λ-Networking has paved a path for business viability.

Customer Requirements

The following is a summary of customer requirements:

Single service provider deploying and managing services end to end

Different aggregation speed, ranging from 56 Kb/sec to 155 Mb/sec (OC-3)

Internet access

VPN services

Voice and video services

Web-hosting services

Online SLA reports

Single bill

The market sectors for these services are small to medium enterprises, large enterprises, and the public sector. Customer applications include Web browsers, email, videoconferencing, imaging, electronic file transfers, and voice. λ-Networking studied the market and found that approximately 45% of the small to medium enterprises wanted a bundling of local and long-distance services because of the desire to work with a single provider for service delivery. These customers are frustrated by service complexities, such as different billing from different providers, exacerbated by regulatory complexities (as addressed in Chapter 1). These customers further would prefer to have a single service provider capable of offering value-added services like Internet access, corporate IP-VPN, Web hosting, voice-over-IP, and so on. Customers representing this market have felt ignored by providers since they do not belong to the large, multinational enterprises coveted by existing service providers. Conversely, large enterprises want to see an established track record from a service provider before any significant business can be successfully negotiated.

λ-Networking also includes the government sector in its portfolio, covering federal, state, and local agencies. The company's market research determined that the federal telecommunications market in the United States is approximately \$6.5 million, with an annual growth rate of about 4.5%. As λ-Networking owns its network infrastructure, extending fiber to the public sector—which requires high bandwidth for such applications as videoconferencing, military imaging, and medical imaging—enables the company to implement a last-mile strategy of bringing the network directly to the customer without connecting via competitors.

Customer requirements include the ability to support different access speeds, ranging from 56 Kb/sec to 155 Mb/sec to the service provider, services that provide Internet access, and corporate VPN access, voice and video services, Web-hosting services, and online SLA reports. Customers require that these services be offered and implemented by a single service provider to manage an SLA end to end—that is, avoiding third parties that can impact the service levels. By avoiding third parties, customers expect that a service provider will consolidate services on a single bill.

λ-Networking, Inc.'s Strategic Objectives

In order to develop and deliver its service portfolios, the company identified its own set of strategic objectives, summarized as follows:

Scalable network (to support hundreds of customer connections)

Reliable network (to offer high availability—99.999%—to customers)

Security for customer data (in the sense that traffic from one customer is not visible/accessible to another customer)

Differentiated services (in terms of bandwidth and delay) for premium customers

SLA reporting to customers

A reliable network operations center (NOC)

λ-Networking has been building a network capable of evolving with future technologies. Constructing a network where the infrastructure can be enhanced and not replaced is the crux of scalability for the company.

An advantage for λ-Networking is that it has no legacy infrastructure. (Why a legacy infrastructure is a liability is discussed in Chapter 4.) The infrastructure technology of choice impacts the scalability issue. One element that affects scalability is the capacity required to support customer access speeds, ranging from 56 Kb/sec to full OC-3 surrounding the 60 national metro locations. Interconnecting eight data centers via OC-12 to the metro PoPs is also a requirement for the company. The national core network must not be a bottleneck for performance and therefore should be capable of supporting multiple aggregation speeds, ranging from OC-3 to OC-12, and the traffic that is switched across the core must be IP only.

λ-Networking standardized on a single protocol, IP, for transporting traffic, voice, video, and data. The strategy for the company is to build an "IP central office" architecture that accepts IP traffic from the metropolitan fiber ring and transports it end to end, the advantage being a single network that can support multiservices (as discussed in Chapter 5).

As there will be customer mission-critical applications on the network, ensuring reliability is also a key requirement for λ-Networking. This means that the core should provide 99.999% availability. There should be redundant fiber connections from the metropolitan PoPs to the core, located in different conduits. The platform components, hardware, and software should not negatively impact network reliability. In case of a component failure, transparent rerouting should be available and not result in loss of connectivity at the application layer.

λ-Networking will not enforce what the company has termed "complex" SLAs. Either the service works or it does not. To avoid customer churn, λ-Networking offers a customer satisfaction guarantee in the first three months of a new service delivery. If the customer is not satisfied within the first three months, the company will switch the customer back to the original carrier free of charge. Should the customer experience a problem after three months, λ-Networking will negotiate a service credit.

Security is a requirement for λ-Networking because a common network infrastructure is used to offer services to multiple enterprises. The same core network of the service provider is used to deliver traffic from multiple services and multiple customers. The network cannot be compromised such that a loss of service is due to unauthorized and miscreant attacks. VPN services to business customers must be delivered with a minimum set of security features, such as IPSec tunneling.

Provisioning differentiated services onto a common backbone infrastructure is also a requirement for λ-Networking. Voice, videoconferencing, and data cannot be treated identically, as these applications possess different QoS requirements for latency, with voice receiving the highest priority in terms of packetized traffic across the backbone. (These QoS requirements are discussed in Chapters 6 and 7.) The base technology implemented by λ-Networking must allow for the support of differentiated services.

Finally, all services must be mapped to a common billing system for unified invoicing and reporting. The unified billing is a value proposition for the end customer. The customer must be able to order a service and view the bill via a secure Web interface. These features must be integrated into the OSS architecture of λ-Networking. (OSS is discussed in Chapters 2 and 6.)

The company must develop and deploy these services quickly, so as to gain revenue and sustain growth and profitability. Performing a due-diligence exercise on these service packages is essential in order to determine whether or not money can be made. The next steps are balancing the costs for the network infrastructure build-out, the costs required to support the services, and operational expenses with revenue gained on a quarterly basis.

8.1.3 Services

λ-Networking developed its service packages in the first six months of the year 2000 while simultaneously building out its metro and national infrastructures. The approach was quick market entry and penetration. The strategy for this quick market entry was to identify a set of service packages that could be readily adopted by the company's target market. The services are voice (local and long distance); Internet access (up to full OC-3); VPN; metro Ethernet services (up to 1 Gb/sec connectivity); Web hosting; managed server; and customer server co-location facility.

Service pricing is designed to be attractive for bundled services. The goal is to assure a 10% to 30% discount, assuming that the entire package is purchased. Price variations depend upon regional access rates. These rates can be granted on a corporate basis or on a per-individual basis. The metro Ethernet service is priced on a per-port basis. Managed server hosting consists of a series of options, depending on the operating system, amount of memory desired, applications, and bandwidth. The pricing includes a one-time installation fee ($700 to $3500), with a monthly price ranging from $700 to $25,000 (if in excess of 10 Mb/sec). The VPN service is also offered in a bundled package where connectivity options range from dial-up at 56 Kb/sec to a full T3 dedicated link. The service can be managed by λ-Networking. The VPN service offered by the company sets it apart as a leader in the market because this service similarly uses bundling and value-added service options to up-sell to customers features like

Table 8.1   Bundled option example for a small to medium enterprise.

Basic Option	Enhanced Option	Supreme Option
Corporate VPN	Corporate VPN	Corporate VPN
Internet access *DSL up to 400K*	Internet access *Leased line up to T1*	Internet access *Leased line up to OC-3*
Web hosting *(hard disk)* *250 MB*	Web hosting *(hard disk)* *500 MB*	Web hosting *(hard disk)* *1 GB*
Voice	Voice	Voice
Local—unlimited	*Local—unlimited*	*Local—unlimited*
Long distance—5000 minutes	*Long distance—10,000 minutes*	*Long distance—15,000 minutes*

Internet access together with VPN service, as an example. The competition tends to sell these services separately.

Table 8.1 depicts a typical bundled option menu targeted to a small to medium enterprise. A customer can order these services via the Web, and the invoicing is a flat rate based on the bundle selected.

Bandwidth Increase

One key driver behind the λ-Networking build-out of its infrastructure has been to provide large amounts of bandwidth in service packages, due to the need to support applications such as videoconferencing and medical imaging. The metropolitan PoP aggregation, reflecting thousands of end-customer connections, is also a factor for bandwidth increase. For example, the gigabit Ethernet service that extends customer LANs remotely requires high bandwidth.

8.1.4   Service Implementation Model

λ-Networking put a priority on developing the OSS architecture in order to facilitate order entry, billing, and reporting. The key was to be able to produce a single, consolidated invoice that reflected multiservice bundles to its customers. The company also added the option for usage-based invoicing and reporting to its system. The platforms are redundant and installed in data centers (with a backup data center for disaster and recovery). Customer interface is Web-based, for order entry by the customer and secure access to provide online billing and reporting.

The sales force uses the sales database that is part of the OSS architecture to forecast sales and to compare performance to date by region. A modeling tool is available for the sales team to work with a customer to compare the costs and benefits of a competitor provider with those offered by λ-Networking. The product management team uses the service creation database for service development: A new service or service extension is entered into the service development database. If the service is new, a flag is sent out and a service development process is launched. If the requirement is a service enhancement, a flag is indicated as "enhancement," and a quick feasibility study is executed to determine time, resources, and expected date of enhancement (this is all available to engineering and network operations as well as to sales and marketing).

λ-Networking believes that the OSS architecture is a cornerstone of their business operations. Everything is automated, from order entry to provisioning. In providing a single OSS for multiservices based on IP, the company views this strategy as vital in reducing operating expenses.

8.1.5 Company Performance

λ-Networking, as a new entrant in the market, has embarked on a strategy to construct its own multiservice networking infrastructure. By investing in a high-performance, IP-based platform developed on top of fiber optics, the company believes that the network will be adaptive to multiservice requirements like voice, videoconferencing, data, and so on. The key difference between λ-Networking and its competitors, specifically incumbents, is that λ-Networking has developed the network and services within approximately one year. The company sees its competition struggling, trying to enable legacy infrastructures for IP-based service offerings without disturbing their very large customer bases. The company, however, realizes that it is only a matter of time before the competition starts to widely develop and deploy IP-based services. Thus, the strategy is to penetrate the market rapidly by gaining and keeping customers.

How did the company perform between 2000 and 2001? The reported revenue from these new service packages at the end of 2000 was approximately $850 million. The reported revenue at the end of 2001 was approximately $2 billion, demonstrating both an increase in revenue and a reduction in operating expenses. λ-Networking is paving a growth path toward profitability. In fundamental business language, the continued improvement in results indicates that the strategy to build out a high-performance, IP-based infrastructure for multiservices is starting to reap benefits.

8.1.6 Alternatives Considered

λ-Networking had considered being only a bandwidth broker as an alternative to developing and deploying IP-based services. The strategy, however, was to address the requirements of small to medium enterprises for bundled value-added services. The market research and corresponding revenue results indicated that there was an opportunity for revenue. The company later extended to its customers bandwidth services as an enhancement to the bundled service offering. Finally, λ-Networking offered a separate bandwidth service offering that is not part of the bundled package.

The company could have constructed separate networks for its services—like PSTN for voice and frame relay and ATM for data and videoconferencing. This would have required separate billing systems as well as dedicated network operations personnel. The probable operating cost would have been negative. By offering bundled services, the company was able to penetrate the market more quickly and to sign up customers interested in having a single service provider that offered value-added services and managed the service levels end to end. λ-Networking built a network that is flexible enough to deliver multiple services invoiced on a single bill, a customer requirement. The company further recognizes that its competition, namely, incumbents, are struggling to evolve multiple networks toward a convergence-like platform. For λ-Networking, the investment in a network asset that will evolve in the future was the only alternative.

8.1.7 Vendor Selection Process

λ-Networking had stated that the network infrastructure must support multiple vendors. Once the company had settled on a strategy for a high-performance, IP-based network and an OSS architecture that would be key to the development and deployment of value-added services, it invited three select vendors to its laboratory. These vendors were selected on the basis of technology leadership, market position, and installed base in a service provider environment. The testing was to narrow down the vendors to two partners for delivery of the core infrastructure. A third-party vendor for OSS integration was selected to ensure that the architecture components such as network management, configuration management, performance management, billing management, service management, and so on were developed and validated.

The lab testing included basic functionality tests for compliance with published specifications; performance testing against load; reliability; environmental factors such as heating, power supply, and card redundancy; and interoperability. Interoperability testing was based on published specifications for standard compliance. λ-Networking stated that the selected vendors must interoperate and assure interoperability in the future—this meant that the vendors would have to work together such that they would not lose the customer for lack of interoperable compliance. λ-Networking also specified that the OSS architecture must be built on open standards in order to assure integration of key components that were nonproprietary. Dependence on any one vendor was to be avoided by the company in order to emphasize open interfaces on new products.

The company lab team conducted further sets of tests like provisioning, reporting, and performance, for validating the services from the vendors.

Finally, after three months of testing, two vendors were selected for the core and edge network infrastructure: one would be positioned in the core network and the other at the edge network. λ-Networking established a strategic relationship with the two vendors in order to develop products necessary for service development. One of these vendors was also selected to deliver the CPE for the managed VPN service. Providing minimal software and hardware upgrades was also a factor in the vendor selection, as the company simply could not afford to change software frequently because a feature was lacking or because of instability. λ-Networking reiterated that these two vendors must work closely together in order to have the business: the vendor contract was explicit on this point of interoperability.

8.1.8 Technical Aspects

λ-Networking needs a network that can deliver all the services discussed in Section 8.1.2 and can meet the company's requirements in terms of scalability, reliability, security, operational aspects, and cost-effectiveness. The company has PoPs in 60 cities distributed all over the country. Assuming that fiber is available between these locations, the network has to be designed for reliability and to avoid single points of failure in the network.

Figure 8.1 gives an overview of the services that λ-Networking wants to offer to its customers: IP-VPN, voice-over-IP, Internet access, and Web hosting. The IP services are based on top of the company's IP network. The IP network is used to deliver the traffic from all of these IP services.

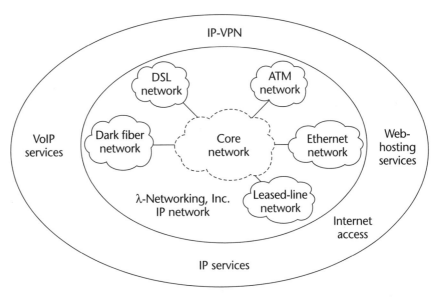

Figure 8.1 Overview of services offered by λ-Networking.

Network Architecture

λ-Networking wants to build a network that is scalable, stable, and reliable. The network must be hierarchical so that it is scalable. It must support redundancy and must not have single points of failure because of the SLA agreements with customers. (The terms *scalable, stable,* and *reliable* are discussed in Chapter 5.) *Scalable* implies that the core network must be capable of supporting several customers and that enough resources (e.g., of bandwidth, memory, routing table) are available to support all of the services. *Stable* means that changes (e.g., topology, addition of new networks) in the customer premises, access, and edge networks do not have any implications for the core network. *Reliable* means that the network does not have single points of failure (both for network links and network nodes).

A good starting point for the network architecture is to use the model described in Section 5.2, based on access, distribution/edge, and core (see Figure 8.2). The access network provides the connectivity between the customer premises and the service provider network. The edge network (in each location where λ-Networking has a PoP) is used to concentrate all of the customer connections and also to provide intelligence to

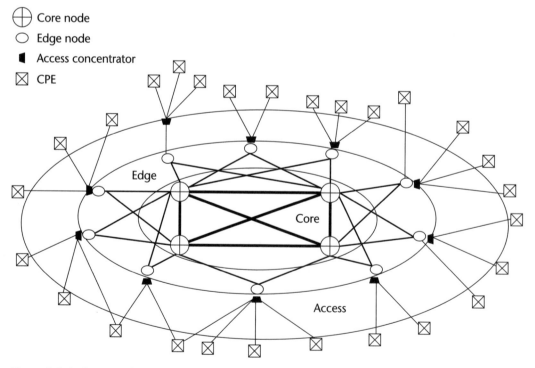

Figure 8.2 Architectural overview of the network.

implement the services offered to the customer. The core network provides connectivity between the different PoPs located in 60 cities.

Access Network

The access network is used to provide connectivity between customer premises and the service provider network. λ-Networking has fiber and copper connections between the network edge and its customers' premises, and in other cases, the telephone line is used to provide connectivity. The company decided to implement the access network using the following technologies in order to meet the different speed requirements, costs, and physical network infrastructures at each customer site:

- *ISDN:* This technology provides up to 56 Kb/sec and is useful for small to medium enterprises and mobile customers. It will not be possible to limit the Layer 2 bandwidth available to the customer.
- *DSL:* This technology provides up to 2.3 Mb/sec and is useful for the residential market, small enterprises, and the small offices of large companies. It is possible to limit the Layer 2 bandwidth available to the customer and also to bill the customer based on usage.
- *Leased lines using T1:* This technology can provide up to 1.54 Mb/sec. It is possible to limit the available bandwidth used by the customer, to increase the available bandwidth-on-demand, and to bill the customer based on link utilization.
- *T3 links using fiber:* This technology provides up to 45 Mb/sec. It is possible to restrict the available Layer 2 bandwidth and also to increase the available Layer 2 bandwidth-on-demand. This can be used for business customers.
- *OC-3 connection:* This technology provides up to 155 Mb/sec using fiber connection. Depending on the Layer 2 technology (limited to ATM but not possible for POS), this technology can be used to restrict the available Layer 2 bandwidth and also to increase the available Layer 2 bandwidth-on-demand (up to the maximum limit). This technology can be used for customers who require high-speed connections for their headquarters.
- *Ethernet using fiber:* This technology can provide bandwidth up to 1000 Mb/sec. The bandwidth can be provided in three steps: 10 Mb/sec, 100 Mb/sec, and 1000 Mb/sec. Available bandwidth cannot be restricted at Layer 2. (Layer 3 techniques are required to restrict the bandwidth available to a customer.)

Access concentrators are required to terminate the multiple access connections from different customers and connect them to the nearest edge device. The location of the access concentrators depends on the access technology. ATM connections can be terminated on an ATM switch before they are connected to the edge device, and it is best to place the concentrator as close as possible to the edge device. The best place for the DSL concentrator is near the telephone switch where the splitters are located. Ethernet switches can be used to concentrate multiple Ethernet connections from a single customer site, and it is best located on the customer premises.

Edge Network

The edge network provides connectivity between a customer's premises and the backbone network of λ-Networking. It is also used to concentrate multiple connections on a single edge device: several customer connections are terminated on the same device. Depending on the technology and the number of customer connections, several edge devices are required in a location (PoP).

Each edge device is connected to two different core devices. This redundancy is necessary to make the edge network reliable and to avoid single points of failure. The edge device also provides the intelligence required to build an IP network that can deliver IP-based services. The functionality required on the edge device to deliver the differentiated services includes the following:

1. Restricting Layer 3 bandwidth available to a customer connection when the access network does not have capability to restrict the bandwidth at Layer 2.
2. Implementing the VPN technology to provide logical (Layer 3) separation between the different Layer 3 connections that terminate on the same edge device.
3. Implementing QoS functionalities like marking, policing, and queuing.
4. Implementing accounting mechanisms like link utilization for billing purposes.

Based on the requirements of each service, λ-Networking decided to use a separate edge device for each of its services, namely,

Internet services, Web-hosting services

VPN services

Services like voice and video that have QoS requirements

Taking all of these requirements into account, λ-Networking has two choices of technology for the connectivity between the edge devices and core devices: Ethernet and POS. Table 8.2 compares the two technologies. Based on the comparison, the cost issues, and the QoS requirements, λ-Networking decided to use the following strategy:

1. Use packet-over-SONET when the edge device is used to support voice and video services.
2. Use Ethernet for edge devices that support all other services.

Table 8.2   Comparison of Ethernet and POS for connectivity between edge and core devices.

Characteristics	Ethernet	POS
Cost	Cheap	Expensive (approximately 35% more than Ethernet)
Speed	Up to 1000 Mb/sec	Up to 2.4 Gb/sec
Layer 2 Failure Detection	No, must depend on Layer 3	Yes
Aggregation	Yes, multiple edge device can connect to a single interface of core device	No, point-to-point technology
QoS Support	Does not meet all QoS requirements, especially when aggregation is used	Meets all QoS requirements of λ-Networking

Core Network

The core network has 60 core locations, separated into two categories:

National core location (12)

Regional core location (48)

Each regional core location is dually connected to the nearest national core location, and each national core location is connected to at least two other national core locations.

The core network is built in a hierarchical manner. There are regional core networks, consisting of one national core location and several regional core locations. There is one national core network, consisting of all the national core locations. In total, the core network has 12 regional core networks and 1 national core network. The topology of the entire network has the following characteristics (see Figure 8.3):

- There are two links between two directly connected core locations.
- There are multiple paths between any two core locations.
- The maximum number of hops between any two core locations does not exceed six. This is required to meet the end-to-end delay requirements of some of the services, like voice and video.

λ-Networking has a DWDM network interconnecting all 60 core locations that can support up to 10 Gb/sec. Currently, λ-Networking has decided to use 10 Gb/sec links between all the national core locations. The connection between the national core location and the regional core location is either 2.4 Gb/sec or 622 Mb/sec, depending on the number of edge devices at each core location and the volume of traffic. Based on the

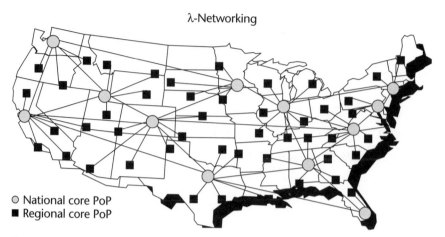

Figure 8.3 Core PoP locations of λ-Networking.

utilization of the links between the regional core and the national core, these links may be upgraded from 622 Mb/sec to 2.4 Gb/sec.

Technologies to Support Service Creation

λ-Networking has decided to use the same core network to transport traffic from all the services. This reduces the cost of the network infrastructure. The company will use specific technologies to support various services. The following is a brief description of each of these technologies and the services that they can support.

MPLS

MPLS is enabled on all the links in the core network and the links between the edge and core devices. MPLS helps to maintain a stable core network. Changes in the edge and access networks or an increase in the number of customers connected to the network will not have an impact on the core network. Moreover, MPLS helps to support VPNs based on MPLS, and also helps to enable traffic engineering in order to spread the load onto all the core links.

MPLS-VPN

MPLS-VPN helps λ-Networking to offer VPN services to the customers using the same core network, as opposed to VPN services based on Layer 2 technologies like frame relay or ATM. Multiple customers requiring VPN services can be connected to the same core network.

IP Security

While MPLS-VPNs guarantee that data from one customer is not visible or accessible to another, it does not guarantee any security for the contents of an IP packet. In order to provide additional security for the contents of IP packets, λ-Networking offers IPSec features on top of MPLS-VPNs. IPSec not only guarantees data security, it also guarantees integrity of the data and ensures that a third party cannot illegally access the data even if they can access the IP packet. By using IPSec, λ-Networking can enhance their service portfolio with additional security features.

QoS

QoS features help λ-Networking to offer differentiated services to their customers. Customers who require guaranteed bandwidth, guaranteed end-to-end delay, and so on, get preferential treatment over those who require only best-effort services. QoS features are also required for services (e.g., voice) that have strict delay requirements and those (e.g., video) that have guaranteed bandwidth requirements.

λ-Networking will enable QoS using the differentiated services model (see Chapter 7 for more details). Enabling QoS means implementing the following mechanisms:

- Marking customer traffic based on the services requested by the customer
- Classification of customer based on the DSCP value in the IP header
- Policing the Layer 3 traffic based on the bandwidth contract signed by the customer
- Drop mechanism to ensure that every class gets its share of the bandwidth in case of congestion in the links
- Queuing mechanism on all devices so that traffic with strict delay requirements is prioritized over other traffic and to minimize end-to-end delay

Classification and policing are applied on the interfaces of edge devices connected to the CPE. This has to be done to the edge device in case the CPE is not managed by λ-Networking.

Queuing mechanisms are implemented in the core network and also on the links between the core and edge devices. They are required because the core links and the link between the core and edge devices are shared by several customer connections. In order to meet the QoS requirements of the different classes, it is necessary to implement queuing mechanisms.

QoS features like policing at Layer 3 help to limit the bandwidth available to customers for access technologies that do not support policing at Layer 2. For example, Layer 2 technologies like Ethernet have no policing mechanism at Layer 2. So a user with 100 Mb/sec can send data at 100 Mb/sec, and it is possible to restrict that to 10 Mb/sec at Layer 2. Using Layer 3 policing mechanisms, it is possible to restrict the amount of bandwidth available to customer connections.

SLA Reporting

As part of the services offered to customers, λ-Networking has identified several SLAs, which are reported to customers on a periodic basis. The SLAs include

Availability

Guaranteed bandwidth

End-to-end delay

In order to verify that the SLAs of the customers are being honored, λ-Networking collects information from the network devices and uses it to calculate the SLAs and generate reporting. SNMP is used to collect the information from the network devices. The information is then fed into an automatic SLA reporting program. These reports are posted on a Web server, from which customers can directly access them.

Network Management and Operations

Managing the λ-Networking network plays an important role in providing reliable services to customers. The NOC is the place from which the entire network is operated and managed. All OSS servers and tools required to monitor, maintain, manage, and upgrade the network are located in the NOC. The NOC plays a crucial role in the success of the company. It is operational 24 hours a day to monitor the network. As a result, it is critical that the NOC has redundancy not only in terms of connectivity to the entire network but also in terms of location.

Redundancy

λ-Networking decided to have two independent NOCs that are physically located in two different locations. One of them is active and has connectivity to the network. The other is used to back up all of the data from the active NOC and becomes active when the active NOC loses connectivity to the network.

Activities

The NOC is responsible for a variety of activities, including

- Monitoring all the devices in the network and raising alarms when the devices are not reachable
- Monitoring the utilization of network resources, like link capacity
- Monitoring resources on network devices, like available memory and CPU usage
- Configuring new network devices and customer connections
- Upgrading customer connections to higher speeds
- Performing software upgrades on network devices

Service Implementation Model

As mentioned in Section 8.1.5, one of the key features of the OSS systems is automation. λ-Networking wants to automate service provisioning, service upgrades, SLA reporting, and various other activities so that it can increase its customer base rapidly and also penetrate the rapidly expanding market. This section presents an example of how a company automates service upgrade requests.

Service Upgrades

λ-Networking will provide customers with a Web-based interface to upgrade their services. One such service upgrade is the bandwidth requirement between the CPE and the edge device. Customers get a periodic report of the link and bandwidth utilization, after which they can decide to upgrade the link speed to a higher capacity. This can be easily done using a Web-based interface (compared to a manual upgrade by an operator) because the Web-based interface helps to automate the service upgrade and reduce the risks of errors due to manual intervention. (See Chapter 6 for more information on this topic.)

The following steps are involved in an online service upgrade (see Figure 8.4):

1. Customer logs on to the Web-based tool using a login name and password.
2. Customer chooses the link that requires the bandwidth upgrade.
3. The new link bandwidth is specified by the customer.
4. The tool verifies that the new bandwidth is applicable to the link and that there is enough available capacity on the link.

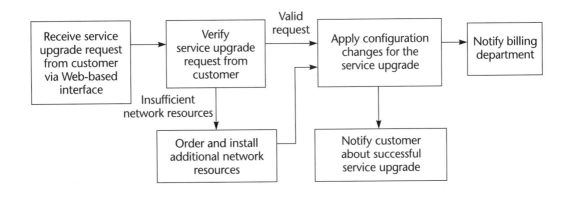

Figure 8.4 Steps involved in a service upgrade.

5. The new configuration is created for both the edge and CPE devices.
6. An SNMP-based tool applies these changes to the concerned devices.
7. A report is sent to the customer and to the billing department once the service upgrade is completed successfully.

The entire service upgrade, starting from the customer's request up to notifying the customer and billing department, should not take more than 30 minutes. Thus, such a Web-based interface will reduce the time required to upgrade a service, compared to upgrading manually, which may take as long as a week before the upgrade information is sent to all the relevant departments and the customer. The Web-based interface will also help to reduce the mistakes due to manual configuration. This in turn will help λ-Networking to rapidly deploy services and have a larger share of the market. In conclusion, a fully automated OSS system is crucial for rapid deployment of IP-based services.

8.1.9 Assessing Project Risks

Building a new backbone, developing new services, and contracting with customers to buy these services is risky for any Greenfield service provider, since these factors require an investment in resources such as infrastructure, people, and return on this investment. Some risks in the λ-Networking project include lack of technology and products to deploy services, insufficient customer base to buy the services, and lack of money to continue the business. Lack of name recognition is also a risk for a Greenfield service provider such as λ-Networking since customers can be reluctant to contract with an unknown alternative provider. Applying due diligence to the marketing plan and business case are ways to mitigate the risks. As an example, it is not enough to build a backbone and hope that customers will throng, often termed in the telecommunications environment as a "build and they will come" approach. Confirming that there is a business opportunity via services is the key to risk reduction.

8.1.10 Lessons Learned

The λ-Networking strategy is aggressive and high-risk. The company embarked on its approach since it believed (and still does) that it is only a matter of precious time before incumbents start to deploy a wide range of services, especially bundled options based on IP. The λ-Networking experience outlined in this case study is a composite of the experiences of several CLECs that have undertaken a similar strategy. It is not IP-based technology that drives sound business practices but rather solid corporate governance.

8.1.11 Future Plans

The company continues to work with their select technology leaders in order to assure that the network will evolve with the required services.

This translates to having not only the technology available but also the vendor products needed to support future services. The company plans to extend the network internationally at a later stage and expects to enhance its product portfolio to include e-commerce, specifically offering a managed e-commerce portal service as an extension to Web hosting.

8.1.12 Conclusion

The λ-Networking experience shows how IP is the driver for building services and can be used to deploy services. In the case study, IP-based services catalyzed revenue and cost improvements for λ-Networking. The next section presents a conceptual case study depicting an incumbent. The incumbent example considers other challenging issues, such as the existence of multiple networks, legacy infrastructure, and millions of existing customers. How can IP possibly be implemented to develop and deploy services without adversely impacting these existing customers? What approach can be taken, if any? These questions and alternatives are explored in the next section.

8.2 Conceptual Case Study—Incumbent

The company in this conceptual case study is one of the oldest incumbents in the United States. The case study examines how IP-based technology has driven the development of new services and created better uniformity of operations and delivery of these new services to transform the company's business from a focus on voice-only services to a focus on value-added services such as Internet access, Web hosting, corporate VPNs, and e-commerce.

8.2.1 Background

The company in this case study is an East Coast–based incumbent that consists of separate business subsidiaries with a focus on wireless, broadband, and retail, as well as data and voice (as opposed to wholesale services such as selling bandwidth only). The company is referred to as Traditiontel, Inc. It has approximately 85,000 employees, and its stock is traded openly on the stock market. In 1997 Traditiontel, Inc., had reported that voice, namely, long distance, dominated the data services that were emerging at that time. From 1998 to the end of 2001, the company experienced a decline in long-distance voice and an increase in data, or packetized, traffic. This decline translated into an approximately $18 billion loss. The increase in data traffic is attributed to the enterprise customers driving e-business applications such as CRM, converged voice and data, and so on, since these customers are pressured to execute business applications efficiently in order to minimize costs and maximize revenue.

The alternative for Traditiontel customers is to maintain separate corporate networks for such applications.

Traditiontel possesses legacy infrastructure and a large customer base of over six million customers, both domestic and international. This legacy infrastructure consists of PSTN for voice, frame relay and ATM for data access, as well as broadband and wireless. The focus of this case study is on the company's decision to embark on a "nondisruptive" service consolidation strategy of *cap and grow*—that is, retaining the existing infrastructure but growing new services on a next-generation, multiservice, high-speed IP backbone. Traditiontel launched this strategy at the beginning of 2000.

Traditiontel constructed an IP-based national infrastructure between 2000 and 2001 that includes multiple OC-48/STM-16 (2.5 Gb/sec) and OC-192/STM-64 (10 Gb/sec) interoffice trunk facilities. The core topology consists of approximately 80,500 kilometers (50,000 miles) of fiber-optic cable and approximately 75 SONET rings that offer self-healing capabilities. The company has been enhancing this network to include an additional 29,000 kilometers (18,000 miles) of fiber capable of operating at OC-192 as well as OC-768/STM-256 speeds.

The target customers for Traditiontel's IP-based services are small to medium enterprises as well as large enterprises. The company offers Web hosting, managed host services, VPN service of intranets and extranets, voice-over-IP, IP-enabled faxing, and so on. These service packages may be purchased as bundled services. A consolidated bill for bundled services is not yet available. Traditiontel plans to have a consolidated invoicing system in place at the end of 2002. Billing is either flat rate, usage based, or a combination, depending on such factors as number of users within an end-customer environment. Price discounts are available, and these vary with both volume and usage.

This conceptual case study represents an incumbent approach to using IP for evolving a current business strategy based on legacy systems, and repositioning a company as a state-of-the-art service provider using IP-based technology to develop and deploy services. This state-of-the-art character manifests itself in the home page of the service provider, where a customer can place orders, participate in a tutorial on a specific technology, and study white papers written about technical issues and service applications. There is an interactive question-and-answer application for the customer to use that is online. Measuring the profitability impact of these services is also part of this conceptual case study.

8.2.2 Business Aspects

Traditiontel has been in a transformation process that commenced in 1998. The company introduced new leadership at that time to enact much-needed change. It had been focused on long-distance voice, but customers were requiring more and more data services. In response to these market requirements, the competition was developing digital network infrastructures, while the long-distance voice was becoming a commodity, resulting in revenue loss for Traditiontel. The company was further burdened with an inflated cost structure in comparison to its competition.

The company at that time decided to convert its network into a packet-based network with intelligence located at the edge. Traditiontel transformed its disjointed local, analog cellular systems into a digital wireless network. To address the inflated cost structure, it removed about $3.5 billion in costs out of the core long-distance business over a period of approximately four years. Toward the end of 2000, the company created four business units, focused on wireless, broadband, residential, and business.

Customer Requirements

The Traditiontel strategy is to retain its current business customer base while attracting new customers. Current business customers typically subscribe to several services, such as frame relay and ATM as well as IP-based VPN and managed hosts. These customers require both a bundled service option and a single bill. This requirement is actually no different from the target customer base of the CLECs and applies therefore to all potential customers. Finally, the price structure must not be complex, especially for value-added services such as metro Ethernet or business-class VPN. Customer requirements may be summarized as follows:

Bundled service option with single bill

Security and reliability

Cost-effective propositions for value-added services

Less complex dealings that do not impact capital expenditure

The customers range from small and medium enterprises to very large enterprises. Customer applications include data, voice, email, Web browsing, videoconferencing, and e-commerce applications. The customers require that the VPN service be secure, reliable, and capable of service differentiation between voice and data. They do not want to subscribe to a service that is feature-rich but difficult to implement. They want to understand whether or not a VPN-like service is appropriate to their own networking environment and expect recommendations from the service provider about the appropriateness of a VPN service within an existing customer network. This requires that Traditiontel understand the end-customer business drivers in order to act in an advisory capacity. Finally, migrating a customer network to an IP-based service should not result in additional capital expenditure for the end customer.

Traditiontel's Strategic Objectives

The top strategic objectives for Traditiontel may be summarized as follows:

Scalability

Integration

Security

Reliability

Traditiontel intends to be a low-cost service provider that offers an end-to-end service portfolio to its customers. The network infrastructure must scale to both domestic as well as international enterprise business customers. For Traditiontel, the customer forecast is approximately one billion customers worldwide. The company has observed that in the domestic market, IP connectivity (VPN, Web hosting, managed host services) has grown over 200% from 2000 to 2001. Because of the transition from voice to IP and the wide use of e-business applications, scalability is a key requirement for Traditiontel, as evidenced by the growth trends.

Integration for Traditiontel means the capability to develop and support multiservices based on IP. Providing an integrated service bundle with a single bill is a requirement for the company. The OSS billing component must be able to invoice for IP-based services. The mediation system has to create price records based on IP-centric elements such as bytes, ToS (for QoS) instead of the traditional voice minutes rating structure. An extended requirement for Traditiontel is to be able to create an electronic bill, or e-bill, that will have the look and feel of a credit card invoice.

Security is a requirement for Traditiontel since it is using a shared infrastructure to develop and provision services for multiple customers. Because IP is used as a base to develop these service packages, customers want the assurance that these services are as secure as the existing frame relay and ATM. Customer VPNs must not be compromised due to miscreant users. Note that the service provider may compromise a frame relay customer VPN due to a misconfiguration. Whether frame relay–based or IP-based, the integrity of the overall network infrastructure must not be destroyed due to security violations or service provider–induced misconfigurations.

Finally, reliability is an important requirement for Traditiontel since it offers a minimum of network availability of 99.99% to its customers. In order to assure the network availability target, redundancy in both fiber installations as well as in PoPs must be implemented. Vendor software and hardware must be "carrier class." This means that failure in a vendor component or software cannot adversely impact the overall function of the network. Traditiontel offers SLAs to its customers with low-latency guarantees that average between 70 milliseconds nationally between two locations. Finally, the company guarantees that domestic average packet loss will not exceed 0.5%.

8.2.3 IP-Based Solution

The IP-based solution for Traditiontel consists of several facets, including business, technology, and the service architecture. The pivotal business aspects driving the IP-based solution service architecture for Traditiontel include a shift from voice to IP and the impact of this shift on the service creation model. Under the shift from voice to IP, the subsequent packaging of IP-based services for the end customer is examined. The impact of IP-based services on the overall OSS architecture as it pertains to the service creation model is also explored.

8.2.4 Services

The business transformation that commenced in 1998 has been rapid for such an old incumbent provider. At the end of 2000, as the high-speed IP-based infrastructure was being constructed, Traditiontel planned a series of IP-based service packages to be created and launched throughout 2001 and 2002. The clear motivation of this strategy was to address pressure on cash flow resulting from the commoditization of long-distance voice. The services range from IP-VPN with an option for integrated voice to e-commerce services. Services, particularly the integrated managed bundles, offer unlimited domestic on-net and off-net calling to end customers. These services are managed IP-VPN with options for voice-over-IP, video-conferencing, and fax-over-IP, as well as Internet access; managed Internet with options for voice-over-IP; managed firewall hosting with network-based, router-based, and server-based options; managed intrusion detection and scanning services; LAN management; and managed host services that include e-commerce options.

Customer access possibilities for IP-VPN services are leased line, frame relay, ATM, Ethernet, and integrated voice and data. Usage reports are available to the customer via a Web interface. The managed service provides 24/7 coverage. The SLA to the customer is that if Traditiontel misses a performance target, the company will reimburse the end customer by providing a three-day credit to the monthly connection charge. The company guarantees a T1 Internet access within 30 business days, a T3 Internet access within 40 business days, and an OC-3 Internet access within 60 business days. Failure to provision within these specified intervals will result in a credit for the installation fee that is subject to regulation. Bandwidth-on-demand service options will be available at the end of 2002. Table 8.3 depicts a service bundle example for e-commerce and hosting for the small to medium enterprise segment.

The bundled e-commerce and host option permits an enterprise to sell products directly to its customers via a Web site hosted by Traditiontel.

Table 8.3   E-commerce and host option.

Basic	Enhanced	Premium
Email accounts: 20 accounts **Data transfer:** 20 GB **Data storage:** 200 MB **Price:** $20/month **One-time charge:** $65 **Add-on options available**	**Email accounts:** 40 accounts **Data transfer:** 40 GB **Data storage:** 400 MB **Price:** $45/month **One-time charge:** $70 **Add-on options available**	**Email accounts:** 60 accounts **Data transfer:** 60 GB **Data storage:** 600 MB **Price:** $115/month **One-time charge:** $70 **Add-on options available**
1–25 e-commerce products $45/month	**1–25** e-commerce products $55/month	**1–25** e-commerce products $110/month
26–100 e-commerce products $65/month	**26–100** e-commerce products $75/month	**26–100** e-commerce products $110/month
101–250 e-commerce products $95/month	**101–250** e-commerce products $105/month	**101–250** e-commerce products $185/month
251–500 e-commerce products $110/month	**251–500** e-commerce products $120/month	**251–500** e-commerce products $195/month
Price package available for additional products	Price package available for additional products	Price package available for additional products

The service supports real-time credit card transactions for the end customer's products, which are to be sold via this hosted site. With regard to Web hosting, Traditiontel sponsored a study that indicates that a typical Web surfer who attempts to navigate will lose interest after approximately 10 seconds. After that time, a number of these users will either go to another site or abort the transaction. Both actions result in a loss of potential revenue for Traditiontel (estimated revenue loss is approximately $4 billion). In response to this performance factor, Traditiontel has evolved traffic management from frame relay and ATM to IP. The company is moving to traffic management above IP in order to examine the packet layer, thus creating a content-aware traffic management service architecture. An enterprise customer may also order a dedicated server for a Web site and have this server delivered within 30 minutes of placing the order.

Traditiontel offers a metro Ethernet service over its high-speed, fiber-optic network that also has self-healing SONET rings available in 120 metropolitan areas in 40 states. *Self-healing* means that the rings are able to recover in case of a network failure, so there should be no service loss to customers. (This is further explained in Chapter 5.) The Ethernet connectivity is up to 500 Mb/sec. Table 8.4 depicts an example of the metro Ethernet service connectivity options.

The customer selects a connectivity option (e.g., between two locations point to point) and chooses the bandwidth required between these

Table 8.4   Metro Ethernet connectivity and bandwidth options.

Connectivity Options

Between two companies, point to point

Between a company and an interexchange carrier

Between a company and an access supplier

Bandwidth Options

50 Mb/sec

150 Mb/sec

250 Mb/sec

500 Mb/sec

Full gigabit Ethernet (future)

locations (e.g., 50 Mb/sec). The customer can select bandwidth up to 500 Mb/sec with a full gigabit Ethernet to be a future offering. The self-healing characteristic of the network that provides this service ensures network reliability by providing redundancy. Network reliability is dependent on the architecture. The high-speed, IP-based network infrastructure has redundant fiber connections that do not traverse the same conduit. The PoPs in the core as well as the metro areas are redundant such that a failure in one area does impact the service in another area.

This network architecture has been constructed with scalability as a basis for servicing approximately 20 million customers. The high-speed fiber optics is OC-768–capable and enhances the scalability feature of the network infrastructure. The national network is coast-to-coast OC-192 backbone.

Traditiontel subscribes to quarterly security audits on its network infrastructure for assessment of the best practices and implementations required for its customers. The IP-VPN service also includes an IPSec option. Disaster recovery for managed data servers is possible with four mirrored data centers located in the East Coast, Central, South, and West Coast regions.

8.2.5 Service Implementation Model

The problem with enhancing the legacy OSS infrastructure is that there are multiple systems that correspond to separate services. Traditiontel felt that it would be effective and least disruptive to existing services to construct a next-generation OSS architecture. The task has been most challenging as the company had to outsource the architectural development to third-party vendors with an expertise in OSS. The key requirement for Traditiontel is nondependency on vendor-proprietary applications. The new OSS architecture includes customer care, business engineering, billing, reporting, and new service creation.

At the end of 2000, Traditiontel planned to launch three services per year. This requirement meant that the service creation process had to be fully automated across the business organization and not limited to geographic locations. A service to be created is triggered by a Traditiontel product manager articulating a need that was expressed by a customer. (This customer can request a service online, and this service request is then sent to the product manager). The user interface is Web based. A business opportunity profile pops up as a window for the product manager to complete. Parameters include whether the service is new or an enhancement; revenue opportunity between 9 and 12 months; customer profile, such as key customers requesting the service; the account team driving the service creation; proposed service description and pricing (draft format); identification of competitors; base technology; known suppliers offering a product that can be used to develop the service; and, finally, estimated cost to develop the service and the required timing for it to go to market. The proposed service should also specify the target customer segment.

The completed profile is routed to the heads of sales and marketing, engineering and services architecture, service and network management, and business engineering for review, approval, and resource reservation. Turnaround time for a yes or no response is 10 working days. If the response is yes, a meeting is organized using collaborative tools to launch the service development project. If the response is no, the service request is filed on a *dashboard* indicating date and reason for an audit trail in case the subject surfaces in the future.

Traditiontel expects that any new service pilot is not to exceed one month in order to validate the overall service model and to assure that the invoicing processes are ready. There is a service life cycle profile that the product manager completes. It includes such parameters as testing and validation, service launch, full service acceptance by the market, commoditization (when competitors flood the market with similar offerings), and service end. These are estimates based on experience and market trends. The output is distributed to the vice presidents of sales and marketing, engineering and services architecture, and operations. These managers execute a due diligence on the new service in order to minimize possible negative impacts on Traditiontel.

Two key profiles are completed at the same time by the product manager: a business opportunity profile and a service life cycle profile. These two profiles represent the business case. Other profiles, such as new service training and provisioning requirements, are also integrated into the

Traditiontel service creation model. The service creation model also includes an application for the sales force that automates responses to requests for proposal.

In 2001 Traditiontel launched four main services: the business-class IP-VPN with options; managed hosting with options; integrated voice and data; and Internet with option for voice-over-IP. The single bill for bundled services will be available at the end of 2002. Traditiontel is planning to move from a bandwidth-based tariff structure to a transaction-based model. An example of this model would be a customer who needs to set up a videoconference in one hour; the customer pays for the bandwidth use during that hour.

8.2.6 Company Performance

How did Traditiontel perform from 1998 to 2001, with the new-services launch in 2001? The company spent three years upgrading its network infrastructure and building a new core and metro edge. A new OSS infrastructure was also developed and deployed during this period. The company spent approximately $30 billion during this period and experienced a shift in revenue from long-distance voice to IP. The volume of IP data doubled in 2000 from 1999. The IP-based traffic growth averaged a 200% increase from 2000 to 2001. The managed hosting growth averaged 50% quarterly over the year 2001. Finally, from 2000 to 2001, the quarterly average revenue increase was 50%, in sync with the customer traffic pattern.

Traditiontel observed a continued trend toward debt reduction from 2000 to 2001 and believes that its business transformation strategy has paid off. The company has evolved from a long-distance voice-centric company to an IP-based services company. The company used this period to assure that the business-engineering processes were common across the organization. Finally, essential to this business transformation was the emphasis on the OSS architecture and infrastructure. Service creation has been automated to facilitate the target of three new services per year.

8.2.7 Alternatives Considered

Rather than build out a new network infrastructure, Traditiontel could have considered investing in its legacy infrastructure to support these IP-based services. The company evaluated this alternative but concluded that it would be too complex for integration, as well as possibly disruptive to existing customers. The legacy services have been performing well for Traditiontel, but the company decided not to invest further in the legacy infrastructure. The pivotal driver was OSS: These services have separate OSS systems, and integrating these OSS systems was not possible due to the existence of vendor-proprietary applications.

8.2.8   Vendor Selection Process

Traditiontel has a multiple-vendor policy. The company does not want to be tied to a specific vendor, since this dependency carries risks (e.g., longevity of the supplier in the market, product pricing). Traditiontel suppliers are selected on the basis of technology and product leadership; established presence in the service provider market; commitment to developing products that will assure new service creation; and product and support pricing that will not be prohibitive to end customers. Interoperability as per open standards is a requirement for Traditiontel.

The company has established relationships with the some of these suppliers. For this project, Traditiontel sent out an RFI to five suppliers. (RFIs are discussed in Chapter 3.) Based on the response, the list was narrowed down to three. A similar process was also launched for the new-generation OSS architecture. Three supplier candidates were invited to present to upper management as well as to the service creation team members. The RFI scope was for core and metro-edge network infrastructure as well as OSS architecture.

After the presentations and internal discussions, Traditiontel selected two suppliers, a primary and a secondary. This selection was based on supplier response as well as Traditiontel agreement. A primary systems integrator was chosen to deliver the OSS architecture. Traditiontel stipulated that OSS must be part of the service lab testing and validation. The core and metro-edge primary and secondary suppliers must also prove interoperability in the Traditiontel labs for service rollout.

8.2.9   Technical Aspects

The IP-based network of Traditiontel has to support several services. Reliability, scalability, and stability are some of the factors that must be taken into account when designing the network. A hierarchical approach (similar to the architecture in Figure 8.2) is the best solution to make the network reliable, stable, scalable, and capable of supporting multiservices (see Section 8.1.8; this is also discussed in Chapter 5).

Network Architecture

Traditiontel has OC-192 links in the core, which gives about 10 Gb/sec between the core locations. The fiber-optic network is capable of supporting up to 40 Gb/sec, which allows for future expansion. This makes the network scalable because it allows the addition of new customers without additions of new links or bandwidth upgrade to the core network.

Multiple connections between core locations make the network more reliable and avoid single points of failure (link and node failure) in the network. Any single link or node failure will not partition the network. This means that end-to-end physical connectivity is not affected by failure of any single link or node.

Limiting the maximum hop count between core locations also helps to place a deterministic bound on the maximum end-to-end delay. Delay-sensitive applications such as voice have requirements like upper bounds on the end-to-end delay. One of several factors that affect end-to-end delay is the number of hops between the source and the destination. By limiting the number of hops between core locations, it is possible to predict the maximum end-to-end delay between any two points in the network.

OSS Architecture

The OSS architecture is critical for the development and deployment of IP-based services. Given the time frame required to develop such services, the OSS architecture plays a crucial role in the success of providing IP-based services to customers. Its departments include

- *Business and marketing:* Responsible for defining the business aspect of the service like pricing, service options, time to market, and so on.
- *Sales:* Responsible for selling the IP-based services to customers, maintaining customer contact, and getting the requirements and information from customers that are necessary for implementing the services.
- *Engineering:* Responsible for developing and testing the technical solutions.
- *NMS:* Responsible for developing the NMS tools required for mass deployment of the service, service upgrades, billing, and SLA reports.
- *NOC:* Responsible for deploying the service, monitoring the network, and ensuring that the SLAs are reported to the customer.
- *Billing:* Responsible for billing the customer for the IP-based services.

The OSS architecture must be capable of supporting the needs of all of these departments. It is responsible for ensuring that information from one department is readily available to other departments. The information flow and communication between the various departments is the key to the successful, rapid development and deployment of new services. (More details about OSS requirements are discussed in Chapter 6.)

Automation

Automation plays a key role in the OSS architecture. Manual intervention or interpretation can be cumbersome and time-consuming and is also prone to mistakes. Information from several departments must be processed and verified for consistency. Information flow from one department to the other must also be automated. The output from the processes of one department is the input to the processes of another department.

Automating this information flow can help to reduce the time required to develop and deploy services. The following sections give some examples to highlight the role of information-flow automation in the OSS architecture.

Device Configuration

The engineering department has the ownership of the configuration guidelines for the network devices for each service. These guidelines are finalized based on tests performed in the engineering labs. The configuration on the device for each service is tested extensively in the labs for correct functionality. The configuration guidelines are then forwarded to the NOC to be implemented into the deployment tool, which is responsible for configuring the network devices. Automation of this process will help to reduce the time required to generate the configuration for the network devices once the guidelines are finalized. It also helps to reduce the time required for modification when the engineering department proposes new configuration guidelines for all the network devices.

Service Deployment

Traditiontel wants to offer fast service deployment with penalties (see Section 8.2.4). This means that if the service deployment is not performed within the specified time period, Traditiontel has to give credits to the customer. In order to ensure that service deployment proceeds on time, it is important to have available all the information that is required to deploy the service for a new customer.

As an example, an IP address plan is an important input that is required to finalize the configuration of the network devices before a service can be deployed for a new customer. This information is provided by the customer to the sales department. Most of the time, lack of an IP address plan is the cause of delay for service deployment. This information has to be provided to the deployment tool in order to generate the configuration for the network devices that are relevant to the new customer. The sales process must be automated such that the IP address plan from the customer is available to the OSS system early enough. The deployment tool can then generate the configuration for the network devices and help to deploy the service for the new customer on time.

Service Upgrades

Traditiontel also wants to minimize the time required to perform a service upgrade. The customer is provided with a Web-based interface to upgrade services. Once a request is received from the customer, the OSS system proceeds with the upgrade, updates the SLA reporting tool for the customer (if it is relevant), and informs the billing department about the upgraded service so that the customer can be billed accordingly.

As described in Section 8.2.4, a customer wants to add a new server for Web hosting, and within 30 minutes after placing the order, the server is made available to the customer. Unless the OSS system is integrated with the Web-based system that takes the service upgrade request from the customer, it will not be possible to perform the service upgrade in 30 minutes.

In conclusion, the OSS architecture plays a key role in developing new services and also for rapid deployment of new services. An integrated, fully automated approach to the OSS system is a must in order to achieve the target for delivering IP-based services. Web-based interfaces will make life easy both for customers and Traditiontel.

8.2.10 Assessing Project Risks

Similar to the Greenfield service example, lack of vendor product, technology availability, and customers to sign up for these new IP-based services are risks for an incumbent. Another risk factor includes service differentiation against Greenfield service providers, who offer similar services (termed in marketing the "me too" strategy). Emphasis on providing value-added services reduces this risk for both incumbents and Greenfield service providers. Finally, outsourcing the development of a next-generation OSS architecture to a third party has risks, such as managing the project itself and ensuring that development is per specification, within budget, and as per the project plan. There is also risk of revenue loss in not using IP to develop value-added services, as the company had been losing revenue on long-distance voice over a period of several years. A clear vision of the company business, due diligence on the marketing plan and business case, and acting decisively in order to mitigate risks are success factors in this project.

8.2.11 Lessons Learned

The business engineering processes have to be aligned with transforming a business strategy. This requires a person with experience in multiservice operations and service management who is both technically and business savvy. One recommendation is to include personnel with established backgrounds in operations at the senior management level in order to facilitate changes—for service management, for example, a senior vice president of operations. This person should drive the goal to unify operations via IP-based technology. To evolve a business strategy based on IP means training the personnel who will support these new IP-based services, as some of them will have a background in other technologies and services like ATM, frame relay, and voice. This is important to successful IP-based service development and deployment.

8.2.12 Future Plans

Traditiontel plans to reduce capital expenditure throughout 2002. At the same time, new IP-based services will continue to be developed and launched. A single bill for bundled services will also be available in 2002. In 2003 and beyond, Traditiontel has a target to be number one in non-voice business by capturing the most customers.

8.2.13 Conclusion

The Traditiontel case study is an example of how an incumbent uses IP to transform a conservative business. There are general perceptions that an incumbent is slow and burdened with heavy processes that may need to be linked across the company. While some of this may be true, leadership at a company like Traditiontel can jump-start the necessary changes.

The next section presents a real-life case study of a European incumbent that embarked on a road similar to that of Traditiontel. Why did a conservative incumbent in Europe want to develop IP-based services? What was the motivation for this change in strategy? What were the issues? The challenges?

8.3 Real-Life Case Study

The conceptual case studies in the previous sections are composites from actual deployments, based on the experiences of U.S. service providers. This section presents an anonymous real-life case study. It looks at an incumbent in Europe and, as a real case study, provides more details into the organizational dynamics of developing IP-based services. (Nondisclosure agreements prevent us from actually naming the service provider.) The case is an example of an early adopter of IP-based services by an incumbent in Europe. The processes that resulted in a decision to develop and deploy IP-based services are also discussed. Finally, the impact that IP-based service has had on this company is also discussed. This case study applies globally and is not restricted to Europe.

8.3.1 Background

We refer to the European provider in this case study as Meta Telecom. Meta Telecom is a European incumbent with 100 years of history and 90% of the domestic market for telecommunications services. It is based in central Europe and has approximately 20,000 employees. One competitive driver to open up the domestic market to new competition is the decision by the European Union as well as the national regulatory agency to unbundle the local loop. Meta Telecom has resisted this requirement and has requested implementation delay from the national regulatory agency.

The case study commences at a time of change for Meta Telecom. The impetus of this change was from company leadership, who wanted rapid privatization of the provider, believing that a totally private company could be flexible enough to compete in a market that was becoming open for new players.

At the end of 1998, Meta Telecom consisted of several business divisions, such as carrier, wholesale, mobile, and enterprise. The carrier group provided transmission and voice services; the wholesale unit offered infrastructure services for telehousing, broadband connectivity, and bandwidth reseller services; the enterprise group provided Internet access, frame relay, remote access, and LAN connection-over-frame relay.

Meta Telecom had been reviewing its cost structure for services such as voice and data. There had been discussions regarding the network infrastructure requirements for the future Universal Mobile Telecommunications System (UMTS). UMTS is a third-generation technology that is capable of delivering broadband at speeds of up to 2 Mb/sec in the form of voice, data, audio, and video. These services were to be available at the beginning of 2002. Discussions pursued a "what if" exercise for a converged voice, data, and UMTS platform.

Service creation was cumbersome and not standard across the business units. The enterprise organization implemented the concept of tollgates (as discussed in Chapter 2). No collaborative tools other than email and file sharing were implemented by Meta Telecom during this period. A company intranet was under development at the end of 1998. The enterprise sales force was frustrated with the service development process as it was "too slow" and took an approach of aggressively selling customized solutions in order to pull the service development process. This translated to "selling a solution now" and "developing the service later." This approach frustrated the service development team, which consisted of engineering, operations, and product management, since the approach conflicted with defined processes. Consequently, there was infighting between the sales and service development teams.

It is in this environment that a very strategic customer, an international bank, approached Meta Telecom with a proposition. The proposition was to engage Meta Telecom as a business and service partner over a period of five years to develop and deploy IP-based services. The customer referred to this value proposition as the "multimedia plug." The term depicts multiservices over one physical connection. The customer wanted the first service fully deployed by the end of September 1999.

8.3.2 Business Aspects

At the end of 1998, Meta Telecom entered into a contract with the strategic customer to develop this multimedia plug. In January 1999, a project team consisting of various members from Meta Telecom business units was created with a goal to develop the first IP-based service. The cross-functional team members were from sales and marketing, product management, engineering, operations, and finance, and the team had executive sponsorship at the CEO level. This meant that resource issues would be resolved with full management support, escalating directly to the CEO. Meta Telecom engaged a consulting company to work with the project team on the financial analysis for the service development initiatives as well as expected revenues from these services over the next three years. The financial analysis methods included net present value and return on investment, in order to determine whether to retain the existing infrastructure or construct a new network.

Customer Requirements

The customer subscribed to LAN connection-over-frame relay serving numerous locations. The business database applications of the customer were based on proprietary protocols. Two main requirements emerged from this customer: The first was a decision to migrate the business applications from proprietary protocols to IP. This decision was motivated by the fact that the costs for application and operating system licensing were increasing. There was a need for an open architecture to support a variety of groupware applications such as hypertext for linking text documents to each other for multiple-person access (e.g., the Web; collaborative writing systems, workflow systems, newsgroups, electronic whiteboards, and video communications). The strategic customer had just merged with an international insurance company, driving the requirement for collaborative tools. The company knew that a migration to IP would require an evolution strategy.

A second requirement was to provide service-rich connectivity that supports multiservices such as any-to-any connectivity, bandwidth upgrades, voice-over-IP, and so on. The first service was to provide "any-to-any" communications to numerous locations, in the thousands. This service was to be attractively priced—that is, a minimum of 10% cheaper than the LAN connection-over-frame relay service. Bandwidth should be able to provide 155 Mb/sec access. The customer also wanted to change its bandwidth via a Web interface with the bandwidth change to occur within 24 hours. Finally, the delivery of the new services and their enhancements should be quicker than the LAN connection-over-frame relay service by 50%—instead of eight weeks for provisioning, a minimum of four weeks.

Table 8.5 provides an overview of the old service, LAN connection-over-frame relay. The service prices are depicted in Table 8.6. The pricing reflects recurring base charges only for 200 remote sites for the customer. The monthly recurring charges for this customer were $1,100,000 per month:

- $3500 × 200 (remote sites) = $700,000
- 2 Mb/sec with 512 Kb/sec CIR—two other primary headquarter sites for 200 remote sites at 5 sites/connection, $10,000 × 40 = $400,000 (this is without oversubscription of frame relay bandwidth)

The connectivity was based on hub-and-spoke topology, with no requirement for the other sites to communicate with one another. The customer requirements may be summarized as follows:

Migration from proprietary protocols to IP

Service-rich offering

Bandwidth support for 155 Mb/sec

Ability to change bandwidth on demand

Minimum of 10% less expensive than LAN connection-over-frame relay

Reduction of provisioning time by 50%

Any-to-any connectivity

As stated, the first service had to be ready in nine months to start the provisioning for the new locations. The existing customer frame relay sites were to be migrated upon completion of the new locations. Total

Table 8.5   LAN connection-over-frame relay.

Provisioning	Eight weeks
Contract Period	One to five years
Access	64 Kb/sec to E3 (34 Mb/sec)
Features	Ethernet 10/100 Mb/sec Token Ring 4/16 Mb/sec
Service Management	24-hour help desk; SLA as per contract with compensation

Table 8.6   LAN connection-over-frame relay price structure.

LAN Connection-over-FR	2 Mb/sec with 64 Kb/sec CIR	2 Mb/sec with 512 Kb/sec CIR
FR Access/Monthly	$3500	$10,000

provisioning was to be completed by the end of March 2000, with service sign-off on April 1, 2000. All locations were domestic.

Meta Network

The primary goal for Meta Telecom was the time to market for this new service as per contract. Failing to deliver this service would result in the loss of a very strategic customer. A secondary goal was to ensure that there was a wider market for these IP-based services. The main issue here was to understand the market requirements as an input to the network architecture. How scalable must this network be? A third goal was that the new service must not cannibalize the existing LAN connection-over-frame relay service. Service positioning must be clear. LAN connection-over-frame relay still was in demand with over 10,000 customer sites connected. A fourth goal was that a new network infrastructure would be used as the base for converging services over time, as determined by each business case. Finally, the OSS architecture had to support the development and provisioning of these new IP-based service packages. Meta Telecom goals may be summarized as follows:

Service time to market for the strategic customer

Wider market for the new service

Not to cannibalize LAN connection-over-frame relay

Network infrastructure to be a base for service convergence

OSS architecture for new IP-based service development and deployment

Quick service delivery for the customer without sacrificing reliability was also an important factor for Meta Telecom, who had a target to maintain 99.99% service availability. The team recognized that the overall project would change Meta Telecom as a company. This project was the first one involving all of the major cross-functional entities of Meta Telecom and had visibility at the CEO level.

Service Time to Market

The requirement for this new service to be ready by September 1999 was daunting. This fact was due to the lack of consistent service development processes across the company. Meta Telecom not only was confronted with a service target but also had a requirement to quickly define a cross-organizational service development process that would achieve the time-to-market goal.

Wider Market

In January 1999, the project team requested a list of the top 10 customers for the first IP-based service, called *LAN connection-over-IP*. Sales and marketing forecasted the quantity of connections per customer over three years, and these connections exceeded 100,000: 600 connections were expected at the end of 1999, 10,000 were anticipated at the end of 2000; 50,000 were expected at the end of 2001; and 70,000 were expected at the end of 2002. The conclusion by the team was that there was a wider market for these IP-based service packages.

Scalability

These connections were used to derive the network architecture requirements for scalability. Frame relay was discounted as a base architecture due to the service bandwidth requirements of 155 Mb/sec and the any-to-any connectivity that would have made the cost prohibitive. The team evaluated ATM for the core architecture. The ATM network had been relatively unused at the time. Meta Telecom wanted a single supplier that was a market leader in high-speed IP routing for the core.

LAN Connection-over-Frame Relay Cannibalization

The LAN connection-over-frame relay service represented about 35% of the revenues for the enterprise division in 1999. A requirement for Meta Telecom was to ensure that the emerging IP-based service would not cannibalize this service: creating a new LAN connection service based on IP must not erode this revenue stream. Positioning these services and assessing at which point cannibalization would make business sense were steps for the company.

Network Infrastructure for Convergence

The requirement for Meta Telecom to use the network infrastructure as a basis for service convergence was driven by previous exercises on this topic. Meta Telecom viewed this project as an opportunity to remove the political deadlock related to the convergence topic. The project had a larger scope than to deliver the first IP-based service by the end of 1999. This scope was to induce cultural buy-in within the company and to result in cultural convergence as well.

OSS Architecture

As there were separate OSS architectures corresponding to the various services such as voice and data, the new OSS architecture needed to develop and provision IP-based services. The specific requirement was to align the cross-organizational business-engineering processes into a new OSS architecture. The Meta Telecom project team viewed this alignment as a necessary step toward eventual convergence.

8.3.3 Technical Aspects

Meta Telecom has a legacy frame relay and ATM network. This Layer 2 network is used to implement the LAN connection service. The IP network for each customer is built on top of the Layer 2 network. The Layer 2

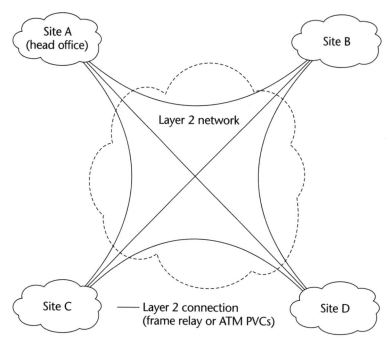

Figure 8.5 Layer 2 network architecture for LAN connection service.

network provides the logical separation between different customer networks. Since a separate Layer 3 network is built for each customer, traffic from one customer network will never be forwarded to another customer.

Network Architecture

The Layer 2 network is used to provide connectivity between different sites (see Figure 8.5). Meta Telecom uses frame relay and ATM for the Layer 2 networks. An IP network (for each customer) is built on top of the Layer 2 network (see Figure 8.6). Each IP network is connected to the NOC of Meta Telecom.

One of the disadvantages of the legacy VPN service is that a separate Layer 3 network has to be built for each customer in order to ensure data security; Layer 3 devices cannot be shared among all the customers. Figure 8.7 shows two VPN customers (indicated as dotted and dashed). A separate IP network is implemented in order to ensure data security. This makes the service expensive for customers, because they have to invest in a lot of equipment. Meta Telecom also has to manage more devices.

Network Management and Operations

Figure 8.6 shows the NOC connected to the customer network. All the devices are monitored from the NOC. Proprietary and vendor-specific

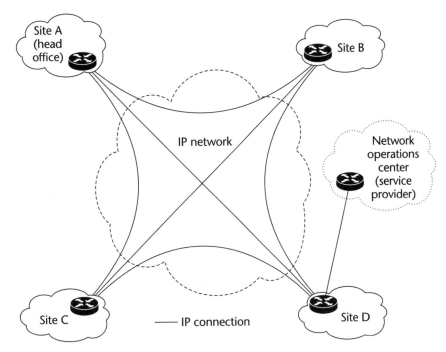

Figure 8.6 Layer 3 network architecture for LAN connection service.

applications are used to manage the network. The NOC is also involved in the following activities:

1. Monitoring the status of each network device
2. Collecting SLA information and generating SLA reports
3. Upgrading the link speed in the Layer 2 network when the customer wants more bandwidth
4. Configuring devices when new customers are added to the network

The time required to install and configure new sites for a customer is about four weeks. It involves the following activities: \

1. Installing the devices in the new customer site
2. Modifying the configuration of some of the existing devices
3. Including the new devices in the monitoring system
4. Modifying SLA reports to include the new devices

8.3.4 IP-Based Solution

Meta Telecom's IP-based solution consists of several elements, including business, technology, and the services architecture. The company culture played a key role in this project. The performance of Meta Telecom in achieving both the customer requirements as well as its own goals is

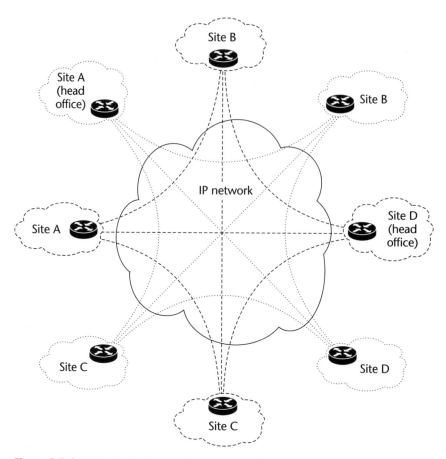

Figure 8.7 Separate Layer 3 network for each customer.

discussed. The transformation of the company in the process of delivering this project is also examined. The case study concludes with a discussion of the future plans of Meta Telecom for IP.

8.3.5 Services

Meta Telecom decided to build out a new network infrastructure based on IP, due to the time-to-market factor. The project team felt that it would be "too process-intensive" to try to develop and deploy the new services on the legacy infrastructure. The problem for the Meta Telecom project team was that the legacy infrastructure was still operated by different groups within the company. There was a view taken by the team that building out a separate network would actually be faster than trying to bridge operational groups across the company. The service development aspect was to include a base IP service development on top of which value-added services such as LAN-over-IP could be developed. Figure 8.8 depicts this model. The core of the services building-block diagram describes the concept of using IP-based technology to build services. The service provider develops the services, then deploys them to the customers, as represented by the larger circle. This decision was made in January 2000.

The Meta Telecom project team examined the network infrastructure elements required for scalability. Based on the input from sales and marketing for expected customer connections over the next three years, the team determined that the core needed to support OC-48/STM-16 bandwidth by the end of 1999 and OC-192/STM-64 by the end of 2002. Because the core supplier could not deliver ATM at speeds of OC-48 since the technology was unavailable, the team decided on a packet-over-SONET/SDH core (POS). The core would consist of 40 domestic locations with link speeds at OC-48 by the end of 1999.

The edges were to aggregate speeds of up to 622 Mb/sec from the access via ATM and eventually leased lines. Approximately 40 domestic aggregation devices were to be installed by the end of 1999. Finally, access would be provided either via POS or DSL. Meta Telecom had been in the process of installing its broadband infrastructure targeted for the wholesale

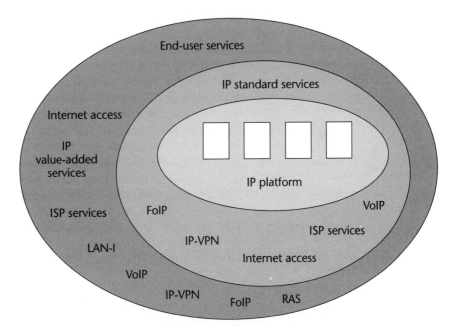

Figure 8.8 Meta telecom IP services building block.

market. At the end of 1999, 1000 DSL PoPs were to be installed. The new IP-based service would use this broadband infrastructure for access. The architecture was to support edge and access growth, and would expand with increased customer connections. The core network would remain small and high-speed in order to accommodate the aggregated traffic flows. The core network was not to be the source of congestion and therefore would be overengineered, as QoS implementations were relatively unavailable in the beginning of 2000. Figure 8.2 depicts this new architecture generically.

To summarize the network architecture, key components include a small and high-performing core, an intelligent edge, and access for aggregation as well as accommodating customer growth. Intelligent edges are the sources of accounting and customer information needed for billing and reporting. The revenue potential is in the access, where the end customers are. Having drafted the generic network architecture, positioning services was the next step for the Meta Telecom team.

Product and service positioning between LAN connection-over-frame relay and LAN connection-over-IP was an important requirement for Meta Telecom. The company also needed to position the emerging IP-based services. LAN connection-over-frame relay is targeted for customers without any-to-any connectivity. The LAN connection-over-IP is for customers who require this any-to-any connectivity. The customer additionally has the capability to order bandwidth-on-demand from 64 Kb/sec to 155 Mb/sec and have this provisioned within 24 hours. This capability is not available for LAN connection-over-frame relay customers. Figure 8.9 depicts the IP-based service product positioning of Meta Telecom. These building blocks reflect the company's IP-based service portfolio.

Financial Aspects

Meta Telecom's primary requirement was to determine that a new revenue stream from IP-based services was possible. The project team examined domestic service trends from 2000 to 2004 as part of market research and ran a series of detailed financial analyses examining capital expenditure, operating expenses, net present value over three years, and pricing models for the new services. Finally, the team explored the OSS architecture's financial aspects in terms of capital expenditure and operating expenses over a period of three years.

We present a high-level view of some of the analysis that was performed, commencing with the trends toward domestic service usage, with a focus on data services from 2000 to 2004 and the compounded annual growth rate. The data in Table 8.7 was used by the Meta Telecom project team as an overall market input confirming the growth rate possibility for IP-based services. The next step was to look at the capital expenditure and operating expense results. Table 8.8 presents a high-level summary of the

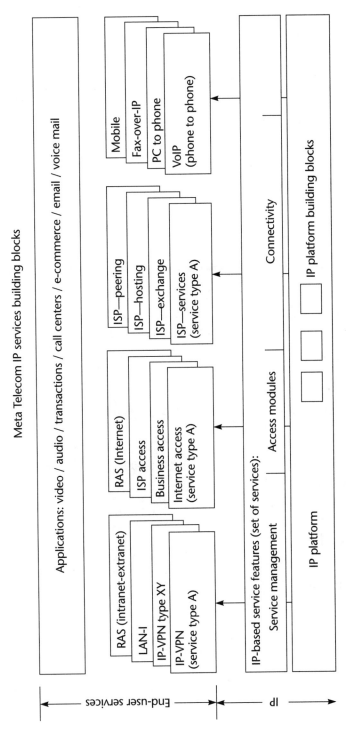

Figure 8.9 Meta Telecom: positioning of IP service products.

Table 8.7   Domestic service trends.

Service	2000 ($ million)	2001 ($ million)	2002 ($ million)	2003 ($ million)	2004 ($ million)	Estimated compounded annual growth rate
FR	20	40	58	80	100	30%
ATM	100	150	170	200	250	25%
x.25	8	6	5	4	3	−12%
ISDN	20	22	23	24	22	5%
IP	30	50	60	90	100	35%
IP-VPN	6	15	25	35	50	58%
VoIP	15	35	58	90	110	60%

Table 8.8   High-level ROI analysis of Meta Telecom.

Capital Expenditure	New Build-Out	Upgrade of Existing Network
Equipment	$60,000,000	$75,000,000
Spares	$20,000,000	$19,000,000
Facilities (racks)	$1,000,000	$1,000,000
Operational costs (monthly)		
Power	$85,000	$70,000
Cooling	$30,000	$35,000
Additional costs	$10,000	$10,000
ROI (three years)		
Capital expenditures	$81,000,000	$95,000,000
Equipment	$80,000,000	$94,000,000
Facilities	$1,000,000	$1,000,000
Operational costs	$4,500,000	$4,140,000
Power	$3,060,000	$2,520,000
Cooling	$1,080,000	$1,260,000
Additional costs	$360,000	$360,000
Total Costs	$85,500,000	$99,140,000
Savings	About 9.9%	

general analysis for the core, edge, and access as discussed previously and compares expenditures for a legacy network infrastructure upgrade as part of due diligence performed by the project team.

The Meta Telecom project team confirmed both market trends as well as the savings for a new network build-out, as opposed to upgrading its legacy networks. These conclusions were derived from market research, the marketing plan, and the financial analysis. In fact, the legacy network, ATM, would be used at the access. The next step was to evaluate a potential pricing model for the new service that would not cannibalize the LAN connection-over-frame relay but would also be attractive for the customer as well as the market. This model would serve as a basis for extrapolating the potential revenue streams for the new IP-based service.

As a result of field research, Meta Telecom decided to price the LAN connection-over-IP service at 10% below the LAN connection-over-frame relay. Such pricing would not introduce cannibalization and was aligned with what the strategic customer wanted. The decision was based on results from market research. Table 8.9 depicts the pricing elements of the managed LAN connection-over-IP service. The pricing is flat-fee based.

The port and access lines are combined for simplicity for the customer. The port fee also includes any class-of-service requirements. The Meta Telecom team applied the pricing model to the expected number of connections, which were further divided by port and access speeds and had, as expected, variable results. Table 8.10 depicts these forecasts at 2 Mb/sec.

Table 8.9 Managed LAN connection-over-IP price model.

LAN-over-IP	64 Kb/sec	256 Kb/sec	2 Mb/sec	34 Mb/sec
Managed CPE	$110	$350	$700	$1200
Access line	$230	$450	$1500	$7000
Port fee	$95	$230	$700	$4200
Total monthly fee	$435	$1030	$2900	$12,400

Table 8.10 Meta Telecom customer connection forecasts and revenue estimate at 2 Mb/sec.

2000	2001	2002
10,600 $36,888,000/year	50,000 $1,920,000,000/year	70,000 $2,436,000,000/year

These are clearly estimates. The exercise approximates the revenue for a single service, LAN connection-over-IP. Meta Telecom concluded that IP-based services could generate revenue. The following discussion examines how all of these factors came together for Meta Telecom to develop and deploy IP-based services. The OSS architecture capital expenditure and operating expense has to be evaluated before deriving this conclusion. Table 8.11 provides a high-level view of the Meta Telecom OSS architecture financial analysis. Meta Telecom assumed approximately 20% systems integration in these figures. The systems integration included the development of an intranet-based, object-oriented system.

To complete the OSS architecture analysis, Meta Telecom evaluated both the yearly cost breakout as well as the yearly savings. Table 8.12 depicts this analysis. The majority of the costs are experienced in the first year with a yearly increase in net savings. Meta Telecom took the information from the ROI build-out, the revenue approximation for LAN

Table 8.11   Meta Telecom OSS architecture financial elements.

Capital Cost, about 15% of Project Cost	Estimated Hourly Downtime Cost, $25,000	Availability at 99.99%	Core Size Medium (40) with 20% Growth
Year	2000	2001	2002
Customer devices	10,600	50,000	70,000
Summary results	Software cost $3,000,000 Hardware cost $10,000,000	OSS savings Provisioning Staff Uptime Avoided truckroll	$35,700,000 $10,000,000 $800,000 $100,000 $1,000,000
		Net savings Break-even days	$22,700,000 270

Table 8.12   Meta Telecom OSS cost savings breakout.

Factors	2000	2001	2002
Software costs	$2,200,000	$450,000	$430,000
Hardware costs	$8,200,000	$950,000	$820,000
Cost savings	$10,000,000	$11,500,000	$15,000,000
Net savings	$1,800,000	$10,550,000	$14,050,000

connection-over-IP, and the OSS architecture analysis and concluded that the company could make money from IP-based services. Finally, using a single infrastructure, Meta Telecom prepared to launch its second IP-based service at the end of 2001 with the addition of voice-over-IP. No additional investments in the new infrastructure were required for this second service launch.

8.3.6 Project Execution and Results

The Meta Telecom project team started in January 1999, and the network build-out, including the OSS architecture, was completed at the end of August 1999. Intensive training of the operational team occurred between March 1999 and May 1999. The staff was largely familiar with managing a PSTN network and voice services and required IP training. Vendors worked on-site with the project team for testing. The project time line is depicted in Figure 8.10.

LAN connection-over-IP was launched on time in September 1999, with the pilot for the strategic customer. The service deployment occurred in record speed for this incumbent. By the end of 1999, the entire project organization consisted of 100 people, with the majority from service management. The project team reflected the functional organization that Meta Telecom wanted to activate after the project end. Creating the IP-based service organization occurred in 2000. The project team was disengaged and integrated into a new IP service organization at Meta Telecom.

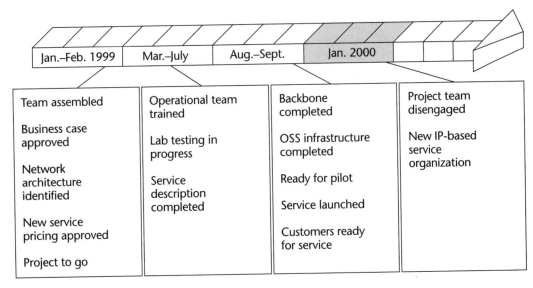

Figure 8.10 Meta Telecom project time line.

Factors that contributed to the rapid execution were the cross-functional composition of the project team and upper-management support. Finally, frequent communications between the strategic customer and the suppliers facilitated the deployment. The customer was clear about its expectations, and the supplier delivered the infrastructure as required.

8.3.7 Service Implementation Model

The main function for the new Meta Telecom OSS architecture was IP-based service development and deployment. The business-engineering processes needed to be defined by the Meta Telecom project team to support IP-based service development and deployment across the company. Figure 8.11 depicts these processes, which provide interfaces between IP-based service creation and the OSS architecture. The IP-based service portfolio is linked to the architecture. With the business-engineering template and the OSS architecture, IP-based service development is accelerated. Meta Telecom launched the second service, voice-over-IP, in the fall of 2001. This service development commenced in July 2001, a total of five months from beginning to end. The first service, LAN connection-over-IP, took nine months (from January 1999 to the end of September 1999). As this was the first IP-based service, the service creation architecture had to be developed and implemented simultaneously. Finally, at the end of 2001, the provisioning function of the architecture has been optimized to deploy approximately 50,000 connections per year.

8.3.8 Alternatives Considered

Using the legacy network to develop the IP-based services was considered, but only for a short period. The constraint was due to the requirement by the team to have a single vendor, a leader in high-speed IP routing. The ATM network has been used at the IP-based service access points. Toward the goal of convergence, Meta Telecom is currently planning for the migration of its leased-line services to the IP-based network infrastructure.

8.3.9 Vendor Selection Process

Meta Telecom required a single vendor for the core, edge, and access aggregation. The DSL vendor is a market leader. The network infrastructure, in fact, supports two vendors. Meta Telecom requested, as an early adopter of the technology, access to the vendor developers for the core, edge, and access aggregation. This exchange provided valuable communications for technology applicability as well as how the technology and product was being used for IP-based services. Meta Telecom had a direct feedback loop to product development. (An example of this feedback loop is described in Chapter 2.) These developers had access to the Meta Telecom service development lab. Other European service providers requested Meta Telecom

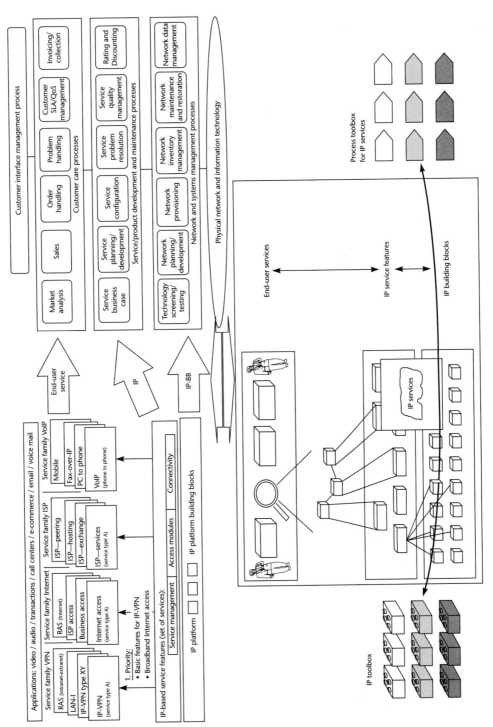

Figure 8.11 Meta Telecom business engineering for IP-based services.

for reference visits to share the IP-based service development and deployment experience.

8.3.10   Technical Aspects

Meta Telecom wants to offer LAN connection service using the new IP network to corporate customers to provide IP connectivity between various locations of the company that are scattered across many cities. Meta Telecom has PoPs located in most of the cities. Some of the features offered by the new LAN connection service include

1. CPEs managed by the service provider
2. Uninterrupted connectivity between all the small satellite sites and the main sites
3. SLA-guaranteed minimum downtime (four to eight hours) for the small sites
4. SLA-guaranteed downtime of less than one hour for main sites
5. Guaranteed bandwidth (in several values, ranging from 64 Kb/sec to 100 Mb/sec) for any site
6. Internet access
7. SLA reporting providing details about link utilization and service availability on a weekly basis

Meta Telecom has decided to use ATM, frame relay, and ADSL in an access network based on the available network infrastructure in most customer sites. Some customers have copper connections, while others have fiber connections to the nearest service provider PoP. ATM is used for sites that have large bandwidth requirements (up to 155 Mb/sec); frame relay is used for sites that have medium bandwidth requirements (up to 30 Mb/sec); and ADSL is used for small sites that have only a few users and small bandwidth requirements (not exceeding 512 Kb/sec).

Network Architecture

Figure 8.2 shows the network architecture. This hierarchical architecture is in line with the architecture adapted by several service providers. It makes the network scalable, stable, reliable, and capable of supporting multiservices. Figure 8.12 shows the LAN connection service using the new IP network. In contrast with the implementation using the legacy network (see Figure 8.7), it can be clearly seen that the same IP network can be used to support multiple customers. The NOC of the service provider requires only one IP connection to manage the entire network.

Network Management and Operations

The NOC plays a major role in providing the LAN connection services using the new IP network. Its activities include provisioning the service,

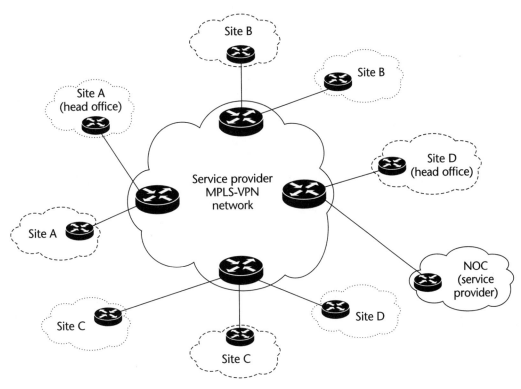

Figure 8.12 LAN connection service using the new IP network.

monitoring the network, generating SLA reports, and so on. Following are brief descriptions of the activities of the NOC.

Implementation and Provisioning

Guaranteed bandwidth is implemented, using the features provided by ATM, frame relay, and ADSL. The maximum link capacity from each site is restricted to the supported guaranteed bandwidth by using the throttling features supported by ATM, frame relay, and ADSL technologies. In order to provide a flexible solution, interconnectivity between the sites is provided using MPLS-VPN. Routing protocols are implemented between sites and the service provider network to get and distribute routing information of a customer's sites.

Provisioning a customer site for the LAN interconnection service requires

1. Establishing Layer 2 connectivity between the customer site and service provider PoP; this requires Layer 2 connectivity to be established in the access network

2. Restricting the bandwidth to the guaranteed bandwidth supported for that site
3. Activating IP connectivity between the CPE and service provider PoP
4. Activating the routing between the CPE and the service provider PoP and ensuring that the new site has connectivity to all other sites

In order to provision several sites within a short time, tools based on SNMP can be used to configure all of the devices in the network. A database provides all of the relevant information for each customer site. The software tool interacts with the database to extract the information that is relevant for each site and configures all of the necessary devices. Software tools help to reduce the time required to configure devices and also to minimize the faults due to manual configuration.

Network Monitoring

In order to guarantee minimum downtime, the NOC must periodically monitor all of the devices in the network. SNMP-based tools can be used to monitor the devices and to receive alarms from the network devices. A good database system with all relevant information about the network will help to monitor the network and also to provide information for troubleshooting in case of the malfunctioning of some of the devices. A visual topology of the network can be of great help for troubleshooting problems in the network.

As part of the fault-monitoring system, error logs must be periodically checked to see if there are any signs of trouble. Automated tools to scan the logs for well-known problems (related to service) can help in reducing the time that is required to detect and isolate faults. These tools are a part of the OSS architecture.

SLA Reporting

The use of SNMP-based tools to periodically collect statistical information about link utilization can aid in generating SLA reports for customers. These tools can be automated to periodically collect this information and save it in a database. Other tools to generate Web-based reports for the customer can use this information. The billing department also uses this information to charge the customer based on link utilization.

OSS Architecture

Meta Telecom has invested time and money to build an OSS architecture that can aid in rapid service development and deployment. The OSS system is built using third-party applications. The architecture helps the various departments to exchange information and also to ensure that information is valid and consistent. The information is accessible to all of the departments electronically, which minimizes manual intervention to extract and manipulate the information once it has been registered in the OSS system.

For example, in the legacy system, the IP addressing plan was exchanged between various departments using Excel sheets. Each department manually extracted the IP address plan from the Excel sheet and then entered it into their own system. The new OSS architecture overcomes this problem. Once the IP address plan of the customer is made available to the OSS system, it is then available to all departments. Since all departments make use of the same OSS system, there is no need to extract the information and enter it into several databases.

Web-Based Tools

Using Web-based tools can help to make the task of provisioning easy for the operator who is responsible for provisioning new customer connections. It can also help the operator to monitor the health of the network and the status of individual devices with a few clicks of a mouse. Meta Telecom intends to provide Web-based online SLA reports to its customers. This will make it easy for customers to get information about their network. Information related to link utilization can help customers in doing capacity planning and ordering more bandwidth for sites that have very high link utilization.

Meta Telecom provides a Web-based interface to customers for requesting service upgrades. One such service upgrade is to increase the link capacity when the link utilization reaches a threshold value. Customers can order more link bandwidth using the online Web-based interface. The link upgrade is performed within 24 hours (if enough network resources are readily available), and a notification is sent to the customer about the successful upgrade.

8.3.11 Assessing Project Risks

Building a new backbone and developing new services in time for the strategic customer's deadline was a big risk taken by Meta Telecom. The time required to build the new IP backbone and to implement the service was extremely short compared to the usual time required for a service development cycle within Meta Telecom. Building the services based on technologies (like MPLS-VPN) that are relatively new is a risk, as the technology is not mature and can have bugs in the implementation. This requires a close working relationship with the vendor. Another risk faced by Meta Telecom was that the new LAN connection service over IP could cannibalize the older LAN connection service over frame relay. This could result in losing customers for the older service and thereby make it less profitable to maintain. The legacy OSS infrastructure was another risk factor that could have slowed down the development of new IP-based services: it could have slowed down the service implementation phase and resulted in the loss of customers (and hence revenue) for Meta Telecom.

8.3.12 Lessons Learned

What went right for Meta Telecom? A strategic customer requesting the development of the "multimedia plug" propelled Meta Telecom into this evolutionary phase of the company. A cross-functional team that included sales and marketing and upper-management support removed the political obstacles that had precluded the company from moving forward. Technology and product availability, as well as a valuable exchange between the vendor developers and the service architecture team aided the project. Finally, the emphasis that the OSS architecture is important to IP-based service creation was perhaps the most significant success factor in the Meta Telecom project.

8.3.13 Future Plans

Meta Telecom has launched three new IP-based services in 2002. These are IP-VPN, remote access, and Internet access. The company is considering off-loading its voice transit switches to the IP backbone by the end of 2003. The IP backbone will be used for the emerging mobile UMTS service packages by the beginning of 2004. The strategy toward service convergence onto a single infrastructure is in progress.

8.3.14 Conclusion

The Meta Telecom experience is a success, demonstrating how IP-based technology has unified a company's operations to develop and deploy IP-based services, reduce costs, and reduce service-provisioning time. The customer no longer has to wait eight weeks for provisioning—the average provisioning time is now four weeks, a 50% improvement in deployment. Most important is that these IP-based services have catalyzed revenues; the company has reported a yearly increase in revenues from service launch. The case study is a model for IP-based service creation and an example of an evolutionary approach to change.

8.4 Chapter Review

The conceptual case studies and the Meta Telecom experience have drawn a picture of the business and technical aspects associated with IP-based service creation. There are common success factors in all three examples that include upper-management support and vision to use IP technology to transform a company, the redefinition of business-engineering processes for company-wide IP-based service development and deployment, an emphasis on OSS architecture as the base for service creation, and, finally, the positive interaction between customers, service providers, and vendors. With these interrelationships, you can ask the appropriate questions as they pertain to IP-based service development. These questions are to your vendor, to your customer, to your service provider. Are you ready to develop and use IP-based services?

Closing Remarks: Remaining Competitive with IP

The previous chapters presented business motivations not only for using IP-based technology to develop services but also for incorporating IP as a philosophy in developing and deploying those services. Rapid service development and implementation is possible for both Greenfield and incumbent operators and can be achieved by using the models proposed in this book. However, quick and efficient service development is not a given. Service providers must apply resources to the creation of the IP-based toolbox, an essential foundation for an electronic development (e-development) strategy. Once IP-based services are in place, service providers can begin offering solutions to customers and achieving a competitive edge.

Let us once again visit the requirements of today's customers, end users, and service providers. Based on the information presented in the previous chapters, let us see whether an IP network can meet all of the requirements. Customer requirements can be summarized as follows:

Connectivity

Multiservices using a single connection

Guaranteed throughput

Minimal delay

Minimal delay variation (jitter)

Security

High availability (99.999%) of the service

SLA reports on a periodic basis

Cost savings

Fast service

Staying ahead of the curve

IP definitely satisfies the connectivity requirements of today's applications, most of which are based on TCP/IP or UDP/IP. As a result, an IP network can easily meet the applications' connectivity requirements.

IP can also provide connectivity over a number of Layer 2 technologies and acts as a melting pot to provide connectivity between users with different access technologies. As seen from the access technologies discussion, an IP network can be used to provide multiservices (voice, video, and data) over a single connection to the customer site. The QoS discussion shows that IP networks can definitely meet the QoS requirements of voice, video, and data applications, such as guaranteed bandwidth and minimal delay and jitter.

Layer 3 VPNs help a service provider to use the same backbone for multiple VPNs and at the same time ensure that each VPN has its privacy so that IP packets from one VPN do not get forwarded to another. Layer 3 VPNs have an advantage over Layer 2 VPNs based on ATM or frame relay in terms of scalability of the core network. IPSec can supplement the security requirements by ensuring data confidentiality in addition to data integrity. Encryption features provided by IPSec can help applications, like e-commerce and e-banking, and customers, like banks, by ensuring that confidential data can be transported using the IP network without any worries about the data being intercepted by unauthorized parties.

Using redundancy, IP-based networks can be used to provide services with high availability. SNMP-based tools can be used to provide SLA reports on availability and network utilization to the customer.

IP helps to provide multiservices (voice, video, and data) using the same physical connection between the service provider PoP and the customer site. This helps the customer to reduce their costs on network connectivity and contributes to the customer's business profitability. For the service provider who offers value-added services based on IP, this can result in both new customers and customer loyalty.

The goals of service providers can be summarized as follows:

Scalable and stable core network to support a large number of customers

Multiservices using the same network

Easy network operations for maintenance purposes and for upgrading/ modifying customer requests

Short time for developing and deploying IP-based services

Fast time to market and cost savings

Scalability and reliability are key issues for service providers. As long as the core network is scalable, it permits the service provider to offer many IP-based services (and hence have more customers) using the same core network. Technologies like MPLS help in designing and implementing scalable and reliable core networks. Traffic engineering (using MPLS) helps to make efficient use of the bandwidth in an IP network.

Reliability can be achieved by using redundancy to avoid single points of failure. IP networks can provide redundancy. Routing protocols help to reroute traffic when a single component or multiple components fail in the network. High availability is provided by having redundant paths in the core network and between the customer site and the service provider PoPs.

Voice, video, and data are some of the different networks owned by service providers. Typically, they would like to reduce the cost of maintaining these networks and at the same time be able to offer all the services required by their customers. Technologies like voice-over-IP and video-streaming help providers to offer these services using a single IP network and thereby reduce the cost of building and maintaining several networks.

An efficient network operations center (NOC) plays a key role in running and maintaining a large IP network that supports several IP-based services. Good NMS tools can assist operators in the NOC to manage the network, detect and diagnose faults in a timely manner, and take preventive actions to avoid network outages. NMS tools also play a key role in provisioning new customers and upgrading the services of existing customers. Provisioning a large number of customers in a short period of time is the key to rapid deployment of new IP-based services and having a competitive edge in the market. The challenge lies in having a good OSS architecture to help reduce the time required to provision new customers and services. IP and IP-based services can definitely help service providers in rapid development and deployment.

Using IP to automate tools and best practices for marketing and business engineering reduces the time to market for a new service because the processes are not done manually; however, an organization must first review its service development process regarding any optimization before automating the process itself. IP-based technology also contributes to cost savings for a service provider by reducing operating expenses in collapsing multiple services and corresponding network management systems to a single, multiservice architecture, thus eliminating separate networks and separate network management organizations. With IP-based technology, the trend is from fast service to self-service for "real-time" service development and deployment as initiated by the customer. Self-service allows the customer to be the key stakeholder for new services: the customer determines the services to be developed and deployed.

Where does one go from here? Clearly, IP-based services will play a huge role in enabling future services. Enhancements are being made to IP in order to provide an equivalent voice QoS and corresponding CoS similar to traditional switching networks like ATM, frame relay, and voice. Certainly, this industry is embarking on changes not seen since the onset of the telephone itself. Challenging service providers to review their own service development and deployment processes has been a common thread throughout this book. Demonstrating how IP-based technology can facilitate the processes is the crux of this book. The challenge now is to activate this model.

Will IP be replaced? Intelligence is certainly moving down to the physical layer in the service provider backbone. For example, optical networking is becoming a more widely adopted transmission technology because of the bandwidth problems it solves. With the rapid emergence of optical networking technology, IP is seen as the protocol that will run directly over an optical transport network like DWDM with an IP-based control plane (GMPLS) used to control the optical networks. This reduces the overhead of the intermediate layers, like SONET/SDH and ATM, and helps to speed up the emergence of IP as a protocol that runs over an optical network.

A consolidation in the industry will precipitate the deployment of IP-based services. The reality is that existing service providers need to reach profitability, funding for new players is lacking, and only a few large suppliers will exist as a result of industry shakeouts. It is not enough to provide innovative hardware but rather IP-based OSS architecture. Given the drive for the supplier requirements for "critical mass," efficiency in research and development, and sales and product depth, coupled with tighter capital markets, the industry will be more concentrated in this consolidation trend, that is toward IP-based solutions in products. IP-based technology will play a key role in this effort.

The most important characteristic of IP is that it is an open protocol, and as a result, it is commonly used in day-to-day operations, whether looking at real-time stock quotes or sharing a presentation via the Web. The future of IP looks good. If anything, for a service provider, the transmission layers like ATM, frame relay, and SONET that exist between IP and the physical layer will be collapsed to a maximum of two; IP will be one of these layers, and the physical layer will be an optical network.

Finally, looking forward, we see how the Web has been a key beneficiary of IP. The Web is an information resource for the world in all areas. For example, the medical profession is using the Web for research, while patients use it to search for information on diseases.

IP-based technology is changing the way people learn: universities and corporations are using it to develop and deploy e-training for customers and employees. Lectures and information are literally being brought to the home, thus eliminating the requirement to physically be at a location to receive information. Developing countries are exploring IP-based technology for information sharing and training in companies and schools. Society is now electronic, an e-society using IP-based technology for communication and information. All of this presents opportunities for service providers. While IP-based technology does not replace the value of human-to-human communication, it can facilitate the way people work and learn by making content available when and where people need it.

We anticipate that the next service you will develop and use will be based on IP. We wish you a successful journey designing and implementing IP-based services!

Acronyms

3G	third-generation wireless network
AAL	ATM adaptation layer
ABR	available bit rate
ADM	add-drop multiplexer
ADPCM	adaptive differential pulse code modulation
ADSL	asymmetric digital subscriber line
AH	authentication header
APS	automatic protection switching
ARP	address resolution protocol
ARPANET	Advanced Research Projects Agency Network
ASN	Abstract Syntex Notation
ASP	application service provider
ATM	asynchronous transfer mode
B2B	business-to-business
B2C	business-to-consumer
BBAC	Bandwidth Broker Advisory Council

BECN	backward explicit congestion notification
BGP	border gateway protocol
BRI	basic rate interface
BSS	Business Support System
CAC	call admission control
CAP	carrierless amplitude and phase
CATV	cable television
CBDS	connectionless broadband data service
CBT	core-based tree
CDMA	code-division multiple access
CDPD	cellular digital packet data
CE	customer edge
CELP	code-excited linear prediction
CEO	chief executive officer
CIR	committed information rate
CLEC	competitive local exchange carrier
CLI	command line interface
CLNS	Connectionless Network Service
CLP	congestion loss priority
CODECs	coder-decoders
CoS	class of service
CPE	customer-premises equipment
CRC	cyclic redundancy checksum
CRM	customer relationship management
CSMA/CD	Carrier Sense Multiple Access with Collision Detection
CSP	content service provider
CU	currently unused
DARPA	Defense Advanced Research Projects Agency
DCE	data circuit-terminating equipment
DDP	Datagram-Delivery Protocol
DES	data encryption standard
DHCP	dynamic host configuration protocol
DLCI	datalink connection identifier

DMT	discrete multitone
DOCSIS	data-over-cable service interface
DoS	denial of service
DSCP	differentiated services code point
DSL	digital subscriber line
DTE	data terminal equipment
DVMRP	distance vector multicast routing protocol
DWDM	dense wavelength-division multiplexing
EHDR	extended MAC header
EPD	early packet discard
ERP	enterprise resource planning
ESP	encapsulated security payload
ETTB	Ethernet to the business
ETTH	Ethernet to the home
EVA	economic value-added
FC	frame control
FCS	frame check sequence
FDDI	fiber distributed data interface
FDMA	frequency-division multiple access
FECN	forward explicit congestion notification
FIB	forwarding information base
FoIP	fax-over-IP
FR	frame relay
GFC	generic flow control
GMPLS	generalized multiprotocol label switching
GRE	generic routing encapsulation
GSM	global system for mobile communication
GSP	gaming service provider
GW	gateway
HAN	home area network
HCS	header check sequence
HDLC	high-level datalink control
HDSL	high bit-rate digital subscriber line

HEC	header error check
HFC	hybrid fiber coax
HSP	host service provider
HW	hardware
IANA	Internet-assigned number authority
ICMP	Internet Control Message Protocol
ICV	integrity check value
IETF	Internet Engineering Task Force
IGMP	Internet group management protocol
IGP	interior gateway protocol
IKE	Internet key exchange
ILEC	incumbent local exchange carrier
IP	Internet Protocol
IPD	intelligent packet discard
IPv4	Internet Protocol version 4
IPv6	Internet Protocol version 6
IPX	Internet Packet Exchange
ISAKMP	Internet security association and key management protocol
ISDN	integrated services digital network
ISI	Information Sciences Institute
IS-IS	intermediate systems-intermediate systems
ISP	Internet service provider
ISS	Internet security system
ISV	independent software vendor
IT	information technology
ITU	International Telecommunications Union
IXC	interexchange carrier
LAN	local area network
LDP	label distribution protocol
LED	light-emitting diode
LFIB	label forwarding information base
LMDS	local multipoint distribution service
LSP	label switch path

LSR	lambda switching router
MAC	media access control
MAE	metropolitan access exchange
MBGP	multicast border gateway protocol
MD5	message digest algorithm
MFG	Modified Final Judgment
MIB	management information base
MOSPF	multicast open shortest path first
MP-BGP	multiprotocol border gateway protocol
MPLS	multiprotocol label switching
MSDP	multicast source-discovery protocol
MSP	multiple switching protection
NAP	network access point
NAS	network access server
NAT	network address translation
NMS	network management system
NNI	network-to-network interface
NOC	network operations center
NPV	net present value
NSP	network service provider
NT	network termination
OC	optical carrier
OSI	open systems interconnection
OSPF	open shortest path first
OSS	operations support system
OTN	optical transport network
OXC	optical cross-connect
P	provider
PBX	private branch exchange
PC	personal computer
PCM	pulse code modulation
PDH	plesiochronous digital hierarchy
PE	provider edge

PHB	per-hop behavior
PIM-DM	protocol-independent multicast—dense mode
PIM-SM	protocol-independent multicast—spare mode
PoP	point of presence
POS	packet-over-SONET
POTS	plain old telephone service
PPP	point-to-point protocol
PRI	primary rate interface
PSTN	public-switched telephone network
PTI	payload type indicator
PTT	post, telephone, and telegraph
PVC	permanent virtual circuit
QAM	quadrature amplitude modulation
QoS	quality of service
QPSK	quadrature phase shift key
RAS	remote-access services
RBOC	regional Bell operating company
RD	route distinguisher
RFC	request for comments
RFI	request for information
RIB	routing information base
RIPE	Réseaux IP Européens
ROI	return on investment
RPF	reverse path forwarding
RSVP	resource reservation protocol
RT	route target
RTP	real-time protocol
SA	security association
SCM	supply chain management
SDH	synchronous digital hierarchy
SDSL	symmetric digital subscriber line
SHA	secure hash algorithm
SIP	session initiation protocol

SKEME	secure key-exchange mechanism
SLA	service-level agreement
SMDS	switched multimegabit data service
SMI	structure of management information
SNAP	subnetwork attachment point
SNMP	simple network management protocol
SONET	synchronous optical network
SPT	shortest path tree
SRP	spatial reuse protocol
SSP	storage service provider
STM	synchronous transport module
STS	synchronous transport signal
SVC	switched virtual circuit
SW	software
SWOT	strengths, weaknesses, opportunities, and threats
TA	terminal adaptor
TCP	transmission control protocol
TDM	time-division multiplexing
TDMA	time-division multiple access
TDP	tag distribution protocol
TE	terminal equipment
ToS	type of service
UA	user agent
UAC	user-agent client
UAS	user-agent server
UBR	unspecified bit rate
UDP	user datagram protocol
UMTS	Universal Mobile Telecommunications System
UNE	unbundled network element
UNI	user-to-network interface
URL	universal resource locator
VAN	value-added network
VBR	variable bit rate

VCI	virtual channel identifier
VDSL	very high speed subscriber line
VLAN	virtual local area network
VoIP	voice-over-IP
VPI	virtual path identifier
VPN	virtual private network
VRF	virtual routing and forwarding
VSP	vertical service provider
xSP	x service provider
WAN	wide area network
WDM	wavelength-division multiplexing
WISP	wireless Internet service provider
WSP	wireless service provider

Bibliography

Aaker, D., and G. S. Day (1990). *Marketing Research.* John Wiley & Sons.

Abstract Syntax Notation One (ASN.1) "Constraint Specification," ITU-T Rec. X.682 (1997) | ISO/IEC 8824-3:1998.

Abstract Syntax Notation One (ASN.1) "Information Object Specification," ITU-T Rec. X.681 (1997) | ISO/IEC 8824-2:1998.

Abstract Syntax Notation One (ASN.1) "Parameterization of ASN.1 Specifications," ITU-T Rec. X.683 (1997) | ISO/IEC 8824-4:1998.

Abstract Syntax Notation One (ASN.1) "Specification of Basic Notation," ITU-T Rec. X.680 (1997) | ISO/IEC 8824-1:1998.

Baker, F., C. Iturralde, F. Le Faucheur, and B. Davie (2001). "Aggregation of RSVP for IPv4 and IPv6 Reservations," RFC 3175, September.

Banerjee, A., J. Drake, J. P. Lang, B. Turner, K. Kompella, and Y. Rekhter (2001a). "Generalized Multiprotocol Label Switching: An Overview of Routing and Management Enhancements," IEEE Communications, January.

Banerjee, A., J. Drake, J. P. Lang, B. Turner, K. Kompella, and Y. Rekhter (2001b) "Generalized Multiprotocol Label Switching: An Overview of Signaling Enhancements and Recovery Techniques," IEEE Communications, January.

Black, U. (1993). *Emerging Communications Technologies.* Prentice Hall.

Blake, S., D. Black, M. Carlson, E. Davies, Z. Wang, and W. Weiss (1998). "An Architecture for Differentiated Service," RFC 2475, December.

Braden, R., L. Zhang, S. Berson, S. Herzog, and S. Jamin (1997). "Resource ReSer-Vation Protocol (RSVP)—Version 1 Functional Specification," RFC 2205, September.

Burris, A. (2002). *Service Provider Strategy Proven Secrets of XSPs*. Prentice Hall.

Case, J., R. Mundy, D. Partain, and B. Stewart (1999). "Introduction to Version 3 of the Internet-Standard Network Management Framework," RFC 2570, April.

Case, J. D., M. Fedor, M. L. Schoffstall, and C. Davin (1990). "Simple Network Management Protocol (SNMP)," RFC 1157, May.

Cavanaugh, J. P. (1998). *Frame Relay Applications Business and Technology Case Studies*. Morgan Kaufmann Publishers.

Comer, D. (1995). *Internetworking with TCP/IP, Vol. 1: Principles, Protocols and Architecture*. Prentice Hall.

Davidson, J., and J. Peters (2000). *Voice over IP Fundamentals*. Cisco Press.

Davie, B., and Y. Rekhter (2000). *MPLS Technology and Applications*. Morgan Kaufmann Publishers.

Doraswarmy, N., and D. Harkins (1999). *IPSec, the New Security Standard for the Internet, Intranets, and Virtual Private Networks*. Prentice Hall.

Downes, K., M. Ford, H. K. Lew, S. Spanier, and T. Stevenson (1998). *Internetworking Technologies Handbook*, 2nd ed. Macmillan Technical Publishing.

Ginsburg, D. (1990). *Implementing ADSL*. Addison Wesley Longman.

Guichard, J., and I. Pepelnjak (2001). *MPLS and VPN Architectures*. Cisco Press.

Harkins, D., and D. Carrel (1998). "The Internet Key Exchange (IKE)," RFC 2209, November.

Heinanen, J. (1993). "Multiprotocol Encapsulation over ATM Adaptation Layer 5," RFC 1483, July.

Heinanen, J., F. Baker, W. Weiss, and J. Wroclawski (1999). "Assured Forwarding PHB Group," RFC 2597, June.

Jacobson, V., K. Nichols, and K. Poduri (1999). "An Expedited Forwarding PHB," RFC 2598, June.

Kent, S., and R. Atkinson (1998). "IP Authentication Header," RFC 2202, November.

Kent, S., and R. Atkinson (1998). "IP Encapsulating Security Payload (ESP)," RFC 2206, November.

Kikki, K. (1999). *Differentiated Services for the Internet*. Macmillan.

Koller, R., A. Arrigoni, R. Faes, and G. Schiller (2001). *Der Service Provider Guide*. Switzerland: B. Com International.

Malis, A., and W. Simpson (1999). "PPP over SONET," RFC 2615, June.

Maughan, D., M. Schertler, M. Schneider, and J. Turner (1998). "Internet Security Association and Key Management Protocol (ISAKMP)," RFC 2208, November.

Muller, N. (2000). *IP Convergence: The Next Revolution in Telecommunications*. Artech House.

Nichols, K., S. Blake, F. Baker, and D. Black (1998). "Definition of the Differentiated Services Field (DS Field) in the IPv4 and IPv6 Headers," RFC 2474, December.

Peter, J. P., and J. H. Donnelly, Jr. (1992). *Marketing Management*. Richard D. Irwin.

Postel, J. (1981). "Internet Control Message Protocol," RFC 792, September.

Rose, M. T., and K. McCloghrie (1990). "Structure and Identification of Management Information for TCP/IP-Based Internets," RFC 1155, May.

Rosen, E., and Y. Rekhter (1999). "BGP/MPLS VPNs," RFC 2547, March.

Shepard, S. (2001). *Optical Networking Crash Course*. McGraw-Hill.

Stallings, W. (1998). *SNMP, SNMPv2, SNMPv3, and RMON 1 and 2,* 3rd ed. Addison Wesley Longman.

Taylor, E. (2000). *Networking Handbook,* McGraw-Hill.

Tomsu, P., and C. Schmutzer (2001). *Next Generation Optical Networks,* Prentice Hall.

Tsiang, D., and G. Suwala (2000). "The Cisco SRP MAC Layer Protocol," RFC 2892, August.

Vegesna, S. (2001). *IP Quality of Service,* Cisco Press.

Vijayananda, K. (1996). "A Framework for Diagnosis of Faults in Communication Protocols," Ph.D. thesis, Swiss Federal Institute of Technology, Lausanne, Switzerland.

Walker, O., H. W. Boyd, Jr., and J.-C. Larnéché (1992). *Marketing Strategy Planning and Implementation.* Richard D. Irwin.

Wang, Z. (2001). *Internet QoS, Architectures and Mechanisms for Quality of Service.* Morgan Kaufmann Publishers.

Wijnen, B., D. Harrington, and R. Presuhn (1999). "An Architecture for Describing SNMP Management Frameworks," RFC 2571, April.

Williamson, B. (2002). *Developing Multicast Networks,* Vol. 1. Cisco Press.

Wroclawski, J. (1997). "The Use of RSVP with IETF Integrated Services," RFC 2210, September.

Index

Symbols and Numbers

λ-Networking, Inc. *See* Greenfield service provider case study (conceptual)

1Disk, 38

3DES, 191

A

AAL1 to AAL5 (ATM adaptation layers), 109–110

Abstract Syntax Notation (ASN), 139, 143

access control service (SNMPv3), 146–147

access methods for network management, 159–160

access networks
defined, 80
in Greenfield case study, 233–234
overview, 81–82
POS in, 99
QoS requirements and, 82

acronyms, glossary of, 285–292

activation of services, 151

ADMs (add-drop multiplexers) in POS, 96

ADPCM (adaptive differential pulse code modulation), 182

ADSL (asymmetric digital subscriber line)
aggregation, 116, 117
data encapsulation, 116, 117
multiservices using, 132, 133
service creation, 132, 133
summary of features, 121–122

technology, 115
transport mechanism, 115–116

Advanced Research Projects Agency Network (ARPANET), 2

advertising in marketing plan, 43

aggregatable global address (IPv6), 201

aggregation
ADSL for, 116, 117
ATM for, 112–113, 133, 134
Ethernet for, 103–105, 106
frame relay for, 106, 108

AH (authentication header) for IPSec, 192–193

A-law PCM, 182

alternative technologies
Greenfield case study, 229–230
for Greenfield service providers, 48–49
incumbent case study (conceptual), 249
for incumbent service providers, 65
in Meta Telecom case study, 270

Amazon.com, 39

America Online (AOL), 39

anycast addresses (IPv6), 201–202

any-to-any connectivity, 8

AOL Time Warner, 4, 36

application-layer services
IP network for data delivery, 79
QoS requirements, 77–78

ARPANET (Advanced Research Projects Agency Network), 2

ASN (Abstract Syntax Notation), 139, 143
ASPs (application service providers), 37
asymmetric digital subscriber line. *See* ADSL (asymmetric digital subscriber line)
AT&T, 39
ATM (asynchronous transfer mode)
    adaptation layers, 109–110
    as ADSL transport mechanism, 115–116, 117
    aggregation, 112–113, 133, 134
    cell, 108–109
    for Greenfield service providers, 48–49
    for incumbent service providers, 61, 65
    IP-based services as unsuitable for, 2–3
    Layer 3 routing capabilities on switches, 70
    multiservices using, 133
    overview, 108
    QoS, 134–135
    service classes, 112
    service creation, 133–135
    summary of features, 121–122
    switching, 110–111
    traffic management, 112
authentication
    IPSec, 190–192
    key exchange, 191–192
    SNMPv3 service, 146–147
authentication header (AH) for IPSec, 190, 192–193
autoconfiguration in IPv6, 205
automation
    in incumbent case study (conceptual), 251–252
    IP for, 282
    as OSS requirement, 165–166
    service development and, 27, 28–29
    of service implementation, 28, 165–166
    of service upgrades, 29
availability, 8

B

B2B (business-to-business), 33, 53–54
B2C (business-to-consumer), 33, 53–54
Baby Bells, 62
bandwidth. *See also* guaranteed bandwidth
    defined, 172
    Web hosting requirements, 52–53
Bandwidth Broker Advisory Council (BBAC), 37
bandwidth brokers, 5, 37. *See also* Greenfield service providers
bandwidth management, MPLS for, 124
bandwidth-on-demand, 219
Baran, Paul, 2
base station (LMDS), 209
basic rate interface (BRI), 114
BBAC (Bandwidth Broker Advisory Council), 37
best-effort services, 7, 78
Birch Telecom, 36
BlueStep, 39–40
BRI (basic rate interface), 114
budget in Greenfield service provider marketing plan, 43
bundled services, 5–6

business case
    draft of, 16
    factors, 18
    full, 17
    preliminary, 17
    scope of deliverables and, 27–28
business model, as vendor requirement, 45
business viability, as vendor requirement, 45
business-to-business (B2B), 33, 53–54
business-to-consumer (B2C), 33, 53–54

C

cable access networks
    components, 118
    data over cable modem, 120–121
    data-over-cable service interface (DOCSIS), 119–120
    frame control (FC) field, 119–120
    hybrid fiber/coax (HFC) systems, 118
    MAC_PARM field, 120
    multiservices using, 132, 134
    overview, 116, 118
    quadrature amplitude modulation (QAM), 119
    quadrature phase shift key (QPSK) modulation, 119
    service creation, 132, 134
    technology, 118–119
    transport technology, 119–120
cable companies, 4, 36
cable television networks. *See* cable access networks
CAC (call admission control), MPLS for, 85
cap and grow strategy, 70
CAP (carrierless amplitude and phase), 115
capability statements (SNMPv2), 145
capacity planning, network statistics for, 158
case studies. *See also specific case studies*
    Greenfield service provider (conceptual), 222–241
    incumbent service provider (conceptual), 241–254
    Meta Telecom (real-life incumbent), 254–276
CATV networks. *See* cable access networks
CBTs (core-based trees), 95
CE (customer edge) device, 88
CELP (code-excited linear prediction) voice compression, 182
CEO responsibilities, 20
challenges
    for Greenfield service providers, 48–49
    for incumbent service providers, 72
classification (QoS), 177–178
CLECs (competitive local exchange carriers), 4–5, 36. *See also* Greenfield service providers
CLI (command line interface), 153–154, 160
CLP (congestion loss priority), 108
cMeRun, 37
code-excited linear prediction (CELP) voice compression, 182
communication protocols for network management, 159–160

company performance
Greenfield case study, 229
incumbent case study (conceptual), 249
competition
for Greenfield service providers, 41, 59
in marketing plan, 41
competitive local exchange carriers (CLECs), 4–5,
36. *See also* Greenfield service providers
configuring. *See also* network device configuration
CPE devices, 149–150, 151–153
devices in incumbent case study (conceptual),
252
network devices, 150–155
congestion avoidance techniques, 178
congestion loss priority (CLP), 108
congestion management, 178
connectivity, 6, 8
content service providers (CSPs), 39
control component of network layer routing,
82–83
control plane of optical networks, 214
controls in Greenfield service provider marketing
plan, 43
convergence of voice and data, 31, 187–188
Conxion, 38
Coradiant, 38
core network
defined, 80
in Greenfield case study, 235–236
optical networking application, 219
overview, 80–81
POS application, 97
scalable, 10
core-based trees (CBTs), 95
Corio, 37
cost. *See* pricing
counter data type (SNMP), 143
CPE (customer-premises equipment)
configuring devices, 149–150, 151–153
installing devices, 149–150
IP access network and, 81–82
IP core network independence, 80–81
IP edge network and, 81
LMDS configurations, 209–210
service activation and, 151
Craig Wireless International, 39
creating services. *See* service creation
CRM (customer relationship management), 31
CSPs (content service providers), 39
customer edge (CE) device, 88
customer order process, 41
customer profile
for Greenfield service providers, 43–44
for incumbent service providers, 64
customer requirements
connectivity, 6
as drivers for service development, 19
in Greenfield case study, 224–225
for Greenfield service providers, 44
guaranteed bandwidth, 7, 169–170

high availability, 8
in incumbent case study (conceptual), 243
for incumbent service providers, 64
in Meta Telecom case study, 256–258
multiservices, 8
overview, 6–10, 279–280
privacy, 170
QoS, 7, 169–170
sample customer and requirements, 8–10
security, 7–8, 44, 170
service-level agreement reports, 8
throughput, 6–7
for Web hosting, 52–53
customer service for Web hosting, 53
customer-premises equipment. *See* CPE (customer-
premises equipment)
customers. *See also* customer requirements
benefits as driver for IP-based services, 31
profiles, 43–44, 64
as service development participants, 18
service development politics and, 22
service implementation and, 147–148

D
DARPA (Department of Defense Advanced Research
Projects Agency), 1
data circuit-terminating equipment (DCE), 104,
106
data distribution, 91–92
data encapsulation
ADSL, 116, 117
Ethernet, 103
ISDN, 114–115
data encryption standard (DES), 191
data forwarding in MPLS-VPNs, 88–89, 90
data security, 7–8, 44. *See also* security
data terminal equipment (DTE), 104, 106
data types (SNMPv1), 143–144
database information, provisioning and, 155
database system for OSS, 162, 164
datalink layer. *See* Layer 2
data-over-cable service interface (DOCSIS), 119–120
DCE (data circuit-terminating equipment), 104,
106
delay
defined, 78, 169
end-to-end, 78–79, 173
factors affecting, 78
minimal, as customer requirement, 7
propagation delay, 173
serialization or transmission delay, 173
switching delay, 173
video application requirements, 169–170
voice-over-IP requirements, 169, 180
delay variation (jitter)
defined, 78, 169, 173
minimal, as customer requirement, 7
queuing mechanisms for minimizing, 173
video application requirements, 169–170
voice-over-IP requirements, 169, 180

dense wavelength-division multiplexing (DWDM), 96, 212–213. *See also* optical networking

dense-mode protocols, 94, 95

Department of Defense Advanced Research Projects Agency (DARPA), 1

deployment time, 10

DES (data encryption standard), 191

development. *See* product development; service development

dial-up Internet access, 36

differentiated services code point (DSCP), 175–176

DiffServ (differentiated services model for QoS), 175–177

architecture, 176–177

described, 172

DSCP for, 175–176

IntServ vs., 177

PHB functions, 176

service creation, 179

traffic conditioners, 176

disclosure (SNMPv2 security issue), 146

disk space, Web hosting requirements, 53

DMT (discrete multitone), 115

DOCSIS (data-over-cable service interface), 119–120

Dorado.com, 40

DSCP (differentiated services code point), 175–176

DSL (digital subscriber line). *See also* ADSL (asymmetric digital subscriber line)

ADSL, 115–116, 121–122

as CLEC service, 36

for Greenfield service providers, 48–49

HDSL, 115

for incumbent service providers, 65

IP-based services as unsuitable for, 2–3

overview, 115

SDSL, 115

summary of features, 121–122

VDSL, 115

DTE (data terminal equipment), 104, 106

DWDM (dense wavelength-division multiplexing), 96, 212–213. *See also* optical networking

E

EarthLink, 39

e-commerce portal service, 53–54, 57–58

e-commerce service providers, 39

economic value-added (EVA), 36

edge application of POS, 97, 98–99

edge networks

defined, 80

in Greenfield case study, 234–235

overview, 81

scalable, 10

EMC, 38

encapsulated security payload (ESP), 190, 193–194

encryption (IPSec), 191–192, 193

end-to-end delay, 78–79, 173

end-to-end QoS, 171

end-to-end service ownership, 44

engineering department responsibilities, 21

ERP (enterprise resource planning), 1, 37

error detection and troubleshooting, statistics for, 158

error logs, network, 157–158

ESP (encapsulated security payload), 190, 193–194

Ethernet

aggregation, 103–105, 106

data encapsulation, 103

frame formats, 103

overview, 102

POS vs., 235

summary of features, 121–122

switches, 103–104

transmission technology, 102

for VLANs, 103–104, 105

ETTB (Ethernet to the business), 32

ETTH (Ethernet to the home), 32

EVA (economic value-added), 36

evolutionary strategy for legacy infrastructure, 70–72

extranets, MPLS-VPNs for, 131–132

F

FDDI, 99

feedback loop for product and service development, 47–48

FIB (forwarding information base), 123–124

financial department responsibilities, 21

flood-and-prune principle, 95

forwarding. *See also* routing

in conventional IP networks, 83

in MPLS, 83

multicast, 92–94

overview, 82

reverse path (RPF), 93–94

forwarding plane of optical networks, 214

frame formats for Ethernet, 103

frame relay. *See also* Meta Telecom case study

aggregation, 106, 108

devices, 104

for Greenfield service providers, 48–49

for incumbent service providers, 65

LAN connection-over-frame relay, 32

managed IP-VPN service vs., 66

overview, 104

service features, 106

summary of features, 121–122

switching, 104, 106

virtual circuits, 104

G

G.711 voice coding standard (PCM), 181–182

G.723.1 voice coding standard (audio compression), 182

G.726 voice coding standard (ADPCM), 182

G.728 voice coding standard (CELP), 182

G.729 voice coding standard (CELP), 182

gaming service providers (GSPs), 39

gatekeeper function in H.323, 183

gateway function in H.323, 183–184

gauge data type (SNMP), 143
generalized multiprotocol label switching (GMPLS), 213, 217–218
generic flow control (GFC), 108
Genuity, 39
geographic reach, 64
Get operation (SNMP), 144, 145, 159
GetBulk operation (SNMP), 145
GetNext operation (SNMP), 144, 145
GFC (generic flow control), 108
global unicast addresses (IPv6), 201
glossary of acronyms, 285–292
GMPLS (generalized multiprotocol label switching), 213, 217–218
goals
    marketing, 42, 63
    of service providers, 10–11, 42, 63, 281
    of vendors, 11–12
grafting, 95
Greenfield, defined, 5, 35
Greenfield service provider case study (conceptual), 222–241
    access network, 233–234
    alternatives considered, 229–230
    background, 223–224
    business aspects, 224–227
    company performance, 229
    conclusion, 241
    core network, 235–236
    customer requirements, 224–225
    edge network, 234–235
    future plans, 240–241
    lessons learned, 240
    network architecture, 232–236
    network management and operations, 238
    overview, 222–223
    project risk assessment, 240
    service implementation model, 228–229, 239–240
    services, 227–228
    strategic objectives, 225–227
    technical aspects, 231–240
    technologies supporting service creation, 236–238
    vendor selection process, 230–231
Greenfield service providers. *See also specific types*
    alternative technologies, 48–49
    business aspects, 40–49
    challenges, 58–59
    common characteristic of, 40
    competition, 41, 59
    conceptual case study, 222–241
    customer profile and requirements, 43–44
    defined, 4, 5, 35–36
    feedback loop, 47–48
    IP-based services' applicability for, 34
    marketing plan, 40–43
    overview, 35–40
    request for information (RFI), 46, 47
    service creation model, 49
    service examples, 49–54

    service packaging and pricing, 54–58
    single-vendor vs. multiple-vendor strategies, 46–47
    types, 36–40
    value-added services from, 36
    vendor profile and requirements, 44–45
    vendor selection process, 45–47
    vendor strategy, 46–47
group membership in multicast communication, 92, 94
group mobbing, 22
GSPs (gaming service providers), 39
guaranteed bandwidth
    as customer requirement, 7, 169–170
    at datalink layer, 172–173
    end-to-end, for video applications, 169–170
    at IP layer, 172
    MPLS for, 124, 127, 128
    service implementation, 151, 152

H

H.323 protocol, 180, 183–184
hardware upgrades, network management for, 158–159
HDLC (high-level datalink control), 96
HDSL (high bit-rate digital subscriber line), 115
header error check (HEC), 108
HEC (header error check), 108
HFC (hybrid fiber/coax) systems, 118
hierarchical networks, MPLS for, 85, 86
high availability, 8
high bit-rate digital subscriber line (HDSL), 115
high-level datalink control (HDLC), 96
history
    events fostering IP-based services, 3–4
    of IP, 1–2
horizontal B2B sites, 53–54
Hostway, 38
HSPs (host service providers), 38
hybrid fiber/coax (HFC) systems, 118

I

IANA (Internet Assigned Number Authority), 199
ICV (integrity check value), 190
IGMP (Internet group management protocol), 94
IKE (Internet key exchange), 190
ILECs (incumbent local exchange carriers). *See also* incumbent service providers
    described, 4–5
    as incumbent service providers, 62
    local loop and, 36
implementation. *See* service implementation
in-band network management, 161–162
incumbent PTTs, 4, 62. *See also* incumbent service providers
incumbent service provider case study (conceptual), 241–254
    alternatives considered, 249
    background, 241–242
    business aspects, 242–245

incumbent service provider case study (conceptual)
  (*continued*)
    company performance, 249
    conclusion, 254
    customer requirements, 243
    future plans, 254
    IP-based solution, 245
    lessons learned, 253
    network architecture, 250–251
    OSS architecture, 251–253
    overview, 241
    project risk assessment, 253
    service implementation model, 247–249
    services, 245–247
    strategic objectives, 244–245
    technical aspects, 250–253
    vendor selection process, 250
incumbent service provider case study (real-life).
    See Meta Telecom case study
incumbent service providers
    alternative technologies, 65
    business aspects, 62–65
    case study (conceptual), 241–254
    case study (Meta Telecom), 254–276
    challenges, 72
    customer profile and requirements, 64
    defined, 62
    described, 4–5
    as Greenfield service provider competition, 59
    IP-based services' applicability for, 34
    legacy infrastructure strategies, 70–72
    marketing plan, 62–64
    networks, 61
    service creation model, 65–66
    service examples, 66–68
    service packaging and pricing, 68–70
    vendor profile and selection, 64–65
independent software vendors (ISVs), 37
InetU, 38
Inform operation (SNMP), 145
information modification (SNMPv2 security issue),
    146
installing CPE devices, 149–150
integer data types (SNMP), 143, 144
integrated overlay and IP peer model for optical
    networking, 217
integrated services digital network. *See* ISDN (inte-
    grated services digital network)
integrated services model for QoS. *See* IntServ (inte-
    grated services model for QoS)
integrity check value (ICV), 190
InteQ, 38
interdomain protocols, 95
interexchange carriers (IXCs), 5, 62. *See also*
    Greenfield service providers
Interland, 38
Internet
    history, 1–2
    Telecommunications Act of 1996 and, 3
Internet Assigned Number Authority (IANA), 199
Internet group management protocol (IGMP), 94

Internet key exchange (IKE), 190
Internet Protocol. *See* IP (Internet Protocol)
Internet security association and key management
    protocol (ISAKMP), 190, 191
Internet Security Systems, 38
Internet service providers (ISPs), 39
Internet services on IP-VPN backbone, 77
Internet2 Initiative, 37
intranets, MPLS-VPNs for, 131–132
IntServ (integrated services model for QoS)
    described, 172, 174
    DiffServ vs., 177
    drawbacks, 174–175
    RSVP for, 174
    for voice-over-IP, 175
Invesmart, 40
IP addresses
    aggregatable global (IPv6), 201
    anycast (IPv6), 201–202
    global unicast (IPv6), 201
    IPv4 space limitations, 170, 199
    IPv4-compatible with IPv6, 201, 202
    IPv6 addressing, 200–203
    link-local (IPv6), 201, 202
    multicast, 92, 93, 94, 95, 203
    site-local (IPv6), 201, 202
    unicast (IPv6), 200–201
    unicast vs. multicast, 92
IP Communications, 4, 36
IP (Internet Protocol). *See also* IPv4; IPv6
    best-effort service using, 7, 78
    future of, 282–283
    history of, 1–2
    IPv4, 170, 197
    IPv6, 170, 199–208
    open protocol advantages, 282–283
    optical networking and, 213–218
    role in service development, 27–29
    services not suitable for, 2–3
    time-sensitive applications and, 7
IP layer, guaranteed bandwidth at, 172
IP networks
    access network, 80, 81–82
    architectural overview, 80–82
    core network, 80–81
    edge network, 80, 81
    QoS in, 171–172, 177–179
IP security. *See* IPSec (IP security)
IP state, transition state vs., 23
IP-based services
    bundled vs. unbundled, 5–6
    customer benefits as driver for, 31
    customer requirements, 6–10
    drivers motivating, 29–32
    examples, 5, 32–33
    history of events fostering, 3–4
    multiservices, 77, 280–281
    service provider goals, 10–11
    service provider motivations for, 30–31
    vendor goals, 11–12
    vendor interest as driver for, 32

IPSec (IP security), 189–199
  advantages, 198
  authentication, 190–191
  authentication header (AH), 190, 192–193
  encapsulated security payload (ESP), 190,
    193–194
  encryption, 191
  in Greenfield case study, 236–237
  how it works, 195–198
  IKE, 190
  ISAKMP, 190, 191
  key exchange, 191–192
  MPLS-VPNs vs. IP-VPNs, 198–199
  RFCs, 189–190
  router to firewall security, 195–196, 197
  security associations (SAs), 190, 192, 194–195,
    196
  services offered by, 189
IPv4. *See also* IP (Internet Protocol)
  address space limitations, 170, 199
  IPSec and, 197
  IPv4-compatible IPv6 address, 201, 202
  migration to IPv6, 207–208
  packet header, 203, 204
IPv6, 199–208. *See also* IP (Internet Protocol)
  advantages, 204–207
  anycast addresses, 201–202
  autoconfiguration, 205
  development of, 199–200
  drawbacks, 207
  features, 200–204
  global unicast addresses, 201
  IPv4 address space limitations and, 170
  IPv4-compatible addresses, 201, 202
  link-local addresses, 201, 202
  migration strategy, 207–208
  Mobile IP and, 206
  multicast addresses, 203
  multihomed sites, 206
  packet header, 203–204, 205
  prefix aggregation, 206
  security, 206
  service creation, 208
  site-local addresses, 201, 202
  unicast addresses, 200–201
IP-VPNs. *See also* MPLS-VPNs
  cost as factor for, 50–51, 52
  enhancements, 55, 56, 68–69
  with Greenfield service providers, 50–51,
    55–56
  with incumbent service providers, 66–67
  as IP-based service example, 32
  Layer 2 networks and, 77
  MPLS-VPNs vs., 198–199
  remote-access, for telecommuting, 50–51, 52,
    55–56
  service packaging and pricing, 55–56, 68–69
  as ubiquitous IP plug, 67
ISAKMP (Internet security association and key
    management protocol), 190, 191
ISDN (integrated services digital network)
    basic rate interface (BRI), 114
    as CLEC service, 36
    components, 113–114
    data encapsulation, 114–115
    for Greenfield service providers, 48–49
    IP-based services as unsuitable for, 2–3
    overview, 113
    primary rate interface (PRI), 114
    summary of features, 121–122
    traffic management, 114–115
ISPs (Internet service providers), 39
ISVs (independent software vendors), 37
IXCs (interexchange carriers), 5, 62. *See also*
    Greenfield service providers

J
jitter. *See* delay variation (jitter)
join mechanism, 95

K
key exchange (IPSec), 191–192

L
label distribution protocol (LDP), 83
label forwarding information base (LFIB) table, 83
label switch path (LSP), 87
λ-Networking, Inc. *See* Greenfield service provider
    case study (conceptual)
LAN connection-over-frame relay, 32. *See also* Meta
    Telecom case study
LAN connection-over-IP, 32. *See also* Meta Telecom
    case study
last mile (local loop), 3, 36, 62
latency. *See* delay
Layer 2
    guaranteed bandwidth at, 172–173
    QoS at, 173–174
Layer 2 networks
    for Greenfield service providers, 48–49
    IP connectivity over, 76–77, 280
    IP-based services as unsuitable for, 2–3
    multiservices, 76–77
Layer 3 networks
    routing capabilities on ATM switches, 70
    VPNs, 280
LDP (label distribution protocol), 83
leased lines
    for Greenfield service providers, 48–49
    for incumbent service providers, 65
LEDs (light-emitting diodes), 210
legacy infrastructure, 70–72
    adding IP-based features, 70
    building new IP-based network infrastructure,
      70
    cap and grow strategy, 70
    evolutionary strategy, 70–72
legacy organizations
    defined, 21
    service development politics and, 21–22, 23
Level3 Communications, as NSP example, 39
LFIB (label forwarding information base) table, 83

life cycles
    management as vendor requirement for
       Greenfield service providers, 45
    product, 23–25
    service, 20
light-emitting diodes (LEDs), 210
link capacity (throughput), 6–7
link utilization, statistics for reporting, 158
link-local address (IPv6), 201, 202
link-state protocols, 95
LiveVault, 38
LMDS (local multipoint distribution service)
    advantages, 210
    base station, 209
    components, 208–210
    CPE configurations, 209–210
    described, 208
    origin of acronym, 208
local loop, 3, 36, 62
local telephone service, 36
location servers for SIP, 185
LSP (label switch path), 87

M

MAC (media access control)
    in cable access networks, 119–120
    SRP as MAC-layer protocol, 100
MAEs (metropolitan access exchanges), 39
managed devices in SNMP, 140
managed IP-VPNs. *See* IP-VPNs
ManagedStorage International, 38
management service providers (MSPs), 37–38
marketing plan
    budget, 43
    controls, 43
    goals, 42, 63
    for Greenfield service providers, 40–43
    importance of, 40
    for incumbent service providers, 62–64
    plan summary, 41
    sections, 41
    situational review, 41
    strategic opportunities and threats, 41–42
    strategy, 42–43, 63–64
masquerading (SNMPv2 security issue), 146
MBGP (multicast border gateway protocol), 95
media access control. *See* MAC (media access
    control)
menu-driven CLI for configuring network devices,
    153–154
merging voice and data networks, 31, 187–188
message authentication code, 190
message sequence modification (SNMPv2 security
    issue), 146
Meta Telecom case study, 254–276
    alternatives considered, 270
    background, 254–255
    business aspects, 255–259
    business engineering for IP-based services, 271
    conclusion, 276

    customer connection forecasts and revenue esti-
       mate, 267
    customer requirements, 256–258
    domestic service trends, 266
    financial aspects, 264–269
    future plans, 276
    high-level ROI analysis, 266
    IP-based solution, 261–262
    LAN connection-over-frame relay, 256, 257, 259
    LAN connection-over-IP, 267–268
    lessons learned, 276
    managed LAN connection-over-IP price model,
       267
    Meta network, 258–259
    network architecture, 272
    network infrastructure for convergence, 259
    network management and operations, 260–261,
       272–274
    network monitoring, 274
    OSS architecture, 259, 268, 274–275
    OSS cost savings breakout, 268
    overview, 254
    positioning of IP service products, 265
    project execution and results, 269–270
    project risk assessment, 275–276
    scalability, 259
    service implementation and provisioning,
       273–274
    service implementation model, 270
    service time-to-market, 258
    services, 255, 262–269
    SLA reporting, 274
    technical aspects, 259–261, 272–275
    vendor selection process, 270, 272
    Web-based tools, 275
    wider market, 258–259
method to contract new customers, in marketing
    plan, 43
metro network, 97, 99, 219
metropolitan access exchanges (MAEs), 39
MFJ (Modified Final Judgment), 3
MIB (management information base)
    defined, 140
    managed objects, 141
    overview, 141
    sample tree, 141–142
    SNMP agent and, 139
    SNMPv1 MIB tables, 144
    SNMPv2 MIB modules, 145
Microsoft, 39
migration to IPv6, 207–208
MKL.Net, 39
Mobile IP, IPv6 and, 206
modification of information (SNMPv2 security
    issue), 146
Modified Final Judgment (MFJ), 3
monitoring network devices
    in Meta Telecom case study, 274
    OSS tools for, 164, 165
    proactive, 157, 158

reactive, 156–157
service windows and, 157
MOSPF (multicast open shortest path first), 95
MP-BGP (multiprotocol border gateway protocol), 88
MPLS (multiprotocol label switching)
  advantages, 84–87
  development of, 24
  DSCP and, 175–176
  in Greenfield case study, 236
  for hierarchical networks, 85, 86
  label forwarding information base (LFIB) table, 83
  multiservices using, 123–127, 128
  operation, 83–84
  overview, 82–83, 84
  packet switching, 124, 125
  protocols, 83
  for QoS, 87, 127
  scalable core, 123
  service creation, 123–127, 128
  stable core, 123–124
  for traffic engineering, 85, 124, 126–127, 128
  traffic engineering, 124, 126–127
  for VPNs, 87–89, 90
MPLS-VPNs. *See also* IP-VPNs
  customer edge (CE) device, 88
  data forwarding, 88–89, 90
  defined, 87
  extranets and intranets, 131–132
  in Greenfield case study, 236
  IP-VPNs vs., 198–199
  label switch path (LSP), 87
  MP-BGP for, 88
  MPLS for, 87–89
  multiservices using, 127, 129–132
  provider edge routers (PEs), 87
  provider router (P), 87
  route distinguisher (RD), 88
  route target (RT), 88
  scalable core network, 129–131
  security, 131
  service creation, 127, 129–132
  virtual routing and forwarding (VRF), 88
MSDP (multicast source-discovery protocol), 95
MSPs (management service providers), 37–38
MU-law PCM, 182
multicast addresses (IPv6), 203
multicast border gateway protocol (MBGP), 95
multicast communication
  advantages and disadvantages, 95
  applications, 91–92
  group membership, 92, 94
  multicast addresses, 92, 93, 94, 95, 203
  multicast forwarding, 92–94
  multicast routing, 92, 94–95
  multiservices using, 135
  overview, 89, 91
  service creation, 135
multicast open shortest path first (MOSPF), 95

multicast source-discovery protocol (MSDP), 95
multihomed sites, IPv6 and, 206
multimedia conferencing, 91
multiple-vendor vs. single-vendor strategies, 46–47
multiprotocol border gateway protocol (MP-BGP), 88
multiprotocol label switching. *See* MPLS (multiprotocol label switching)
multiservices
  ADSL for, 132, 133
  application-layer services, 77–79
  ATM for, 133
  cable technology for, 132, 134
  customer requirements, 8
  defined, 75–76, 79
  IP-based services, 77, 280–281
  Layer 2 services, 76–77
  MPLS for, 123–127, 128
  MPLS-VPNs for, 127, 129–132
  multicast for, 135
  service provider goals, 10–11
  using the same network, 10–11
  vendor goals, 12

N
NAPs (network access points), 39
NAT (network address translation), 199
NetLedger, 37
network access points (NAPs), 39
network address data type (SNMP), 143
network address translation (NAT), 199
network device configuration, 150–155
  ATM and, 150
  guaranteed bandwidth service implementation, 151, 152
  matching CPE configuration to, 150–151
  menu-driven CLI method, 153–154
  misconfiguration risks, 151–152
  overview, 150–151
  simplicity in, 153
  SNMP-based interface for, 154–155
  text-based CLI method, 153
  Web-based CLI method, 154
network devices
  configuring, 150–155
  error logs, 157–158
  monitoring, 156–157
  upgrades, 158–159
network management, 155–162. *See also* NMS (network management system); SNMP (simple network management protocol); traffic management
  activities, 156–159
  communication network for, 161–162
  communication protocols and access methods, 159–160
  error logs, 157–158
  in Greenfield case study, 238
  hardware and software upgrades, 158–159
  importance of, 138

network management (*continued*)
    in-band, 161–162
    issues, 155–156
    in Meta Telecom case study, 260–261, 272–274
    monitoring devices, 156–157
    NMS, 11, 139, 140, 156
    out-band, 162, 163
    security issues, 162
    statistical information, 158
network operations center (NOC), 11, 281
network security. *See* security
Nextel Communications, 39
NMS (network management system). *See also* SNMP
    (simple network management protocol)
    communication protocols, 159–160
    described, 139, 140, 156
    off-the-shelf systems, 156
    service provider goals, 11
NOC (network operations center), 11, 281
Novopoint, 40
NSPs (network service providers), 39
Nuclio Corporation, 38

O

Oakley key-determination protocol, 191
object ID data type (SNMP), 143
OC (optical carrier), 211
octet string data type (SNMP), 143
opaque data type (SNMP), 144
open architecture, as OSS requirement, 164
operational failures, customer requirements, 44
operations department responsibilities, 21
operations support system. *See* OSS (operations sup-
    port system)
optical carrier (OC), 211
optical cross-connects (OXCs), 213, 217
optical networking, 210–219
    applications, 218–219
    described, 210–211
    DWDM, 212–213
    GMPLS, 213
    integrated overlay and IP peer model, 217
    IP and, 213–218
    overlay model, 215–216
    peer model, 215, 216–217
    SDH, 2–3, 211
    SONET, 2–3, 211
OSI seven-layer model, 76
OSS (operations support system)
    architecture, 162, 164–166
    automation, 165–166
    business processes and interfaces, 29, 30
    components, 162, 164
    database system, 162, 164
    defined, 138
    described, 2
    in incumbent case study (conceptual), 251–253
    in Meta Telecom case study, 259, 268, 274–275
    network provisioning and monitoring tools, 164
    requirements, 164–166
    responsibilities, 149
    scalability, 164–165
    SLA reporting and billing, 164
    Web-based tools, 166
OTNs (optical transport networks). *See* optical
    networking
out-band network management, 162, 163
overlay model for optical networking, 215–216
OXCs (optical cross-connects), 213, 217

P

packaging. *See* service packaging and pricing
packet delay. *See* delay
packet header
    IPv4, 203, 204
    IPv6, 203–204, 205
packet loss, 78–79, 173
packet switching. *See also* switches and switching
    described, 2
    in MPLS, 124, 125
packet voice network, 180–181
packet-over-SONET. *See* POS (packet-over-SONET)
payload type indicator (PTI), 108
PCM (pulse code modulation), 181–182
PE (provider edge) device, 81
peer model for optical networking, 215, 216–217
PeopleSoft, 37
perfect forward secrecy, 191
permanent virtual circuits (PVCs), 104, 106, 110
PHB functions (DiffServ), 176
PIM-DM (protocol-independent multicast-dense
    mode), 84
PIM-SM (protocol-independent multicast-spare
    mode), 84
ping utility, 160
platform simplicity, 31
point-to-point protocol (PPP), 96
policing mechanisms (QoS), 178
politics in service development, 21–23
    cultural differences, 22, 23
    customers and, 22
    group mobbing, 22
    legacy organizations and, 21–22, 23
    preventing, 22
PoP (point of presence), 76–77
POS (packet-over-SONET)
    in access networks, 99
    core application, 97
    edge application, 97, 98–99
    Ethernet vs., 235
    implementations, 96–97
    metro application, 97, 99
    overview, 96
    summary of features, 121–122
positioning, in marketing plan, 42
post, telephone, and telegraph companies (PTTs), 4,
    62
PPP (point-to-point protocol), 96
prefix aggregation in IPv6, 206
PRI (primary rate interface), 114

pricing. *See also* service packaging and pricing
  for e-commerce portals, 58
  for managed IP-VPNs, 50–51, 52, 55, 56, 69
  in marketing plan, 43
  in Meta Telecom case study, 267
  for Web hosting, 53, 56–57
primary rate interface (PRI), 114
principals (SNMPv3), 146–147
privacy
  customer requirements, 170
  SNMPv3 privacy service, 146–147
privatization of telephone utilities, 3–4
proactive device monitoring, 157, 158
product development. *See also* service development
  cycle, 23–25
  feedback loop, 47–48
  market requirements and, 24
  service development and, 14, 23–25
  technology availability and, 23–24
  time-to-market products, 24
  vendor competition and, 24
product life cycle, 23–25
product management responsibilities, 20–21
products. *See* services
profiles
  customer, 43–44, 64
  vendor, 44–45, 64
project risk assessment
  Greenfield case study, 240
  incumbent case study (conceptual), 253
  in Meta Telecom case study, 275–276
propagation delay, 173. *See also* delay
protocol operations in SNMP, 144, 145
protocol-independent multicast-dense mode (PIM-DM), 84
protocol-independent multicast-spare mode (PIM-SM), 84
provider edge (PE) device, 81
provisioning, 149–155. *See also* network device configuration; service implementation
  CPE device configuration, 149–150, 151–153
  CPE device installation, 149–150
  database information, 155
  defined, 149
  easy and profitable manner for, 137
  in Meta Telecom case study, 273–274
  network device configuration, 150–155
  network management and, 138
  OSS tools for, 164, 165
  service activation, 151
  service modification, 155
  service upgrades and, 138
  simplicity and scalability in, 137–138
  tasks, 149
proxy servers for SIP, 185, 186
PSTN (public-switched telephone network), 61
PTI (payload type indicator), 108
PTTs (post, telephone, and telegraph companies), 4, 62
pull principle, 95

pulse code modulation (PCM), 181–182
PVCs (permanent virtual circuits), 104, 106, 110

Q
QAM (quadrature amplitude modulation), 119
QoS (quality-of-service), 170–179. *See also* delay; delay variation (jitter); guaranteed bandwidth
  access network and, 82
  for application-layer services, 77–78
  ATM for, 134–135
  best-effort services, 7, 78
  classification, 177–178
  congestion avoidance techniques, 178
  congestion management, 178
  customer requirements, 7, 169–170
  defined, 170–171
  differentiated services, 172
  end-to-end, 171
  in Greenfield case study, 237
  integrated services model, 172, 174–175
  in IP networks, 171–172, 177–179
  at Layer 2, 173–174
  MPLS for, 87, 127
  multiservices and, 8
  packet loss, 78–79, 173
  parameters, 172–174
  policing and shaping mechanisms, 178
  resource reservation for, 171
  scheduling mechanisms for, 171
  service creation and, 179
  signaling, 178
  standardization, 172
  transport layer (TCP) provisions, 78
  video application requirements, 169–170
  voice-over-IP requirements, 169
QPSK (quadrature phase shift key) modulation, 119
quadrature amplitude modulation (QAM), 119
queuing mechanisms for minimizing jitter, 173
Qwest, 39

R
RAND Corporation, 1–2
RBOCs (regional Bell operating companies), 3–4
RD (route distinguisher), 88
reactive device monitoring, 157–158
read command (SNMP), 141
real-life case study. *See* Meta Telecom case study
real-time data multicast, 92
redirect servers for SIP, 185
reliability
  defined, 10
  as service provider goal, 10, 281
  Web hosting requirements, 53
request for information (RFI), 46, 47
requirements, customer. *See* customer requirements
requirements, vendor. *See* vendors
Réseaux IP Européens (RIPE), 199
reseller CLECs, 36
resource reservation for QoS, 171
resource reservation protocol (RSVP), 85, 174, 175

retiring a service, 20–21
reverse path forwarding (RPF), 93–94
RFI (request for information), 46, 47
RIB (routing information base), 123–124
ring topology. *See also* SRP (spatial reuse protocol)
    FDDI, 99
    SRP, 99–102
    summary of features, 121–122
    Token Ring, 99
RIPE (Réseaux IP Européens), 199
risk assessment. *See* project risk assessment
ROI analysis of Meta Telecom, 266
route distinguisher (RD), 88
route targets (RTs), 88
routing. *See also* forwarding
    Layer 3 capabilities on ATM switches, 70
    multicast, 92, 94–95
    in optical networking, 213–214
    VRF (virtual routing and forwarding), 88
routing information base (RIB), 123–124
RPF (reverse path forwarding), 93–94
RSVP (resource reservation protocol), 85, 174, 175
RTs (route targets), 88

S
sales and marketing staff responsibilities, 20
SAs (security associations)
    authentication header and, 192
    confidentiality and, 197
    contents, 196
    overview, 194–195
    RFC, 190
    router and firewall agreement on, 196
    transport mode, 195, 196
    tunnel mode, 195, 196
    two-way communication and, 196–197
scalability
    for core networks, 10
    for edge networks, 10
    in Meta network, 259
    of MPLS core, 123
    of MPLS-VPN core network, 129–131
    as OSS requirement, 164–165
    as reason for service development, 14
    as service provider goal, 10, 281
    in service provisioning, 137
scheduling mechanisms for QoS, 171
SCM (supply chain management), 1
scope of deliverables, defining, 26, 27–28
SDH (synchronous digital hierarchy), 2–3, 211. *See also* optical networking
SDSL (symmetric digital subscriber line), 115
security. *See also* IPSec (IP security)
    customer requirements, 7–8, 44, 170
    data, 7–8, 44
    IPSec, 189–199
    IPv6, 206
    MPLS-VPN, 131
    network, 7, 146, 147
    network management issues, 162

    SNMPv2 issues, 146
    SNMPv3 features, 146, 147
security associations. *See* SAs (security associations)
Sega Online, 39
selecting vendors. *See* vendor selection
serialization delay, 173. *See also* delay
service classes in ATM, 112
service creation
    ADSL for, 132, 133
    ATM for, 133–135
    cable technology for, 132, 134
    defined, 14
    in Greenfield case study, 236–238
    Greenfield service provider model, 49
    incumbent service provider model, 65–66
    IPv6 and, 208
    MPLS for, 123–127, 128
    MPLS-VPNs for, 127, 129–132
    multicast for, 135
    QoS and, 179
    as tollgate 1 in service development, 15–16
    vendor product development cycle, 23–25
service delivery. *See* service implementation
service deployment in incumbent case study (conceptual), 252
service development. *See also* product development; service creation
    automation using IP-based technology, 27–29
    basics, 14–15
    business case, 16–17, 18
    delays, reasons for, 26
    feedback loop, 47–48
    final service documents, 17
    implementation automation, 28
    IP role in, 27–29
    OSS business processes and interfaces in, 29, 30
    paper proposal, 16
    participants, 13, 19–21
    pilot, testing, and validation phase, 17
    politics, 21–23
    problems in the process, 25–26
    product development and, 14, 23–25
    scalability as reason for, 14
    scope of deliverables and, 26, 27–28
    service creation, 14, 15–16
    service description, 17
    service implementation, 14
    service launch, 17
    service provider goals, 10
    service upgrade automation, 29
    time required for, 25–26
    tollgates in process of, 15–19
service enhancements, 20
service implementation. *See also* OSS (operations support system); provisioning
    automation of, 28, 165–166
    customer involvement, 147–148
    defined, 14, 147
    departments involved, 148–149
    in Greenfield case study, 228–229, 239–240

guaranteed bandwidth, 151, 152
in incumbent case study (conceptual), 247–249
IP QoS, 177–179
IP-based automation for, 28
in Meta Telecom case study, 270, 273–274
network management, 138, 155–162, 163
OSS, 149, 162, 164–166
POS (packet-over-SONET), 96–97
provisioning, 137–138, 149–155
scalability and, 164–165
service development delays and, 26
SRP topology, 100, 101
service life cycle, 20
service management responsibilities, 21
service packaging and pricing. *See also* pricing
e-commerce portal service, 57–58
for Greenfield service providers, 54–58
for incumbent service providers, 64, 68–70
IP-VPNs, 55–56, 68–69
Web hosting, 53, 56–57, 69–70
service providers. *See also* Greenfield service providers; incumbent service providers; *specific types*
challenges for, 13
defined, 1, 15
goals, 10–11, 281
motivations for IP-based services, 30–31
service development participants, 19–21
value-added services from, 13
service time-to-market (Meta Telecom case study), 258
service upgrades
in Greenfield case study, 239–240
in incumbent case study (conceptual), 252–253
IP-based automation for, 29
as provisioning factor, 138
service-level agreements. *See* SLAs (service-level agreements)
services. *See also* IP-based services; multiservices; service packaging and pricing; value-added services; *specific services*
bundled vs. unbundled, 5–6
defined, 1, 5, 14–15
in Greenfield case study, 227–228
Greenfield service provider examples, 49–54
in incumbent case study (conceptual), 245–247
incumbent service provider examples, 66–68
in marketing plan, 42, 43
in Meta Telecom case study, 262–269
modifying, 155
voice-over-IP services, 187–189
session initiation protocol (SIP), 180, 184–185
Set operation (SNMP), 144, 145, 160
shaping mechanisms (QoS), 178
shared tree for multicast addresses, 93, 94, 95
shortest path tree (STP) for multicast addresses, 93, 95
signaling, QoS, 178
simple network management protocol. *See* SNMP (simple network management protocol)

simplicity
as customer requirement, 44
in network device configuration, 153
platform, 31
in service provisioning, 137
single-vendor vs. multiple-vendor strategies, 46–47
SIP (session initiation protocol), 180, 184–185
SIP URLs, 185
site-local address (IPv6), 201, 202
situational review in Greenfield service provider marketing plan, 41
SLAs (service-level agreements)
described, 8, 14
network statistics for reporting, 158
OSS components for reporting and billing, 164
reporting in Greenfield case study, 238
reporting in Meta Telecom case study, 274
reports as customer requirement, 8
SMI (structure of management information) in SNMP, 143, 145
SNMP agents, 139, 140
SNMP (simple network management protocol), 139–147
components, 139–140
described, 139
as interface for network device configuration, 154–155
MIB (management information base), 139, 140, 141–142
as network management communication protocol, 159–160
NMS (network management system) and, 11, 139, 140, 159
operations, 141
security issues, 146
SNMP agents, 139, 140
version 1, 139, 142–144
version 2, 139, 144–145
version 3, 139, 146–147
snmpget operation (SNMP), 159
snmpset operation (SNMP), 160
snmptrap operation (SNMP), 159
SNMPv1
ASN data types and, 143
described, 142–143
MIB tables, 144
other versions vs., 139, 144
protocol operations, 144
SMI-specific data types and, 143–144
structure of management information (SMI), 143
SNMPv2
capability statements, 145
described, 144
MIB modules, 145
other versions vs., 139, 144, 146
protocol operations, 145
security issues, 146
structure of management information (SMI), 145

SNMPv3
    access control service, 146–147
    administrative framework features, 146
    authentication service, 146–147
    other versions vs., 139, 146
    principals, 146–147
    privacy service, 146–147
    security features, 146, 147
software upgrades
    as multicast application, 92
    network management for, 158–159
SONET (synchronous optical network). *See also*
        optical networking; POS (packet-over-
        SONET)
    IP-based services as unsuitable for, 2–3
    overview, 211
    POS (packet-over-SONET), 96–99, 121–122
source tree for multicast addresses, 93
sparse-mode protocols, 95
speed, Web hosting requirements, 53
Sprint, 39
SRP (spatial reuse protocol)
    applications, 102
    features, 100–102
    implementation, 100, 101
    overview, 99
    packet format, 101
SSPs (storage service providers), 38
stability
    defined, 123
    of MPLS core, 123–124
statistics, network, 158
STM (synchronous transport module), 211
STP (shortest path tree) for multicast addresses, 93,
        95
strategic objectives
    Greenfield case study, 225–227
    incumbent case study (conceptual), 244–245
Streetmail, 39
structure of management information (SMI) in
        SNMP, 143, 145
STS (synchronous transport signal), 211
suppliers. *See* vendors
supply chain management (SCM), 1
SVCs (switched virtual circuits)
    in ATM, 110
    in frame relay, 104
switches and switching. *See also* MPLS
        (multiprotocol label switching)
    ATM, 70, 110–111
    Ethernet, 103–104
    frame relay, 104, 106
    MPLS packet switching, 124, 125
    optical cross-connects (OXCs), 213, 217
    switching delay, 173
SWOT (strengths, weaknesses, opportunities, and
        threats) analysis, 41–42
symmetric digital subscriber line (SDSL), 115
synchronous digital hierarchy (SDH), 2–3, 211. *See
        also* optical networking

synchronous optical network. *See* SONET (synchro-
        nous optical network)
synchronous transport module (STM), 211
synchronous transport signal (STS), 211

T
tag distribution protocol (TDP), 83
target market, 42
TCP/IP (transmission control protocol/Internet Pro-
        tocol), 1–2, 76
TDM (time-division multiplexing), 61, 65
TDP (tag distribution protocol), 83
technology providers, 15
technology suppliers, 15
Telecommunications Act of 1996, 3–4
telecommuting
    managed remote-access IP-VPNs for, 50–51
    as remote access driver, 50
Telia, 39
terminals (H.323), 183
text-based CLI
    for accessing network devices, 160
    for configuring network devices, 153
3DES, 191
throughput, 6–7
time tick data type (SNMP), 143
time-division multiplexing (TDM), 61, 65
time-to-market products, 24
timing modification (SNMPv2 security issue), 146
Token Ring, 99
toll bypass using voice-over-IP, 188–189
total cost of ownership, 44
traceroute utility, 160
Traditiontel. *See* incumbent service provider case
        study (conceptual)
traffic conditioners (DiffServ), 176
traffic engineering
    bandwidth management, 124
    guaranteed bandwidth, 124, 127, 128
    MPLS for, 85, 124, 126–127, 128
traffic management
    ATM for, 112
    ISDN for, 114–115
transition state, IP state vs., 23
transmission control protocol/Internet Protocol
        (TCP/IP), 1–2, 76
transmission delay, 173. *See also* delay
transparency, as customer requirement, 44
transport layer (TCP), QoS provisions, 78
transport mode SAs, 195, 196
transport technologies. *See also specific technologies*
    ATM, 108–113
    cable modem, 116, 118–121
    DSL, 115–116, 117
    Ethernet, 102–104, 105, 106
    frame relay, 104, 106–108
    ISDN, 113–115
    packet-over-SONET (POS), 96–99
    ring topology, 99–102
    summary of features, 121–122

transversal operations (SNMP), 141
Trap operation (SNMP), 141, 144, 145, 159
trees for multicast addresses, 93
triple DES, 191
tunnel mode SAs, 195, 196

U
UAC (user-agent client), 184
UAs (user agents), 184–185
UAS (user-agent server), 184
ubiquitous IP plug, 67
UNEs (unbundled network elements), 36
unicast addresses (IPv6), 200–201
United Online, 39
unsigned integer data type (SNMP), 144
upgrades
    managing hardware and software upgrades,
        158–159
    Web hosting requirements, 53
user agents (UAs), 184–185
user-agent client (UAC), 184
user-agent server (UAS), 184
UUNET (Worldcom), 39

V
value-added services
    as customer requirement, 64
    defined, 15, 36
    economic (EVA), 36
    for networks (VANs), 36
    requirements for developing and deploying, 13
    as service provider objective, 31
    for Web hosting, 69–70
VAN (value-added network), 36
VCI (virtual channel identifier), 108, 110
VDSL (very high speed subscriber line), 115
vendor profile
    for Greenfield service providers, 44–45
    for incumbent service providers, 64
vendor selection
    in Greenfield case study, 230–231
    for Greenfield service providers, 45–47
    in incumbent case study (conceptual), 250
    for incumbent service providers, 64–65
    in Meta Telecom case study, 270, 272
vendors
    as drivers for IP-based services, 32
    goals, 11–12
    profiles, 44–45, 64
    requirements for Greenfield service providers,
        45
    as service development participants, 18
    support as service provider goal, 11
Verio, 38
vertical B2B sites, 53
vertical service providers (VSPs), 39–40
very high speed subscriber line (VDSL), 115
video application sensitivity to delay and jitter,
    169–170

videoconferencing
    bandwidth requirements, 169–170
    with Greenfield service providers, 55–56
    pricing, 56
video-on-demand, bandwidth requirements,
    169–170
virtual channel identifier (VCI), 108, 110
virtual path identifier (VPI), 108, 110
virtual private networks (VPNs). *See* IP-VPNs; MPLS-
    VPNs
virtual routing and forwarding (VRF), 88
VLANs (virtual LANs), Ethernet for, 103–104, 105
voice coding, 181–183
voice-over-IP, 180–189
    call setup, 185–187
    components, 180–185
    H.323 protocol, 180, 183–184
    as IP-based service example, 32
    merging voice and data networks, 187–188
    packet voice network, 180–181
    requirements, 169, 180
    RSVP for, 175
    sensitivity to delay and jitter, 169, 180
    services, 187–189
    SIP protocol, 180, 184–185
    toll bypass, 188–189
    voice coding, 181–183
VPI (virtual path identifier), 108, 110
VPNs (virtual private networks). *See* IP-VPNs; MPLS-
    VPNs
VRF (virtual routing and forwarding), 88
VSPs (vertical service providers), 39–40

W
wavelength routers, 214
Web hosting
    as CLEC service, 36
    customer requirements, 52–53
    dedicated, 51–53
    by Greenfield service providers, 51–53, 56–57
    by incumbent service providers, 67–68
    as IP-based service example, 32
    service packaging and pricing, 53, 56–57, 69–70
    value-added services, 57, 69–70
Web-based CLI for configuring network devices,
    154
Web-based tools
    in Meta Telecom case study, 275
    as OSS requirement, 166
WISPs (wireless Internet service providers), 38–39
write command (SNMP), 141
WSPs (wireless service providers), 38–39

X, Y, Z
xSPs (x service providers). *See also* Greenfield ser-
    vice providers; *specific types*
    described, 5
    as Greenfield service providers, 4
    types, 37–40

About the Authors

Monique Morrow is currently CTO Consulting Engineer at Cisco Systems. She has 20 years' experience in IP Internetworking, including design, implementation of complex customer projects, and service development. Morrow has been involved in developing managed network services such as remote access and LAN switching in a service provider environment. She has worked for both enterprise and service provider companies in the United States and in Europe, and led the Engineering Project team for one of the first European MPLS-VPN deployments in 1999 for a European service provider.

Morrow has an M.S. in telecommunications management and an M.B.A. in marketing and is a Cisco Certified Internetworking Expert (#1711).

Kateel Vijayananda is currently a design consultant at Cisco Systems. He has 9 years' experience in data networking, including the design, implementation, and management of IP networks, and the development of software to implement the OSI protocol stack. He has also been involved in developing managed network services such as LAN switching and LAN interconnect in a service provider environment. Vijayananda has worked as a network engineer/architect for a European service provider where he was part of teams that designed and implemented an MPLS network and that developed and managed IP-based services on top of an MPLS network.

Vijayananda has an M.S. and a Ph.D. in computer science and is a Cisco Certified Internetworking Expert (#4850).